Fossil in the Flagstones

... WHERE THE UNUSUAL IS USUAL

by Lyn Caverhill

Kimberley Australia

Copyright © 2024 by Lyn Caverhill.

All rights reserved. No part of this publication may be reproduced, distributed or transmitted in any form or by any means, including photocopying, recording, or other electronic or mechanical methods, without the prior written permission of the publisher, except in the case of brief quotations embodied in critical reviews and certain other non-commercial uses permitted by copyright law. For permission requests, write to the publisher, addressed "Attention: Permissions Coordinator," at the address below.

Lyn Caverhill c/- Intertype Publish and Print
Unit 45, 125 Highbury Road
BURWOOD VIC 3125
Australia
www.intertype.com.au

Ordering Information:
Quantity sales. Special discounts are available on quantity purchases by corporations, associations, and others. For details, contact the "Special Sales Department" at the address above.

Fossil in the Flagstones / Lyn Caverhill. —1st ed.
ISBN 978-1-7635664-1-5

Contents

Preface 11

The Dream: 1879—1930 15

The Trek 23

Into The Territory 35

Meeting up with Duracks 41

Back to the Trek 45

Destination Reached 49

Addendum 53

Western Australia becomes a State 55

Drovers' 3000-Mile Trip – The Longest Cattle Drive ... 57

Exploration from across the Continent 59

Establishing the Station 61

Charlie Visits Goulburn 67

McKenzies Want Out of Partnership 69

Charlie Appointed a J.P. 71

Willie Marries Ida 75

Achievements of Donald (snr), Charlie & Willie: 81

Duncan and Donald Jnr. (Dan) (1910) 83

Achievements of Duncan and Dan: 85

Mail Service	87
Sale to Kidman	89
Public Auction	91
Second Generation: 1928—1963	93
Bill & Maxine MacDonald	93
Dan Dies	97
Bill is Manager	99
Homestead	101
Jean MacDonald Visits	103
Bill Marries Maxine	107
Popular in Perth	109
Maxine arrives at Fossil	111
Margaret River Runs	115
Fitzroy Crossing Township	119
Old River Crossing	121
Sports	125
Rev. John Flynn	129
Roads	131
The Races	133
Church	135
Mail	137

World War II	139
Building the Homestead	143
Maxine's Touches	147
Blue Mountain Lowries and Budgerigars	151
Aborigines Inspect	153
National Trust and Australian Heritage	155
Native Staff	157
Native Amenities	159
Modern Amenities	163
Visit of Princess Margaret	165
Vlesio Zenelia	167
Bill's Experiments & Publicity for the Kimberley	169
Change of Attitude	171
Stud Cattle	173
Bull shipment makes history	175
Bulls Take Flight	177
Air Beef Scheme	179
Stock horses	181
Walkabout Disease	183
Mules	185
Drought	187

- Excellent Beef Yield ... 191
- Killing Cattle at Broome ... 193
- Beef Roads ... 195
- Conducts Trials ... 197
- Faster Maturing Beef ... 199
- Aerial Seeding ... 201
- Irrigated Lucerne ... 203
- Forward Thinking ... 205
- Future Development of the Kimberley ... 207
- Bruce Gray—Manager ... 209
- Sandy Gray ... 211
- Bill MacDonald Departs ... 215
- Maxine in Charge ... 219
- Vic Jones ... 221
- Debacle ... 223
- Simon Maffey aka Lord Rugby ... 225
- Peter Gray ... 227
- Healthy Soup ... 231
- Chest Deep Freeze ... 233
- Lyn Arrives: 1969—1970 ... 235
- Third Generation: 1967–2015 ... 243

John & Annette Henwood	243
The Pastoral Award	249
Efficient Equipment	253
Future Farming at Fossil	255
Droughtmasters	257
BTEC	259
Dung Beetles	263
Corroboree	265
River Runs	267
Amber & Norman	269
My Name Now Is...	271
Killing the Snake	275
Rain Stones	277
The Rain Game	279
'Millsy'	281
Mt. Hart	283
Rowing the River	285
Moonlight Magic	287
Personalised Plates?	289
Penicillin Vaccinations	291
Medico Madness	293

Adenoids Removal 297

24 Gallons of Curry 299

Muludja 301

Aborigine boys 303

No Pot Luck 305

Merilee and the Males 307

Kimberley Wet 311

Telephone Arrives 313

Contract Musterers 315

Drive to Kununurra 317

Time to go 321

A Week of Drama, Hell, and High Water 323

Bridges or Highway Upgrade? 333

Maxine Departs 337

(Some Of The) Achievements of Bill & Maxine MacDonald 339

Suspension of Live Cattle Trade 341

Epilogue 2014 343

Achievements of John & Annette Henwood 349

ACCOLADES 351

Bibliography 355

GLOSSARY 356

ACKNOWLEDGMENTS

Heartfelt thanks to:
Sunshine Coast Writer's Club, Goodlife Writer's Group,
Ann, Beryl, Judy, Keith, Susie, Tammy,
and John, who drove me to all of the places mentioned.
Most of all, the information from
John and Annette Henwood and Bob MacDonald was invaluable.
Your knowledge, encouragement and insight is
sincerely appreciated.

Preface

The air smelt different. The tropical night air had a dank, yet sweet earthy scent at midnight. Is this how tropical air smells—or is it the surrounding mud flats and mix of the abundant frangipani fragrance which gives Derby its distinctive yet not unpleasant aroma? Derby, 1800 miles north of Perth in Western Australia though, was just a night stop before I flew 200 miles east next morning to a speck on the map called Fitzroy Crossing.

The small mail plane stopped at cattle stations on the way. You could tell it was a mail plane—there were sacks of mail and packages wherever they could be shoved in—on and under the seats. There was no door to the cockpit, so you could see the relaxed pilot reading a book—or was it a flying instruction manual? Staring down at the moving landscape you could make out tiny tracks leading off in various directions in the dry paddocks. Where do they lead? Just prior to landing at a station, the pilot would lean through the opening, and tap his fingers on the *Fasten Seat Belts* sign. At one station, while the freight was being unloaded onto the back of the station ute, his capable flight attendant skillfully managed to produce a very welcome cuppa from a large vacuum flask for us three passengers.

'Private Secretary to Station Proprietress', in the Kimberley region of Western Australia, had been advertised in the Perth daily paper. With confidence, and naivety, I'd felt right for this position. My secretarial skills had been honed in real estate and a legal office, plus private secretarial positions in management, and I'd attended many lectures on raising and judging beef cattle in a young farmers organization. I had a driver's license. That just about covered everything, I thought. So here I was, in 1969, ready to embrace the life on cattle stations I'd read so much about.

Fitzroy Crossing, in the Kimberley, was still a frontier town with just 5 establishments: the Post Office, Police Station and Australian Inland Mission hospital on one side of the rocky tree-lined Brooking Creek—the Crossing Inn, and United Aborigines Mission, including the primary school, on the other side.

'The Crossing appears a bit rugged at first sight, but it grows on you,' commented Jeanette who'd collected me on the dusty airport runway, and whom I was replacing at the Station. 'It's beautiful at Fossil Downs though—a real oasis.' This was the era before the Kimberley had bridges over its enormous rivers, or telephones on the cattle stations, and before air-conditioned four-wheel drive vehicles became *de rigueur*.

Before these now popular four-wheel drives, the mode of transport of the owner of Fossil Downs was an air-conditioned V8 Holden Kingswood sedan. Mrs. MacDonald, who I'd be working with and driving, had had it equipped with an 8-deck cassette tape player under the dashboard, and a 'fridge' in the boot. This was very advanced for the time, and a definite upgrade from the little Morris 1100 I'd driven around Perth. Jeanette and I collected some necessities at Crossing Inn and several mailbags at the Post Office, and proceeded the 26 miles over the then benign 100 yards wide Fitzroy River, and through bush tracks where clouds of fine dust billowed as the occasional vehicle traversed them. After crossing the 80 yards wide Margaret River, we arrived at Fossil Downs Station's ZV5 boundary gate. First lesson about driving in the outback—'Don't open the car door until the dust has gone past.'

Jeanette appeared to have great competence and a wealth of practical knowledge, along with a friendly and easy manner with everyone. She had worked on the station in two separate stints, and was only departing because her family in Perth needed her. How much of her knowledge could be relayed to me in the next two weeks? Would I be able to cope as she appeared to?

We proceeded along the two-mile drive to the station homestead entrance and environs. The impressive pillars on either side of the entrance gates were emblazoned with the MacDonald Coat of Arms, its motto being 'By Land and by Sea'. The MacDonald family had been in possession of Fossil Downs Station since Western Australian explorer Alexander Forrest first surveyed the area in 1879, and discovered the grassy red and black soil plains along the mighty Fitzroy, Leopold, and Margaret Rivers.

Driving through those gates was astonishing. Was this Australia's version of 'Tara' from 'Gone with the Wind'? It was surreal. How had this stylish, grand establishment evolved in such a dry, outback, isolated place? Whose vision and foresight was responsible for the set-up and construction of this 'township', with pink-flowering oleanders in the street's median strip? All the buildings were lined up on either side of this street, many beautifully constructed in local stone. The verandas were supported with moulded cement grecian-style pillars. All roofs were painted green, and the shed walls were pink. Interesting! Who designed and built the stately two-storey home at its apex? Again a green roof, but with white walls. Who kept it all so immaculate? Both an aura and enigma enveloped the orderly affluent surroundings.

Visiting and staying on a variety of rural properties had been usual for me when I'd worked in various farming-type occupations—small-fruit growing, green-paddock dairying and sheep both for mutton and wool all in Victoria, and wheat, oats and barley cropping in Western Australia. Learning how the layouts of homesteads, gardens if any, staff quarters, cookhouses, storage and implement sheds, garages, hay barns, and stockyards evolved was always an interesting study. On most properties surplus machinery and debris is either stacked neatly or, more often, thrown haphazardly into a pile of junk, which might come in handy one day! Fossil Downs was different—no old collapsed sheds or abandoned vehicles or car-bodies, and no rusty corrugated iron or machinery in sight. Everything was immaculate. It melded seamlessly into the environment of the adjacent Geikie Range.

The establishment of Fossil Downs station became an absorbing study. Meticulously kept diaries and scrapbooks, kept up-to-date by monthly newspaper clippings sent from Sydney, were a fascinating source of information. It was part of the secretaries' job description to maintain these records, so gradual scrutiny of these priceless documents, photographs and mementos revealed an amazing series of events over the preceding ninety years, which included numerous firsts. Here was Australian history unknown by most of its inhabitants.

The Dream: 1879—1930

'Did ya hear about Forrest's exploration in the north of Western Australia?' Cattlemen were agog! It was 1879. Western Australian surveyor Alexander Forrest, after making some exploratory trips north of Perth in previous years, had journeyed to the far north of that State, into an area he named 'the Kimberley' which had not been surveyed previously. His published glowing reports and letters had reached the eastern states of Australia. Excitement abounded in the cattle world. 'He says there's millions of acres of green fertile pastures and wide-flowing, permanent rivers and big waterholes.'

Between the Ord and Fitzroy Rivers, Forrest had found more than 25 million acres of empty virgin pastures—miles of open rolling grassland and fertile alluvial flats threaded by wide, deep flowing rivers and studded with lily-covered lagoons.

Forrest had been an independent licensed surveyor working by contract for the Survey Department in Western Australia. Those officials were not expected to profit from their finds. The Forrest brothers, John and Alexander, had already been criticized for their investments in properties where they had surveyed previously—so Alexander set up as a land agent. He was consulted by the Durack, Emanuel and MacDonald families, and many more, who ultimately swarmed to take up over 51 million prime acres of Kimberley pastoral leaseholds by 1883.

Archibald and Sarah MacDonald had sailed from the Isle of Skye, Scotland in 1835, with other free settlers, to seek a life of prosperity on the land in Australia. After arriving they were granted a lease of 100 acres, which they called *Clifford's Creek*, at Laggan, on the Southern Tablelands of NSW. He cleared the trees from the land, built a Scottish-style stone house, and bought both breeding and grazing stock. Then Archibald sent for his younger brother Donald MacDonald, who was awaiting word from him back in Scotland.

Anne McAllum had migrated from the Isle of Mull, in Scotland. She and Donald met in Sydney NSW and, having much in common, married in Goulburn on 10 July 1849.

Initially Donald and Anne worked with Archibald and Sarah, but also acquired their own selection. They built it up by fencing off the abundant grass into paddocks, increased the cattle herd, and purchased some more adjacent blocks. In the next few years, Donald and Anne also built a stone house for their growing family.

They had six sons and two daughters: John, Catherine (Kitty), Charles (Charlie), Archie, Duncan, Ann (Nance), William (Willie), and Donald Junior (Dan). Over time as their family grew, along with their little stone house, they realized the holdings they'd acquired would not be big enough for all their boys to prosper in Australia. More land was needed, but where? All the fertile acreage around them had been taken up. Not all of Australia was fertile, they knew, and sometimes the annual rains failed. If there were big rivers up in the north, as this 1879 report of Forrest's indicated, Archibald and Donald believed that signified rainfall must be regular. 'How much of the land was fertile? How much could be procured? On what terms would it be available?' So mused Archibald and Donald MacDonald.

Donald wrote to Alexander Forrest seeking further details. The pleasing reply still had him cautious. Perhaps the Kimberley was a land of promise, but establishing properties there, 3500 miles away, would be a physically massive, expensive, and unknown undertaking. His sons had inherited the MacDonald physique and grown into tall, broad-shouldered, bearded young men, who had been gold prospecting, cattle and sheep droving and shearing. They had also become good bushmen. They would be capable of overlanding the entire necessary inventory to commence cattle or sheep grazing, he thought, but he needed to be sure the massive effort and expense would be worthwhile. He contacted his youngest son Dan, now in his early twenties, who happened to be gold prospecting in Western Australia at the time, and asked him to do a reconnaissance in the areas recommended by Forrest. In 1882 Dan acquired some horses in Derby and, following the Fitzroy River east from there, travelled out to the newly explored but trackless land to assess the proposed selection.

Dan was so favourably impressed by the fertile, green black-soil plains and the massive abundant rivers, that he immediately applied to the WA State Government for a lease of 100 square miles of land at the junction of the Margaret and Fitzroy Rivers, where Forrest had blazed a tree 'F136'. The ever-reliable grapevine indicated there were many other cattlemen interested in this new region, and he knew the race would be on to secure grass empires.

The Fitzroy River rises at approximately 1300 feet in the Mueller Range in far north Western Australia, and flows southwest through the Kimberley for 455 miles, and into King Sound near Derby. Its catchment occupies an area of 36,228 square miles with 20 tributaries. On 29 May 1879, Forrest named another inland river with 15 tributaries 'Margaret', after his sister-in-law, Margaret Forrest. The area Dan applied for was just north of the confluence of these two mighty rivers. The address was merely 125.89 longitude and 18.17 latitude scribbled on a scrap of paper that Donald had sent him.

Since first hearing Forrest's glowing report, and while he'd been waiting for Dan's assessment, the idea of establishing a cattle station in the Kimberley waxed and waned in Donald Senior's mind, but it never went away completely.

'I wonder if it really is as good as he says. Will this be the means of setting up my boys?' he pondered. When Dan's positive account arrived he excitedly sprang into action. He searched out what primitive maps were available, and sketched out a route. These maps showed rivers all the way, but did they always contain water sufficient for a mob of stock to drink, or were they just wet-weather run-offs or mudholes? Would it be better to send the stock there by ship?

How much would that cost? How many could be transported that way? Where was the nearest port or landfall to their destination? Donald continued working on the logistics of an operation to overland cattle, horses, and the total inventory to start up a station. What would be needed to convey this amount of gear for 3,500 miles through an unknown environment? Would horses or bullocks be best to pull the transporting conveyance? The amount of detail was daunting.

It soon became apparent that if they proceeded with this undertaking it would severely strain the MacDonald's finances, and leave them no leeway to factor in unknown adversities, either on the way, or especially when they arrived at their destination. They also had to continue maintaining the *Clifford's Creek* property at Laggan as John, the eldest son, expressed his interest in retaining and farming it. It had become the family stronghold and Archie and Sarah were close to retiring from active farming. Would all the other boys go to the new property? Of course, their daughters Catherine and Annie would marry locally, and be provided for that way, he assumed.

A financial backer was needed. He felt this should be someone who had the same long-term vision, dreams, and passion to finance an undertaking such as this. It may be a long time before dividends would be payable. After much deliberation Donald, now in his 50s, contacted his close friends and relatives by marriage, Duncan McKenzie, and his sons, Kenneth, William, and Alexander, suggesting to them a joint venture to help finance this undertaking. The McKenzies were situated at *Heather Heath* and *Peelwood* at Hobby's Yards, south of Blayney, NSW, and at *The Junction* on the confluence of Tuena Creek and the Abercrombie River, 30 miles further south in the Southern Tablelands.

Although they were all motivated by an adventurous spirit, it still took some persuading for the McKenzies to link up and become part of the project. They were not wealthy, as they had also acquired and developed extra land locally, but eventually the agreement was that the McKenzies would provide the finances, most of the stock, plant and equipment and some initial labour, and the MacDonalds would undertake the droving and the physical establishment of the station. One of the first expenses was £100 for the first year's rental of the 100 square miles Dan had applied for—Kimberley Leases 705 to 708. The receipt was dated 15 May 1882.

This decision made, the McKenzie women, Ann, Jane, Mattie, Meg and Annie, leapt into action. 'They'll be wanting plenty of good food to keep them fit and healthy on this journey,' they agreed and began producing long lists of food and utensils, which was added to daily. What quantities would be needed for this estimated two-year journey? How many drovers and teamsters would need feeding? Where could further supplies be obtained on the journey? The McKenzie women undertook this provisioning as Ann MacDonald, Donald's wife, had died in 1862, when William was just two, and none of the young men actually contemplating the Kimberley trek had married yet.

The food list began: flour, baking soda, cream of tartar, tea, sugar, table salt, pepper, mustard, pickles, jam, treacle. 'It will have to be packed really well to last that distance without spoiling,' the McKenzie women decided. Large quantities of cooking fat were clarified and sealed in tins. Fruit from their home orchards was dried and packed in calico bags, which were tightly stitched to keep out moth infestation. Biscuits were baked hard so they would remain edible. 'This will be better and more nutritious than the diet of salt beef and damper which drovers usually eat,' Mattie declared. Old ships' tanks were procured, 4 feet high and wide, which were made of thick, heavy flat iron, securely riveted with neatly fitted water-tight lids, and the foodstuffs were packed into those. Camp ovens, frying pans, cast iron saucepans, billycans, plates, mugs, cutlery, and sundry other utensils were assembled. Hammocks for the drovers were created from corn sacks. And, of course, they'd need a compass or sextant to guide them to the supplied co-ordinates. There was no accurate map.

The McKenzie menfolk were also planning and gathering. Tons of equipment and supplies were amassed—axes, saws, picks, shovels, mattocks, crowbars, adzes, hammers, chisels, screwdrivers, planes, braces and bits, a blacksmith's anvil and shoeing gear, plus tools for repairing harness and saddles. 'How are we going to transport all of this equipment and supplies', Donald contemplated. 'What will carry it all and last the distance?' Two bullock wagons were decided on. The MacDonalds arranged for these to be constructed in Goulburn, NSW, by Mr. W. Southall, the local coach, buggy and wagon builder. The wagons needed to be especially strong not only to haul all these tons of equipment but also to take the strain of traversing the continent on rough tracks. Mr. Southall added a unique feature of two large, strong hooks attached to either end of the front axle to assist in difficult conditions, if they arose.

'Where will be the nearest source of supplies when the boys get there,' Donald kept wondering. The little outpost of Derby had only just been settled and was 200 miles distant, to the west of their destination. Dan had alighted there by ship and reported that little gear and supplies would be available from that source. Thus it was decided to take as much as they could to equip the station after they arrived. So they added extra saddles, bridles, halters, spare reins, straps and stirrup leathers. Butcher's knives, cleavers and saws, dog chains and collars, guns, rifles, revolvers and a plentiful supply of ammunition, plus large coils of rope, tarpaulins, boxes of nails, screws, bolts and nuts of various sizes, ladders to climb up onto the wagons to access the items on the top, plus timber for making rafts—the lists continued to grow. Included were spare parts for the wagons as some could wear out on the trek. Additionally they needed yokes, bows, pins, whips and chains for the bullocks pulling the wagons.

Stock was procured in the Laggan area—beef cattle to begin stocking the station, sufficient horses for droving and rounding up the cattle, plus spares for packhorses; bullocks for hauling the wagons, and a couple of milking cows to provide fresh milk on the journey, and when they arrived at their destination. The livestock was assembled at William McKenzie's property *Heather Heath* at Hobby's Yards, and imprinted with his brand, Z over 5.

At last all the stock and the equipment was assembled and piled up at the McKenzies' properties. It would soon be time to depart. The bullocks hauled the wagons from Laggan, along with some of the cattle, and horses, north up and over the steep densely treed range following the Cobb & Co. track, to *Peelwood* and *The Junction* at Tuena, then through the gold-fossicking Trunkey's Creek area and on to *Heather Heath* at Hobby's Yards. Here the supplies amassed by the McKenzie men and women were loaded. It had taken six months to accumulate everything that both the MacDonalds and the McKenzies thought they'd need. Eventually the personnel, stock, and equipment were all packed and loaded on the wagons, ready to leave.

'I've got great faith in you, boys. I know you'll acquit yourselves well. Look after the other men, Charlie, and send us a wire soon's you can after you've arrived,' Donald, the Scotsman, intoned. 'I'll be wanting to visit you there when you're set up.'

With the goodbyes all said, and the last words of advice and cautions repeated, the young men mounted their horses, and thus began perhaps the most underrated achievement of Australian droving. At a time when explorers were dying and disappearing without trace, these determined, resolute and gritty young Australian bushmen cracked their whips and started the cattle moving. On the command of their handlers the bullocks slowly started the wagons moving and hence became part of the greatest recorded cattle drive across Australia. The ultimate destination was the confluence of the mighty Fitzroy and Margaret Rivers in the Kimberley, northern Western Australia. It was 26 March 1883.

Did anyone really understand what that journey would entail, or envisage how it would impact the lives of Charlie and Willie MacDonald, these lovable larrikins? They were popular young men and held in high regard in the Laggan area.

A *Cliffords Creek* neighbour penned the following:
> All honour to that gallant band, who left their homes today,
> To try their fortunes in that land from here so far away.
> To West Australia they are bound, these bold and hardy few,
> And 'mongst these plucky sons are found brave old MacDonald's two.
> And on that day from out the lot who weakness did not show
> As, I believe, that grand old Scot who saw his two sons go.
> And tho it cut him to the heart he stifled e'en a sigh,
> And gravely said as they did part 'God bless these boys: Goodbye'.
> So we will wish them all 'God-speed', young Will and Charlie too
> For whom so many hearts do bleed, they were so kind and true.
> Yet, of the twain, the youngest son the lasses most regret;
> For Willie was so full of fun and quite the ladies pet.
> And in conclusion let us pray this dauntless Scottish band
> Will be successful, and that they will reach their promised land.
> And when arrived that they will find as many friends and true
> As at the Creek they've left behind—including Clermont too.

[1] This poem was signed "J.M.A". Clermont was a property five kilometres down the road and the McAllister family lived there so the poem could have been written by John McAllister, or the contemporary poet J. Murray Allison.

The Trek

On the urging command of 'heyah' from their handlers, the bullocks leaned into their yokes, and began heaving the two massive wagons loaded with the tons of provisions and equipment. Seven drovers and handlers, plus 670 head of mixed cattle, 60 horses and 46 bullocks comprised the entourage as it pulled out of Hobby's Yards after it had all been uplifted from the three McKenzie properties. Emblazoned on the side of the wagon covers was *Bound for Western Australia*. It was a clear autumn morning, and the sun's rays glistened on the dew and the steam rising off the grass as they set off.

Tall, strong Charlie MacDonald, 30, was the drover in charge—Willie MacDonald and Jim McGeorge were assisting. Peter Thompson and Jasper (Jimmy) Pickles were handling and driving the bullock teams, and young John and Duncan McKenzie were assisting as far as Dubbo, where handsome Donald McKenzie would take over from them. Ten-year-old Kenneth McKenzie was home at *The Meglo* bawling his eyes out, as his father wouldn't let him go too.

Charlie had some familiarity with this country. He'd previously trekked to the Palmer River goldfields in North Queensland where his plans to make his fortune panning for gold had come unstuck. But after crossing into Queensland they'd be heading northwest into new territory for him. How familiar was he in navigating by sextant to the co-ordinates they'd been given for F136?

Initially the mixed stock ambled at different speeds, with the cows and calves lagging behind the steers and horses, but after a few days they settled down to a steady ten miles per day. Following their father's sketch map, they travelled from Hobby's Yards through Carcoar, Molong and Wellington. Once over the hills and onto the plains, travelling was relatively easy. On the lush green grass of an abundant season all the stock retained their good condition. These young drovers were living a wonderful adventure. The mild autumn weather was pleasant, and their assorted food provisions were like a well-planned picnic every day. 'At this rate we could get there in a year,' mused Charlie optimistically doing some sums in his head. They reached Dubbo. Here, as arranged, Donald McKenzie joined them and, very reluctantly, John and Duncan McKenzie turned their mounts and headed for home. 'Can't we keep going with you?' they'd pleaded. It was an immensely enjoyable lifestyle.

The cattle strolled along grazing contentedly on the plentiful grass on the plains north of Dubbo. The cortege skirted the Macquarie marshes. Donald, a crack shot, marvelled at the amazing bird life, some of which found its way into their camp oven.

But on reaching the Barwon River near Brewarrina, on the upper reaches of the mighty Darling system, they were mystified. Brown and swirling, the water was running a pea soup banker. Apparently good summer rains had fallen 500 miles away on the western side of the Great Dividing Range to their east, and this was the run-off still flowing down the rivers. Donald suggested they just wait and graze the stock on the good grass until the floodwaters receded. No one knew how long the river would stay at this level, but sanguine Charlie wanted to maintain the good speed. His decision? They would swim the stock across, and then convey all their supplies and equipment over the river by raft. 'After all,' he spelled out, 'we specially brought the timber and tarps for situations like this.' And they still had plenty of energy.

Charlie and Jasper hunted for a suitable crossing place with no snags or unseen holes, while Willie, Donald, and the others constructed the rafts. Tarpaulins were stretched over the lashed logs to make them waterproof. All the tons of supplies and equipment on the wagons were unloaded. 'We'll lead the horses across first', Charlie directed, 'then the bullocks with their yokes and harnesses on. They'll be able to drag the wagons through the water now they're unloaded.' The horses moseyed into the water, and slowly swam to the other side, without drama. With everyone urging, the leading bullocks then plunged into the Barwon and reached the far bank while the wagons were still midstream. Willie and Donald had attached ropes to the provision-laden rafts and these were then hauled over to the northern bank. Finally, a few 'coaxers' (tame cattle) were urged to the far bank as decoys to lure the other cattle, while all hands drove the spelling bullocks and the cattle mobs across, leading the first few and driving the rest. How long did it take? Hours? Days? Whatever it took, exuberant Charlie and Willie were buoyed on by the imagination of their destination—millions of acres of rolling green virgin pastures watered by deep, permanent flowing rivers. With renewed vigour, they reloaded the tons of equipment onto the wagons and headed towards the Queensland border. But this droving adventure would soon be severely challenged again.

A few miles north of Brewarrina the pastures had dried out. 'What do you think's the problem here?' Charlie and Willie began to have unspoken doubts—there'd been plenty of good grazing until now. Hadn't there been the rain they'd encountered further south? Where had all the water at Brewarrina come from? Trudging north, the waterholes were murky, not clear and clean. Here, as arranged before they left Hobby's Yards, they collected what was left of the mob of 500 head of mixed cattle belonging to Samuel Marsden and John Plumb from back at Blayney. These cattle had been driven north previously and were to be delivered to a property in the Kimberley where their owners had also acquired a lease. Their condition was poor, having grazed for some time on the almost non-existent pastures.

'We'll travel as fast as we can,' Charlie intoned cheerfully, trying to keep up the spirits of the team, 'and Cooper Creek will provide better country than this.' But as they headed towards south-west Queensland, they found that good feed was becoming even more scarce with waterholes reduced to small muddy depressions as the channels from further north dried out. Any grass was dry and unpalatable to the cattle—mainly stalks and herbage lacking nutrition.

Queensland separated from the Colony of New South Wales as a self-governing Crown colony in 1859. At Barringun, the Queensland border gate, an officious customs official demanded payment of a tax on each head of livestock before allowing them to cross the border. This unexpected wallop to their finances incurred the wrath of Charlie. The official was left in no doubt what he thought. Begrudgingly the tax was paid—but Charlie made sure their cattle ate every blade of grass in the holding paddocks before they moved on!

Prior to Federation the separate colonies levied tariffs on goods crossing over their boundaries. But 'Living Animals' were on a free list, issued in 1876. Was a customs official—in some cases the police—making something on the side for himself here, or had this list been amended because of the drought? All state border taxes ceased with Federation in 1901.

Charlie, Willie, and the team, now learned the grim news that Queensland was scorching under one of its worst-ever droughts. Their fortitude was dwindling, but doggedly they refused to retrace their steps. 'We can't go back,' Charlie mulled. 'That so-and-so official won't give us our money back for departing.' The next three months were a drover's nightmare as they toiled desperately over bare, baked, parched stock routes. 'How will we get through this appalling situation?' Silently Charlie hid his worried thoughts, trying to keep his team in reasonable spirits, but it was difficult when landholders, understandably, were hostile as they saw the dust of the approaching mob. Charlie observed the 'gentleman's agreement' of advising pastoralists twenty-four hours before they drove past their properties. Understandably they shut their gates to conserve the scarce grass and water for what was left of their own stock. Their stock number dwindled. Their weakened and starving cattle were left to die as they succumbed to the constant 115+°F heat. Every day was heartbreaking.

Trailing up the Langlo River was disappointing, so they veered west towards the Thompson where they found several other mobs of cattle strung along the shrinking waterholes. 'We're not game to move until the drought breaks,' the other drovers confessed. 'Although the water here is foul, at least there's some water.' Contracted drovers are paid on the number of stock they deliver to their destination, hence their decision to stay put. The MacDonald team continued on and staggered through Isisford, Queensland, with approximately 900 head on 1 October 1883.

Charlie sent a scout ahead each day to try to locate any water and fodder, and to explore the best path for the wagons and stock to follow. Often no water was found and they were forced to just keep on going. The mob moved slowly, panting incessantly. The pall of dust generated tortured the drovers' eyes, too. Squinting into the distance, they would see a line of trees indicating a watercourse just up ahead, but as they drew closer the trees melted into the ether like sugar dissolving in tea. It was just another shimmering mirage tormenting them. Their own tongues, like those of the cattle, were swollen and their eyes were red and scratchy from the dehydrated atmosphere as they strained to see through the dust, the glare, and the heat.

The cattle became skittish and nervous. Frequent night attacks by local inhabitants spooked them. They were now in the Kalkadoon mob's country. Their traditional hunting grounds were being jeopardised by the increasing mobs of cattle being driven through Queensland. With their tall, muscular physiques they towered over many of their European opponents, even Charlie and Willie, who also possessed strong, muscular frames. Like the MacDonalds, the aboriginals were all bearded, and their wavy hair frequently had the tail of a dingo woven into it. They were known as fierce, aggressive, independent people, and ferocious fighters. Camped at night, the cattle in their fodder-deprived state provided an easy food target for them. This tribe was becoming accustomed to the flavour of beef. In desperation, Charlie compiled a roster for his men, and they were all allocated a watch, night and day, so beasts and stores were guarded constantly.

Their options were continually examined—they could bargain with landholders with their labour. Seeking rations from one station, they agreed to erect several miles of fencing to pay for these supplies. A few miles west of Winton, in the Diamantina Channel Country, they eventually arranged with the manager of Elderslie Station to camp at the Nine-mile Waterhole situated on his land, then. There they stayed put. Normally it was a reliable water source, but now it was only a short muddy stretch.

'Three rivers join just to the north of us here,' Charlie explained to the team. 'If there's any rain at all to the west, north or east of us, it will eventually flow down here.' He was talking about the confluence of the Diamantina, Wokingham, and Western Rivers. Some time previously an inexperienced drover had allowed his herd to rush the waterhole resulting in about 300 beasts being smothered. Systematically Charlie's team dragged away as many of those stinking, rotting carcasses as they could. At least the huge flat plains adjacent to the Diamantina allowed plenty of room for their cattle to be tailed-out loosely to pick at any herbage to be found. They were brought down to drink at the waterhole in small numbers each day. The MacDonald horses generally were still in fair condition, the bullocks were just surviving, but the cattle were suffering badly and more were dying.

The pesky flies, crawling up their noses and sucking any moisture out of the ringers eyes, and the irritating mosquitoes in the early morning and evening, joined forces to make this one hellish stint. In an effort to keep the men healthy, Charlie or Willie boiled all water for their use, and cleared it with Epsom salts. They'd heard that some men in other droving teams had contracted Barcoo rot (aka scurvy) it was thought from drinking putrid water, or eating food lacking in nutrition.

Of the eighteen months they'd now been on the trek, three of those months were camped beside this Nine-mile Waterhole. So much for their earlier pace, which might have allowed the entire trek to be completed in twelve months! Three months of waiting for the drought to break shortened their tempers. A couple of the men became disillusioned and despaired of ever reaching their goal, and left the trek. The river by then was a stench trench even though they pulled the stinking carcasses of the dead cattle into a heap well away from their camp.

Donald McKenzie and Charlie had for some time suffered a conflict of character. These deplorable conditions would bring out the worst, and shorten the temper, of most people. Utilizing his shooting skills, which he preferred to do, Donald would go off hunting, sometimes not completing his watch. He was attracted to the scenic, multi-coloured low mesas and ranges, south of the waterhole, where there was some birdlife. Charlie conceded at least Donald usually came back with something different to vary their tucker, often pigeons. Donald was handsome, athletic, and Kings School educated, and had a 'lady-killer' reputation. His lifestyle back at home had never enthralled pragmatic Charlie and now rancour over trivialities upset their camp. However, neither would admit defeat nor have it appear they weren't tough enough to handle these appalling conditions. Weren't they both of Scots origin? So Charlie and Donald were each relieved when a telegram finally reached them, via the township of Winton, that Donald was needed back home at *The Junction*, Tuena. Without delay he saddled his horse and headed south. This, after all, was in accordance with the original arrangement—the MacDonalds would be the drovers, while the McKenzies supplied the finance.

Charlie was glad to be rid of the irritation of incompatible company. 'Good riddance' he muttered under his breath as Donald trotted off. Didn't he have enough trying circumstances to contend with, without having to soothe his own nerves and that of the team? Reluctantly he had to pay off Jim McGeorge and Jimmy Pickles as the McKenzie finances were being severely strained—and they too headed south. Charlie and Willie were sorry to see them go. Peter Thompson, the bullocky, was still with them.

They were camped near the area where only twenty-odd years before, the illfated Burke and Wills expedition had traversed. At night camp, Charlie and Willie separately wondered how long they could tolerate this nightmare. How much more of these horrendous conditions could they endure? They hated seeing their cattle suffer and die, and they didn't really know what awaited them at their destination, or even exactly the route they should take to get there. Their brother Dan had made it sound outstanding from his reconnoitre, but where was he? Not here helping! Would their Kimberley destination really be worth suffering this living hell? With bravado, they tried to bolster each other's spirits, but their personal tolerance levels were frequently at breaking point. They were both known in Goulburn for their tidy, well-groomed appearance—now they looked, felt and smelt foul. No water could be spared for washing themselves or their clothes. Positively, the tinder-dry atmosphere dried their perspiration alleviating some odour. Did OP rum, stored in their waterbag, provide some solace?

'What's going on over there?' Willie, on early evening watch, stood up and squinted over the plains when he noticed the cattle staggering to their feet in the heavy, still atmosphere. Some were scuffing up dust. Scratching the back of his head and fearing another native attack, Charlie groaned, 'I'll load the shotgun and fire a warning. Will...get Pete and untie the horses.' They got ready to ward off more harassment.

But no attack eventuated. It puzzled them. Why were the cattle skittish? What was disturbing them? And what could they smell? It was different—not the smell of themselves or rotting carcasses. This was an earthy aroma. 'It smells like rain's coming', Willie commented, tongue-in-cheek, and recalling from a long time ago the petrichor smell emitted from rocks and plants after a prolonged dry spell, just before rain arrives. 'Yeah. Like that's gunna happen,' they mocked. But this was a different smell. Not wanting their hopes to be dashed again, and trying not to get excited, but with hearts pounding, they walked out from their camp staring into the night sky. No stars were visible. There was a distinct scent of rain in the air. Rain? Could rain really be coming? Could it possibly be coming after all this time? Yes, it was! Slowly big beautiful raindrops began thudding into their upturned faces, each one stinging. But they didn't notice that. This was thudding monsoonal tropical rain—unlike the gentle pitter-patter of soft misty drops they'd known on the Southern Tablelands in New South Wales.

Gradually the steamy earthy smell of real rain on parched dehydrated soil permeated everything. Was this really the monsoon arriving? How many months had they been waiting for this to happen? Cheering, yelling, and yahooing gradually spread along the riverbanks and waterholes from the other previously desperate drovers who'd been camped further along the Diamantina. Frogs emerged from their damp hidey-holes, and began croaking their calls of 'ribbit, ribbit'. Charlie and Willie, their emotions pent up for so long, silently and unashamedly gave thanks with their tears. Who cared that they were getting soaked to the skin, their clothes saturated, and their camp was becoming waterlogged?

That beautiful, sweet, monsoon rain fell for days on the warm earth. It banished the oppressive humidity. Small palatable flowers, grasses, and herbage appeared and grew with unbelievable speed. The river plains came alive. Their camp and the cattle were moved to higher ground further back from the river. The cattle had feed to eat and fresh water to drink as, eventually, clear water accumulated from the three rivers to the north of them and flowed down the Diamantina and into the Nine-mile Waterhole. Riders came by with good news from the North. The rain had covered the entire western side of Queensland! All their empty buckets were filled, and they washed and bathed in this precious rainwater which they tipped over each other and which they'd been denied for so long. 'This is the end of our predicament', a happy Charlie and Willie agreed. If only.

At that time, few drovers or overlanders knew the true nature of the channel country—it took many years before it was generally understood. Chris Hammer, in his book *The River*, calls it 'the tin roof country of western Queensland'. 'North-west of Charleville,' he says, 'the southerly extreme of the Asian monsoon falls on land so hard, so unforgiving, that instead of soaking into the earth it runs across the plain, funneling into channels that in turn converge to form a watercourse that becomes definable enough to be given a name. The rivers lose themselves into a series of terminal lakes which quickly explode with plant and animal life'. (*The River*, by Chris Hammer, pp56)

> One hundred years later, when landholders in this area wanted to create a cool garden oasis around their homesteads, they used dynamite to blast holes. They then filled these with truckloads of premium compost and soil to achieve their gardens.

Charlie, with restored physical and mental acumen, took a couple of horses and rode south looking for replacement cattle to purchase. He remembered the good-looking beasts he'd seen on Harry Tyson's *Tinnenburra Station*, near Barringun, when they'd crossed the border into Queensland. At Cunnamulla he telegraphed the McKenzies for money to replenish their herd. How much of the good news of the broken drought did he put in the message? His communications were known for being brief and taciturn. He didn't waste expense— telegrams were charged by the word. Typically a wire would say, 'Will have mob at (name of town) about (date). Send £250 there.' Sometimes he would state the condition of the cattle as 'fairly strong generally'— at other times 'they have lost condition'. The funds having arrived, he also contacted *Tinnenburra*, to arrange purchase of cattle carrying the TY1 brand. Satisfied with the quietness of this newly acquired mob, Charlie hired another drover in Cunnamulla to assist him. When they reached their stock camp back on *Elderslie*, their ZV5 cattle were putting on weight. Excitedly, they prepared to head north again on this constantly interrupted journey. The Nine-mile Waterhole had been their saviour, but it was great to be moving on again, heading towards their Kimberley goal.

Travelling up the Channel Country was effortless compared with what they'd endured for the past six months. Likewise, crossing the

McKinley and Cloncurry Rivers was like their previous holiday adventures. They picked up news of other mobs converging on the Gulf of Carpentaria. Nat Buchanan, renowned bushman and drover, had headed three mobs north from Richmond, Queensland. Charlie and Willie's friends, the Duracks, originally from the Goulburn area too, were ahead with three mobs, totalling nearly 6,000 head, from their *Thylungra* holdings in Queensland. Cooper and Stuckey, pastoralists they knew from the Goulburn district, were also moving their mob north. They were all converging onto the route grandly called 'The Gulf Road'. It wasn't a road, or even a track, but actually a trade route path of the northern aboriginal mobs, which they followed when they traded goods with the Makassan people from Indonesia. The goods these people traded, in return for trepang or beche-de-mer, were basalt spear heads from the Kalkadoons, yellow-red schist from the Arnhem Land groups, and ochre from Central Desert tribes, all bartered across a network established through custom and tradition over thousands of years. Ludwig Leichhardt had followed this route on his epic exploration journey to Port Essington.

Nat Buchanan had taken mobs through previously. Before European settlement, this path may have been four feet wide, and was kept clear with fire and foot traffic. Now, with six thousand-plus head of cattle, the track became a swathe of trampled shrubs and eaten-out grass. Although some local landholders sympathized with the lack of grass for all the mobs coming through, they had to insist the mob only camp for one night on their properties. To ensure this, the manager would deploy one of his stockmen to travel with the mob to stop the temptation of the drovers deviating too far from the track, and/or replacing their previous losses by rounding up some of the pastoralists cattle.

The Leichhardt River was crossed. This red country they were on now, was tougher, treeless, and stony, but there was still plenty of lush tropical coastal growth appearing at the creeks. Compared with what they'd endured further south, it was a land of plenty! It was hard on the feet of the bullocks pulling the wagons though, so Peter

Thompson shod them with half-horseshoes. At the port of Burketown, on the Gulf of Carpentaria, they met Patsy Durack's brother-in-law, John Costello, who was droving 1700 head to flats he'd acquired on the Limmen River. The Duracks were camped at Burketown too, so they all celebrated with an impromptu race meeting—the unspoken inference being they didn't know when, where, or if, they might ever meet again. The unknown still lay ahead of them and it was rumoured that native attacks were plentiful.

While socialising with their friends was an enjoyable diversion, their Burketown experience wasn't totally blissful. They became aware that 'pleuro' (pleurisy) had struck the leading cattle mobs. Apparently, lush young spring growth caused that problem in the area. While there, Charlie and Willie learned how to take blood from some of their cattle less affected by the disease and to separate the serum. This would be injected into the cattle to keep them healthy. Armed with the necessary instruments, they reluctantly headed their mob slightly southwest from Burketown, leaving behind the last real settlement they would see for many months. Temporary brush fences were constructed to hold their mob so they could inoculate them. This substantially hindered their progress, but slowly they made their way behind the other mobs. Those dreaded pleuro camps of the leading mobs with their 'beware' signs had to be avoided. Despite all their precautions, pleurisy still struck some of their cattle.

Into The Territory

Venturing further into swampy country, the salty crocodile infested rivers had to be negotiated. As if the dehydrated bone-dry conditions they endured at the Nine-mile Waterhole weren't bad enough, now opposite wretched conditions prevailed. Humidity, a 90+°F sticky heat, oppressed them during the day. This was the build up season of the tropical North when the humidity intensified before the monsoon rains began. Perspiration dripped from all over their bodies. Merciless mosquitoes gave no respite in the evenings. There was no convivial yarning as they sat around a campfire. Their small netted sleeping tents were their only refuge. There was no repellent. Years later November in the tropics would be referred to as 'suicide month'.

Nights became disturbed and sleepless. Frequently the cattle were either spooked or speared by the locals. The dawn parade was a sorry sight—cattle with torn hides, hanging horns, bleeding wounds. Others were blood-smeared and some were dead. It was heartbreaking. Then came the monsoonal rain, for which they'd longed previously, and it saturated their camp and those on watch at night. For the next four months in the tropical wet season, their herd battled northwest against the muddy terrain and the flooded gulf rivers. They endured the rain and endless humidity, the sandflies and mosquitoes, sometimes held up for weeks at a time. Fever haunted them and they were continually wary of attacks. Crocodiles killed four horses and two steers while they were drinking from a river. Resolutely the team battled across the Calvert, the Robinson, and the

Wearyan rivers. With good reason this area is now known as 'Hells Gate'.

Wearily they trudged on. Eventually a tiny store was reached on the McArthur River where a schooner was anchored, in the area now known as Borroloola. The assisting drover from Cunnamulla, stricken with fever and disenchantment, left them here. Peter 'Bullocky' Thompson, the extremely competent bullock handler and driver who'd been with them from the beginning, became so ill with fever he couldn't carry on. As John Costello had reached his green and grassy river plains a bit further along on the Limmen Bight, Charlie took Peter there for him to rest and recuperate. Returning, he met a Chinese gold digger on his way to Palmerston and, employing his considerable charisma, coerced him into joining them as cook.

Battles with the natives became aggressive, and wretchedly one night this sleeping cook was pinned to the ground with a spear. This was gutwrenching for Charlie and Willie. For the rest of the night they sat, back to back between their wagons, ready to fire at anything that moved. The cattle would rush at the slightest alarm now they were so skittish from frequent attacks. At dawn Willie mustered what remained of the wounded and scattered cattle. Their wagons had been plundered continually, the contents spread haphazardly around their camp. Charlie transferred the most salvageable items from the least roadworthy wagon to the other wagon. Leaving one wagon behind was distressing, considering its sturdy construction and usefulness, but they could not travel quickly enough with two wagons. In the late afternoon Charlie and Willie moved on, just the two of them. Having no alternative to leaving, they left the dead cook where he lay. 'I detest abandoning him', Charlie uttered as they pulled out, 'but we've got no choice. We just have to move away from this nightmarish God-forsaken damned awful place. We'll never survive another night here.'

Reluctantly they headed north towards the Roper River, each of them sleeping only half the night, the other half on watch, then droving, plus bringing up the wagon during the day. It was exhausting and nerve-wracking. Christmas 1884 came and went. They had been on the trek now for 21 months. All Charlie's previous thoughts of a twelve-month trek had been completely expunged. Even though the wet meant they could only move at snail's pace, they finally reached the Roper, where a small community was established. As the river was wide and navigable for several miles inland from the Gulf of Carpentaria, it was a provisioning point for the hardy few that had settled in that area of the Territory.

Matt Kirwan had a store there with bare basics, which allowed Charlie and Willie to replenish their meagre supplies of flour, tea and sugar, but not much else. However, they relaxed and restored some of their *joie de vivre* by spending time with convivial company. The Roper River has a rocky shelf that forms a natural shallow crossing place, with a water hole devoid of crocodiles. A daily soaking of their bodies in this waterhole was bliss. Then, hearing that Charlie and Willie had lost their men, Charles and George Hall left the Cooper and Stuckey party and returned to help them.

All the drovers were following a track that Wentworth D'Arcy Uhr had blazed through the undergrowth 13 years previously. He was the first drover to overland a mob of cattle from Queensland to Palmerston, the freshwater settlement of Port Darwin in the Northern Territory. This followed Ludwig Leichhardt's suggestion to utilise the southern side of the Roper River, rather than the rugged north side in the area now known as Arnhem Land. So they followed the Roper west travelling via Red Lily Lagoon to where springs fed it, described by Charles Hall as '50 acres of beautiful, clear cold water bubbling up from the bowels of the earth'. Paradise! Again, they revitalised their tired bodies by leaping into the springs. After Charlie had washed his hair, beard, and body, along with what remained of his smelly, tattered clothes, he admitted, 'There were times back there I thought we'd never experience this luxury again'. Willie agreed. Their relief to have help, good pasture, and excellent water for the stock and themselves, was immeasurable. It was now two years since they'd departed Hobby's Yards and *Clifford's Creek*.

This area, now known as Mataranka, became immortalised in Mrs. Aeneas Gunn's book, *We of the Never Never*. She had experienced many perilous situations, crossing rivers by slithering up and down banks with her husband, whom everyone referred to as 'the Maluka'.

Just when conditions improved as they'd cleared the Gulf Rivers area, and the constant fear of attack from both natives and crocodiles was abating, Charlie, feeling hot and cold, began shivering and shaking and succumbed to malarial fever. Though fit and strong physically, his metabolism was somewhat susceptible, as he'd previously contracted malaria while gold prospecting at the Palmer River. Their precious supply of quinine was diminishing. Near the Overland Telegraph Line he was so distressed that Willie stepped up, took charge and arranged for him to be taken north to Palmerston. Charlie had been the leader and sheet anchor of the expedition so he pleaded with Willie to carry on with the trek. Still in his mind was the agreement they had with the McKenzies, who had fulfilled their side of the agreement in providing the stock, plant, equipment and finance. It was up to Charlie and Willie to complete their side of the bargain. 'I'll get there even if I finish with only my rifle, and myself,' Willie devoutly promised. But his innermost and unspoken thoughts kept nagging at him about Charlie, 'Will I ever see him alive again?'

Willie detailed Charles Hall to pilot Charlie to get treatment somewhere, possibly Port Essington. Riding beside him, Hall would hold his arm and bridle rein, steadying him in the saddle. After the first day's ride they encountered two prospectors who were also heading north along the rutted but defined track. For a sizeable consideration they agreed to take care of Charlie and see him safely to Palmerston. There a Mr. Sullivan undertook to care for him and brought him over the worst of his fever with a reported temperature of 107.8F°, perilously close to the human limit. The families back at *Clifford's Creek* were so concerned, as Willie had informed them by telegram of Charlie's condition, that Dan was dispatched to Darwin to escort Charlie home. Together they caught a steamer to Sydney, from where they travelled back to *Clifford's Creek*.

Meanwhile Charles Hall had caught up with Willie, George, and the cattle mob now travelling west, making for the Willaroo Station area in the centre of the Territory. At Battle Creek, George Hall was the next to succumb to malaria. He left for Palmerston to receive treatment, too. Willie took on Joe Edmonds, previously the head stockman with the Cooper and Stuckey mob, along with a Chinese cook.

Meeting up with Duracks

Veering to the southwest, the country was first rough and heavily timbered in places, but emerged into excellent savannah plains where the stock had plenty of feed. Creeks provided water, and the pink/mauve/blue hills were scenic. But this pleasant landscape, providing good food for cattle, bullocks and horses, didn't provide anything for the men to eat. Their provisions were low now—salt beef, ships biscuits, and damper made with weevil-infested flour, was their diet. The wonderful provisions initially provided by the McKenzie women were now totally depleted, having either been consumed or plundered. They hadn't been able to re-provision adequately for several months. Auspiciously, then, they came across fresh tracks. Willie construed these to be of the Durack party. Attaching a water canteen to his saddle and leaving Joe Edmonds in charge, he rode ahead hoping to catch up and borrow some supplies. It was late at night before he reached the Victoria River and saw their camp.

'Long Michael' Durack recalls that meeting:

'Now here's something you may never have heard before. Except for a bit of luck I might have gone down in history as "the man who shot Willie MacDonald". All the way along they had kept in touch with the MacDonald party that had at times been only a stage or two behind, and they already knew the story of their many misfortunes. It was late at night when he saw our fire by the riverbank and not wishing to create a disturbance had tied his horse to a tree some distance away and walked up to the camp. He had long since worn out his last pair of stockman's boots and

was barefoot so it was little wonder that I had mistaken the quietly moving figure for a native. I had my finger on the trigger before he spoke up. Willie had eyes like a cat in the dark and he must have spotted me under my net. "Put that rifle away there, Durack" he said. "It's only another poor bloody drover like yourself, and a hungry one at that." We weren't too flush with tucker ourselves, but we gave him enough to carry them on to the Ord.'
'Kings in Grass Castles' by Mary Durack.

'Long Michael' Durack tried to dissuade Willie from continuing the trek with his stock, wagon and encumbrances. 'There's rugged ranges out past the Ord. God knows where you could get through. Forrest is the only one who has and he didn't have cattle and a wagon'. But Willie, barefoot and haggard, was adamant he was going on regardless. He spoke of his promise to Charlie, and his determination touched Michael Durack. 'Can't see a man alone in this country. Bring your mob up and we'll all travel along together.'

So, the merged parties travelled in sync, each striving towards their individual goals of well-watered productive grassy plains. They followed the majestic tree-lined Victoria River, to the junction with the abundant Wickham River, near where Victoria River Downs station is situated now. The only possible course to the other side of the range, though, was through the Wickham Gorge. This awesome place has red, terracotta, and orange-ochre rock walls rising straight up on either side of the river, with a narrow rocky access down one side. Although the cattle were used to rough going, they stumbled along through the unfamiliar sounds echoing in the ravine. They bellowed their misery while the drovers' steadying voices and cracking whips made a confusion of sound. Only the stockmen's skill prevented disaster. 'Take it slowly', Willie directed his men, so they let the cattle pick their way through the gorge, resisting the urge to force them. Progress was slow and cautious as the loose river rock was negotiated, and they slithered on the flat rocks. The cattle's bellows reverberated back and forth in the unfamiliar acoustics of the gorge walls.

The wagon's construction, the drover's skill, and the bullocks' strength, were tested to the limit.

Of all the challenging stages they had travelled, none was more fearful, or beautiful, than the cliffs of Wickham Gorge. Naturally the local indigenous people were terrified. They had never seen or heard anything like this conglomeration. Their defense was to roll boulders over the sides of the cliffs to skitter the cattle. Down-to-earth Willie instructed his men to bide their time, and not to engage in any conflict. 'Take it slowly,' he repeated as they cautiously picked their way along. With so many challenges to overcome, it's doubtful that the overlanders appreciated the colourful and beautiful cliffs of the gorge—it was just another obstacle to be surmounted with a few more challenges thrown in. They were totally focused on accessing the green grassy plains way beyond.

Once through that beautiful but nightmare gorge the next challenge was the Rudolph Range. Fortuitously that proved not so arduous. Once over that range, the vegetation was mainly tea-tree thickets and bulwaddie scrub—they'd left behind the lush growth on the savannah plains in the Territory. But cattle feed was plentiful. Again flat-topped pink/blue/mauve mesas modified these vast, flat plains. Flocks of parrots, cockatoos and wild ducks were abundant. Also finches, wild turkeys, and brolgas, but kangaroos and wallabies were scarce.

Slowly the stock of the respective parties wound their way up and over the ridges into the Victoria-Ord River divide, which was not too challenging. That achieved, they strolled through the beautiful limestone spring country along Black Gin Creek to the upper Ord Valley, and down the Stirling River to the Negri.

Now they were now in Western Australia! Joyfully they reached the Ord River. At its junction with the Negri, Michael Durack dismounted and stood on the land that was his destination. It was 25 September 1885. This emotional moment had been in the planning for more than five years. The Duracks had driven their stock from Thylungra, near Quilpie, in the Channel Country of Queensland.

One hundred years later the Australian public became aware of the nearby amazing geological beehive features of the nearby Bungle Bungle Range, producing its spectacular red, orange and yellow colour show at sunset, in what is now the Purnululu National Park.

After a few days of much-needed rest Willie, Tom Hayes, Long Michael, and Big John Durack rode to Wyndham, which had just been declared a town, Willie taking three packhorses for their supplies. To his immense surprise and delight, young brother Dan was there. 'I've brought funds and news of the family. Charlie's recovered!' he announced. Willie struggled to hold his emotions in check, his relief overwhelming.

With Dan's help they stocked up their provisions and made their way back to the cattle—but now Willie began to falter. By the time he reached the Duracks' land, he was shaking in malarial delirium. He refused to leave but finally the decision was made for him. He was too ill. The last of the original droving team wasn't able to go any further. Leaving strict instructions with Joe Edmonds to hold the cattle there until their return, Dan and Charles Hall escorted Willie back towards Port Darwin. The going was slow, as the wet had set in—again.

They rode on until they reached a rough shanty and here they received food and shelter until a coach conveying gold, with a police guard, agreed to transport them to Palmerston. It was three weeks before a ship was available to convey Dan and Willie back to Sydney. Once on board, Willie's condition improved immediately without the stresses and strains that had been his daily grind for the past two and a half years. Youth was on his side—he was still only twenty-seven.

The Goulburn Agricultural Show was on. Willie and Dan arrived there and revelled in the company and camaraderie of their mates. Charlie joined in too. How long since they'd seen their friends? How much of their nightmarish experiences did they divulge? Weren't their struggles best forgotten?

Back to the Trek

With their health somewhat restored, Charlie and Willie returned to Wyndham by ship and rode south to the Negri River, to collect the waiting cattle. But where were they? The area where the cattle had been camped was trampled and eaten out, but there was no sign of their mob!

This letter from G.O'S, written to a newspaper in 1937, (a full copy is in the addendum) explains: 'I was sent out by MacDonald to assist Joe. Riding from Port Darwin I picked up a blackboy, and arrived at the camp on the Negri on 27 December 1886 [sic]. A week or so later we collected the cattle and made a start, our party consisting of Joe Edmonds, two blackboys, a Chinaman cook, and myself. Besides the cattle and horses we had a bullock team that gave us a lot of trouble, as there was no road after passing Ord River Station—furthermore, we had no maps. All we had to guide us was a scratch plan of the country.' Maybe they didn't have the equipment, or skills, to navigate to the Longitude and Latitude number—if that information had been given to them.

So Charlie and Willie dashed back to Wyndham and caught the *s.s.Menmuir* to Derby, arriving on 13 May 1886. The Derby police records show C. MacDonald, W. MacDonald and a McDonald with no initial, were passengers. It is presumed this was Jack McDonnell—'McDonald' sometimes but no relation—who Charlie and Willie met en route, and who they engaged to help them finish the cattle drive. He stayed on with them for several years.

Acquiring supplies and meeting the few locals in Derby occupied their attention. But Willie, having observed the immense grassy plains of the Durack country, was eager to acquaint himself with the acres waiting for them between the Margaret and the Fitzroy Rivers and to locate their cattle and equipment.

Six days later on 19 May 1886, also recorded by the Police, Joe Edmunds arrived in Derby with some packhorses, having ridden there after delivering the cattle to the confluence of the Fitzroy and Margaret Rivers. Was this the first Charlie and Willie knew their stock, equipment and paraphernalia had arrived at the tree marked F136? What a relief it would be to know for sure.

No time was lost in advising relatives and authorities that their goal had been achieved. A telegram was sent to their family back at *Clifford's Creek*. Learning that the cattle, horses and bullocks were grazing on the abundant grassy plains alongside the Margaret River and that Charlie and Willie were safely back in the Kimberley required a good-spirited celebration! Donald, their father, and siblings John, Catherine, Duncan, and Annie, constantly wondered if this day would ever come. Dan had more confidence, as he'd originally investigated the Kimberley, although he was also aware of the perils and diseases prevalent in the tropics. Hadn't he escorted them both back to Goulburn to recuperate from their significant bouts of malaria? Ann, the mother of this family, had died in 1862 after Dan was born, and brother Archie died when he was 16. The next year, 1887, Donald Senior tragically had a heart attack whilst riding his horse, was thrown off, and died. This brawny, visionary, and enthusiastic Scotsman, who meticulously planned the expedition, never saw the destination or his dream realised.

On 24 May 1886, Charlie sent a telegram to John Forrest, Commissioner of Lands, in Perth:

'I beg to inform you that I have reached my country on the Margaret and Fitzroy Rivers overland from NSW and Qld with 500 head of cattle. This is the first mob that has ever reached the Fitzroy and Margaret country overland and I consider I have opened up a track which was hitherto thought impracticable and the first class condition that my cattle have reached the country will dispel all fears as to the state of the route.'

Did Charlie and Willie feel fulfilled that their historic and unparalleled stock trek had been completed? Willie had left instructions with Joe Edmunds, and the Chinese cook, to hold the stock on the Ord until he arrived back. When another drover arrived with two young native men, did Edmonds think this was the intended droving help? As one of the young men knew the area, they'd rounded up the mob and headed west following first the Mary River and then the Margaret River towards its junction with the Fitzroy. Or had Joe become bored with just tailing out the cattle daily? After all, he was an extremely competent drover.

Destination Reached

It seems 'G.O'S (aforementioned) was camped at the F136 destination with the cattle when Charlie and Willie, along with some others en route to the Halls Creek gold diggings, arrived.

A fresh diary started by Charlie, in a masterpiece of understatement, simply states: 'Arrived here June 3rd 1886 and called it Fossil Downs.' The name ensued from the numerous fossil shells and fish found in the petrified reef that runs through the property. Alexander Forrest had blazed the tree, F136 here, at Longtitude 125.90, Latitude 18.17.

Sheer guts and determination, strength of mind and resolve, fortitude, grit, pluck and stamina, are all appropriate descriptions of the attainment of these two stoic but humble young men. Their achievement has little comparison. It has been described, in *Australian Geographic*, as 'the longest and most tedious journey ever undertaken in the history of Australian pioneering'. Charlie and Willie stuck to the task at hand with never a thought of quitting, despite every adversity imaginable being thrown at them. They endured drought, humid soggy wet seasons, cattle pleurisy, malaria, bodily and mental strain, hostilities at times from both white and black people, bureaucracy, lack of ready communication, lack of funds, their stock perishing, stores being pillaged, and a lack of proper maps and information. Perhaps, also, they lacked an intimate knowledge of Australia's northern dry weather and tropical climate.

In fulfilling their father's dream and vision, the cattle had been driven 3500 miles, taking three and a quarter years. No cattle have ever been overlanded as far before or since. They arrived with 370 head of cattle and 13 horses, plus the bullocks, some of which completed the complete crossing of Australia. The progeny of the original herd, plus purchases on the way, made up the cattle number. One of the milking cows survived the entire journey along with a chestnut gelding with a white star on its forehead on which one of the McKenzie children had previously learned to ride. A wind-up gramophone, along with a leather water bag also survived the journey and both have pride of place now atop the staircase in the Fossil Downs homestead. Although it is always referred to as a 'water bag', Bob MacDonald, a grandnephew, maintains it couldn't possibly have held water. It has rivets in it! That must have held their OP bottled rum.

Naturally as family lore is passed down orally the thread can become distorted in the telling. There are different versions of who arrived at the confluence of the mighty Fitzroy and Margaret Rivers. Were Charlie and Willie imprecise in the details? They didn't seem to consider their achievements particularly notable at the time. They avoided publicity as much as they could.

In *The Longest Cattle Drive*, written one hundred years after the epic trek, Charles Kimberley MacDonald (grandson of Willie MacDonald) states it was Willie who finished the long drive with the cattle. The MacDonald family generally believes this.

However, Keith McKenzie records yet a different account. In his version of the trek, *The Longest Droving Trip*, published in September 1980, pp. 90, he writes:

'Over the years much fiction has been written about the MacDonald expedition.... Not one man who started with the expedition was still with the mob when it reached Fossil Downs. Mr. Charles Hall reported that Willie MacDonald was with him and two others when they came away from the Ord River about March 1886 [sic] [Should be March 1885] to catch a ship at Darwin in order to get back to Goulburn to recuperate. After a few months spell Willie went back and completed the task he set out to do in March 1883, and for the success of the expedition the biggest share of the credit must go to Willie MacDonald.'

But Police records show both Charlie and Willie MacDonald arriving in Derby together on 13 May 1886.

Some possible scenarios:

Willie's grandson, Charles Kimberley MacDonald, contends that Willie arrived with the cattle, but he doesn't give a date. Does he infer that Willie arrived after Joe Edmonds had delivered the cattle? Keith McKenzie says: 'Not one man who started with the expedition was still with the mob when it reached Fossil Downs'. Police records at Derby record both Willie and Charlie arriving there, by ship, in May 1886.

G.O'S, in a letter to the Townsville Daily Bulletin in 1937, (printed in full in the addendum), says he and Joe Edmonds got to F136 with the cattle in April 1886, with the help of two native boys, and they made a camp on the Margaret River flats. Joe took the packhorses and went on to Derby, a ride of three weeks, where he appears to have met both Charlie and Willie in May 1886. Joe didn't return from Derby. Did Joe consider 'the help' had arrived when G.O'S and two native boys turned up, back on the Ord, where the cattle were to be held for the MacDonald's return?

Gordon Buchanan, who became a friend of the brothers, says in *Packhorse and Waterhole*, it was Charlie who arrived with the cattle. Charlie's new diary entry 'Arrived here June 3rd 1886 and called it 'Fossil Downs' raises questions. F136 was 9 miles from the Geikie range where the fossils are most visible. Had Dan discovered them on his reconnaissance and suggested that name to Charlie? Or G.O'S? Without the diaries we can only guess at whom and when.

There could be other scenarios. Historians agree that information is sketchy on the movement of the cattle heading west after leaving the Overland Telegraph Line when Charlie had returned to Goulburn for recuperation.

It's doubtful we'll ever know precisely who arrived with the cattle at Survey Mark F136, Longitude 125.90E, Latitude 18.17S, and on what date. Nevertheless, it still remains a record-breaking trek of epic proportions, the like of which has never been exceeded, and unlikely ever will be. Willie and Charlie MacDonald completed their historic journey almost half a century after Archibald and Sarah MacDonald had sailed in the *Boyne* to a new land. Grandfather Archibald would have been proud of them. If only the diaries, detailing one of the great pastoral journeys of our history, may one day be found.

Addendum

The following letter appeared in the Townsville Daily Bulletin in 1937 and is reproduced in full. It would appear to be written from memory 50 years after the trek, and therefore in two cases the years mentioned are incorrect.

"Re the death of Joe Edmonds, mentioned in a recent 'Track', you state he went out with cattle in the [eighteen] seventies to stock Durack's North-west Australian country, but that is not correct. I went out there at the same time as Joe, and we both joined up with a mob of cattle at Burketown. These beasts were in charge of the late Sam Galloway, and they were being sent to stock the Willeroo country. It was late in 1884 when we started out, but I left the mob at Roper Bar. Joe saw them through to Willeroo, then he joined up with the McDonald Brothers, who were taking cattle out to stock the Fossil Downs country at Kimberley (WA). There were two McDonald Brothers, who were taking cattle to the same place, and Joe got the job because the elder brother contracted fever along the route and had to leave for the south. When they reached the Negri river the remaining brother also went down with fever and went south, leaving Joe Edmonds in charge of the cattle. I was sent out by McDonald to assist Joe. Riding from Port Darwin I picked up a blackboy, and arrived at the camp on the Negri on December 27, 1886. [sic] A week or so later we collected the cattle and made a start, our party consisting of Joe Edmonds, myself, two blackboys, and a Chinaman cook. Besides the cattle and horses we had a bullock team, which gave us a lot of trouble, as there was no road after passing Ord River Station; furthermore, we had no maps. All we had to guide us was a scratch plan of the country. Finding suitable crossings for the wagon delayed us. Anyhow we got through, landing stock and bullock team at our destination

late in April 1886. After we had formed a camp, Joe joined up with some prospectors, taking all the packhorses we had, and they headed for Derby. There he met both of the McDonalds who had come up with the first boatload of diggers for the Kimberley rush. They took Joe's packhorses, and with some other men who had accompanied them from the south, they arrived at the camp in May 1888 [sic], with a good supply of much-needed rations. Joe Edmonds did not accompany them. He took a boat from Derby, and thus ended one of the longest—if not the longest—trips ever connected with cattle. Starting from Goulburn (NSW) and finishing at the Margaret River (Kimberley), the cattle were three years and three months on the road, and not one man that started with them saw the trip through. Joe Edmonds was a splendid bushman, a good tracker, and handy at anything where bushcraft was concerned. He must have been well over 80 years of age at the time of his passing. I only met him on one occasion since those old days, and most of the men we knew so many years back have also passed away. The McDonalds are all dead, and they were fine fellows. There was a big family of them, and they lived at Clifford Creek, 81 miles from Goulburn (NSW)."
Townsville Daily Bulletin Thursday 8 April 1937

G. O'S. Letter (His full name is unknown.) It would seem this letter is written from memory some 50 years later, thus some of the dates don't confirm other dates.

Western Australia becomes a State

The State of Western Australia was gazetted in 1932, but still referred to as Swan River Colony for many years afterwards. Mr. T. Traine, a pioneer of the NorthWest, experienced the rigours of the east-west trek from the Barkley Tableland to Roebourne in 1889. In 1937 he related: 'The first time I saw the name Western Australia was on the side board of a bullock wagon. It was in Goulburn, New South Wales. A wheelwright had just finished painting the words, Bound for Western Australia, on the sideboard when I happened to pass. I was curious to know more and asked him some questions. He told me that two young men were leaving the district in a few days with a mob of cattle to stock country in West Australia. A short time later I saw the party set out with the loaded wagons and 1,000 head of cattle. From what I heard and saw later I am of the opinion that those men did the longest trek ever done in Australia and probably in the world.' *The West Australian 24 February 1937*

The Goulburn Presbyterian Church is situated now where the wheelwright's premises were.

Drovers' 3000-Mile Trip – The Longest Cattle Drive

Mr. Young, secretary of Goulburn and District Tourist Bureau, wrote in 1937: Two brothers, Charlie and William MacDonald, undertook to drove 400 female cattle from Tuena, near Goulburn, to the junction of the Fitzroy and Margaret Rivers (WA), a distance of 3000 miles, and left in March 1883, with 30 horses, two bullock wagons, and cattle. They struck a severe drought in Queensland, and lost many of their cattle, but replenished the herd in Queensland.

They arrived at their destination late in 1886, thus taking nearly three and a half years. This, I think, constitutes the world's longest droving record. In the last six weeks of their journey they moved through unexplored country, and though they encountered many blacks, they made friendships continuing to the present with the natives. The object of the journey was to establish a station, which was called 'Fossil Downs.'

The present manager is a nephew of those two pioneers, and Fossil Downs, with about 1,000,000 acres, is stocked with the progeny of part of the 400 head, which left Goulburn so many years ago. The wagons used on the trip are still at work.

Goulburn is proud of its early settlers. Such names as the Duracks, Costellos, Sheehans, and MacDonalds should be engraved in gold on the pages of Australian history.'

The Burrowa News 26 July 1935

Exploration from across the Continent (From a Correspondent)

There have been many great and thrilling feats of exploration and bushmanship in and about the wilds of Australia recorded, but news has just come to hand of the longest, most extraordinary, and daring, yet successful trip that has ever been or probably ever will be done in this island. It dwarfs and eclipses all others of its kind.

To travel from the frontages of New South Wales through Queensland, the Gulf country, and Northern Territory country, into the heart of the wild and far-famed Kimberley district of Western Australia with packhorses would be a very extraordinary feat indeed; but to travel with something like a thousand head of cattle and other stock, together with a wagon and team of bullocks, and at the same time exploring the country, is truly something wonderful and unparalleled.

This has been accomplished by the well-known Brothers MacDonald of Goulburn, New South Wales, who are real typical bushmen and who possess so remarkably and forcibly the pluck, stamina, and determination so necessary for the undertaking of such a journey. What with long dry stages, severe tropical heat, the dreaded fever and ague, together with the bodily and mental strain, they naturally of course went through some great suffering; but Nil Desperandum was, and is, imprinted on their foreheads and they were equal to their task, which took nearly three years to accomplish. The stock are now located on their country, which is on the Margaret River, Western Australia.

We feel sure all Australia will wish success to such worthy pioneers. Their names will be handed down in the history of exploration and travels of Australia, as they have now opened a route across the continent for stock, which hitherto was generally thought to be impracticable and impossible. They travelled over all descriptions of country, some good, others bad and indifferent. Blacks were on the whole friendly. Wagon, cattle, and teams are all in good order. *Derby (Western Australia) 24th May 1886.*

In the 1950s, Hollywood Westerns made the migrations to Oregon and the northwestern territories of the United States more familiar to many Australians than the exploits of their own pioneers. These tough, laconic overlanding stockmen who drove the first mobs of cattle across the continent without defined tracks and assured watering points, have not always received the recognition they deserve. Nat Buchanan, Patsy Durack, John Costello, Darcy Wentworth Uhr, and the MacDonalds along with many others, pushed huge mobs of cattle over scarcely defined tracks. They covered distances and faced hardships unparalleled in any other country. The seemingly unending droughts in Queensland, fever, and crocodile-haunted swamps of the Gulf country, the spears and fires lit by the understandably savage aboriginal tribes of Queensland and the Northern Territory, were just some of the challenges. Yet, with only coordinates to guide them, and a sketch map—no GPS, or any communication or specific directions—they eventually found their destinations in the Northern Territory and the East and West Kimberley.

Establishing the Station

Now that the brothers were reunited with their cattle and the remaining wagon, and with the excitement of exploring their land, the torrid years on the trek were gradually dissolving in their mind. Willie wasted no time in heading back to Derby. On 5 June 1886 he set out with the wagon to stock up on rations and anything else he found there that would be useful. Three weeks later, the inhabitants of this new settlement mobbed him when he arrived. It's now possible to travel this stage, albeit by a slightly shorter route, in less than three hours. The wagon was the first four-wheeled vehicle to travel from one side of the continent of Australia to the other.

Back at Fossil, how long did it take the brothers to discover the extent of those grassy black and red-soil plains, the abundant rivers and permanent soaks and waterholes, the spectacular ranges, gorges, and gullies? The country is both open downs and hilly, typical of the great Kimberley pastoral topography, and is watered by the Fitzroy, Margaret, and Leopold rivers and several creeks, including Horse, Pothole, Nhilabublica, Middle and Boab, as they were named eventually. The Margaret River borders the southern portion, the Leopold the eastern, whilst the mighty Fitzroy River is its northern and western boundary.

The Louisa River also runs through the property, and bounds the extreme southern end, while Horse Creek runs from east to west watering much of the eastern portion. The southern portion of the lease is a narrow strip of country running due south and only a few miles wide, terminating at the southern turn of the Louisa River. In

2013 this portion was relinquished from the Fossil Downs lease, and taken up by Mt. Pierre station.

When did Charlie and Willie find the recently named Geikie Gorge on their western boundary? Did they know that boundary on the Fitzroy River was ten miles long, while the eastern boundary on the Margaret River was forty-five miles? How much of the run had Dan explored on his reconnaissance trip?

With the addition of other adjacent leases, Fossil Downs eventually became one of the biggest pastoral leases in the Kimberley. It eventually comprised 1,064,000 acres. Bob MacDonald, a grand-nephew of the overlanders, who became the Fossil Downs consultant agronomist in the 1980s, maintains that a third of the station is excellent grazing country, another third is quite good, and the remaining third, being rocky ranges, is too difficult and time-consuming to muster nowadays. 'Abundance of river and bore water is its greatest asset,' he says. Ruefully, though, he wonders why Dan didn't recommend the family apply for the leases further south, where Gogo station is situated. That pastoral lease is not situated near ranges and has more river flats and black-soil plains, and can therefore carry more stock. Dan recommended that area to the Emanuel family. Did he climb the Geikie Range and assume the whole run was like the grassy green plains stretching out before him? Or had he explored those ranges and found all the natural creeks and rivers?

Even in 1886, the year Charlie and Willie arrived, visitors called in. The track to Halls Creek 'where gold was growing' supposedly, ran alongside the Margaret. This unnamed gentleman, writing in a rural paper, was unimpressed with the lack of gold in Halls Creek, but very impressed with the potential at Fossil Downs, and its stock:

> 'I visited the Fossil Downs station, belonging to the Messrs. MacDonald, where I was very kindly entertained by those gentlemen,' he said. 'Mr. Chas MacDonald informed me that the run is capable of carrying from 80,000 to 100,000 sheep all the year round,' he continued, 'so the proprietors can congratulate themselves upon

having secured some of the best country in Western Australia. I was sorry to leave the station'.

What criteria did Charlie use to decide where to set up his house and headquarters? He had little practical knowledge of the seasonal conditions then, and whilst in later years the aborigines would advise on flood levels, at that time relations between white and black were still not cordial, but not because of any hostility intentionally engendered by the brothers. He chose a site near the tree where Alexander Forrest had blazed F136, where there was clear vision in all directions. This homestead structure was made of the ubiquitous galvanised corrugated iron they had carried with them, on the wagon, from Goulburn. The house consisted of a through passage with two rooms on either side of it, a veranda front and back and perched on the black-soil plain. Gradually other buildings and shelters needed for storing their equipment were erected.

However, in choosing the black-soil plain adjacent to the Margaret River for their headquarters, other problems were encountered. When wet, these plains are notorious and impassable to motorised vehicles. Black gluey mud sticks to everything! At that time their transport was by horse. Of greater concern to them was safety and having vision in all directions. The clear plains provided this. Charlie, there by himself once, thought he was about to be ambushed by a posse of natives, which happened occasionally. Preferring to foster good relations with them, he decided against firing a shot, and instead placed the gramophone, which they had brought on the trek, outside on the veranda, wound the handle, and played a shellac-coated record at maximum decibels. The natives had never heard musical sounds like that before and scarpered in fright!

After their tortuous time back in the drought in Queensland, plus attacks by natives and crocodiles, and the prevalence of fever to which they both succumbed, the tranquil abundance of grass and water here for their stock, and the relatively peaceful relations with the indigenous people which they planned to foster, must have helped expunge those nightmare conditions from Charlie and Willie's minds.

Cautiously the aborigines became accustomed to Charlie and Willie's presence, and appreciated the friendly gestures they made by the food they left out for them. This Gooniyandi tribe was generally peace loving, so gradually cordial relations were established. That pattern continued for at least the next 130 years. The indigenous people were always welcome to occupy the land they had roamed for generations, and were never hassled to vacate it.

Mr. George Craig, a representative of the Kimberley Squatting and Investment Company, visited Fossil Downs in 1887. His report of the property was enthusiastic: 'The cattle, which had been driven right through from New South Wales, and their increase, were not only in good condition, but really fat,' he wrote. He commented that the horses also looked well. His inspection of the run revealed salt bush and blue bush in large quantities, plus other fattening grasses, such as Mitchell, blue, burley, couch, silver and a grass much resembling Mitchell grass. He decided to call it 'Kimberley Grass'. *Western Mail Saturday 5 February 1887, Page 19*

After the MacDonald lease on the Lansdowne block on the northeast boundary of Fossil was relinquished many years later, it became part of the Quilty holding. If Rod and Edna Quilty were returning from the Derby direction, they were able to drive right through Fossil, that track being a much shorter route home to Lansdowne for them than round through Halls Creek, and Springvale and Bedford stations. In 1999, after publishing her book *Nothing Prepared Me,* unprompted, Edna commented, 'Fossil Downs was a most beautiful property.' By then, of course, fencing and yards had been constructed, bores drilled, windmills and water-troughs installed, and tracks graded to strategic areas. Or was Edna just thinking of those abundant black soil plains with the waving Mitchell grass?

Crocodile hunters also knew about the track through Fossil, and sometimes requested permission to use it. Saltwater crocodiles could still be hunted until 1970.

In 1893, a horse went missing from the station:

> £10 REWARD. STOLEN, off Fossil Downs Station, one BAY GELDING, about 15 hands high; small star on forehead, branded Z over 5 near shoulder. Any person giving information that will lead to the conviction of the thief shall receive the above reward. E.J.HARRIS, Mt. Andersen, West Kimberley, WA. May 29 1893. Does this indicate stock duffers were around, even then?

Charlie and Willie's 'Ord River' friends, Patrick, and 'Long Michael' Durack had closed a deal to deliver a mob of 500 bullocks to Derby from Argyle and Lissadell stations, 470 miles west from their Negri River holding. From Halls Creek, the East Kimberley station men were on new ground. All their previous trekking had been either north to Wyndham on Cambridge Gulf, or east through the Territory to Queensland, and initially from Goulburn, NSW, when they headed north to take up country near Quilpie in Queensland's Channel Country. Charlie and Willie welcomed them to their modest dwelling and they discussed the problems of the industry. Willie said they had been living on credit since they arrived at Fossil, and looked like continuing to do so for another couple of years. A storekeeper in Derby had carried them all that time, 'But he won't regret it', he avowed. 'Every penny will be paid back now the markets are opening up'.

Initially there was only a small local market for meat—then gold was discovered at Halls Creek! By selling beef to the diggers who were en route to their perceived 'El Dorado', the brothers realized from £30 to £40 per head for their few steers. That rush was soon over, so it wasn't until 1895, nine years after their arrival, that natural herd increases and market conditions enabled a profit, but the two tough overlanders stuck it out. They had a bitter struggle to develop their property, as the country was still wild, their cattle were either attacked or struck by disease, and supplies took months to arrive. But it had wonderful potential.

Advertisements and comments in the Perth papers regarding Fossil Downs cattle invariably commented on their condition. The following is typical re 125 prime bullocks: 'They have been sold to Connor and Doherty, of Fremantle and, as I saw them just lately en route to the port of Derby for shipment, I can only say that when they get south the Southerners will know what fat beef is,' the writer commented. *Daily News, Perth 16 April 1895*

Likewise, the following advertisement in 1895:

'250 PRIME FAT BULLOCKS, Account Messrs. MacDonald Bros., Fossil Downs station, West Kimberley. As the class and quality of Messrs. McDonald Bros. cattle are so well known further comment is unnecessary.' *The West Australian, Friday 11 October 1895*

This was after the cattle had been droved for three weeks to Derby, loaded aboard ship, and sailed the 1800 miles south to Perth.

Charlie Visits Goulburn

The livestock on Fossil Downs thrived and multiplied but lack of good markets hindered a profit being returned. There were years when the cattle were fat but the prices were thin. Perth only had a small population, and freight costs always eroded their returns. But in 1893, Paddy Hannan discovered payable gold at Mt. Charlotte, near present-day Kalgoorlie. There was an instant demand for beef, and fortunes on Fossil Downs turned for the better.

After ten years at Fossil, and thirteen since the start of the trek, Charlie decided to visit the family back in Goulburn. With no time, or maybe with no inclination, to change his rough and ready clothes, (perhaps it was all he had) he joined his friend Isidore Emanuel at Albany, on a ship that also carried the newly appointed Governor of New South Wales and his entourage. It is said that Isidore thought Charlie should keep to himself as much as possible as his old, tattered clothes were not suitable for mixing in esteemed company. Charlie replied, 'If I'm not fit to mix with the other passengers they can put me in the hold!' He was soon one of the most popular passengers in his quiet, laid-back way. His unprepossessing clothes accentuated his fine, muscular physique, tanned skin and long black beard. Searching questions, and his sardonic sense of humour, provoked his remark, 'I suppose you wonder where, when and why I was caught!' Apparently at Port Adelaide a reporter from the local newspaper offered him £500 for an account of his adventures. He dryly replied 'It's worth £5,000 to forget them'.

He zealously guarded the diaries of the trek when he was back at Goulburn. Unlike later relatives, he disliked publicity and resented the continuous attempts of writers and reporters to obtain either an interview with him, or the diaries. Finally, he deposited them somewhere, remarking to the family subsequently, 'Don't worry about the diaries, they're in a safe place.' To this day, these overlanding records, containing authentic, but presumably brief notes of an Australian historic droving event, have not been located. It is understood they were deposited with Mr. Cope, Charlie's solicitor in Sydney. Apparently, when Mr. Cope died his estate, including papers, went to his niece and nephew. But it is also said that there was a fire at the solicitors' premises and the diaries were lost in flames.

McKenzies Want Out of Partnership

For thirteen years, periodical reports had been sent to the McKenzie family on the activities at Fossil Downs. It took several years before the few hundred cattle that survived the overland trip multiplied into the thousands needed to stock the vast area of the station. Only a few cattle were sold and the McKenzies were providing the finance to pay the running costs plus any development work, therefore the venture was a continuous drain on their financial resources.

Was this one of the reasons Charlie had returned to Goulburn? Had he returned to have a meeting with the McKenzies? Would he convince them that, long term, Fossil Downs would be a wise investment for them? Or, did he want to relinquish the need to report regularly and share any profits? The older children of William and Kenneth McKenzie were either working on the properties of their parents, or on the roads driving their father's bullock teams. In accordance with the custom of these times, the only reward the third generation received was their keep. Naturally they felt at times they were working to fund the MacDonalds. When their fathers and their Uncle Sandy spoke of withdrawing from the partnership in 1896, William, 30, the oldest of Kenneth's family, and Kenneth 25, eldest surviving son of William McKenzie, pleaded to be allowed to go to Fossil Downs and make an on-the-spot investigation before dissolving the partnership. Their parents refused them permission. This was a sad error for the future understanding of both the McKenzies and the MacDonalds.

Keith McKenzie, a grandson, writes: 'The relationship between the two families had always been cordial and the McKenzie partners trusted the MacDonalds implicitly. However, some of the younger McKenzies have harboured the feeling that in the haste to withdraw from the partnership, their elders settled for less than just terms, which might have been avoided had young William and Kenneth McKenzie been allowed to make a personal inspection of the property. Their respective fathers and Uncle Sandy were to blame—not the MacDonalds.'

With the McKenzies wanting out, it seems that Charlie, Willie and Dan, agreed to purchase the McKenzies' shares, on terms over a period of years. The price agreed on is unknown. No doubt for the sake of peace and harmony in their families, the senior McKenzie men deemed it wise not to divulge the terms of settlement. That's how family business was conducted then.

Charlie Appointed a J.P.

The better times now afforded Charlie and Willie some time away from the isolation of Fossil Downs. Later, the terms of Charlie's will indicated he also had property at Goulburn. That could have been a bequest from an estate, or had he purchased it prior to commencing the trek to the Kimberley? He also acquired a house in Derby. Now he'd been appointed a Justice of the Peace in the West Kimberley district, perhaps it would be more convenient to carry out his court duties from this location, and possibly some of the business associated with the station. In his laid-back, laconic way, Charlie would not have sought to become a Justice of the Peace. Was it thrust upon him? It's recorded that if he had to make a judgment and fine someone he invariably paid the fine himself—although sometimes he tossed a coin to see who would pay!

In 1900, an offer to purchase the wagon, the first to cross the continent, came from an exhibitor at the Chicago (US) World Fair, but the offer was refused. Was there too much sentiment attached to it? Was the money not needed now? Did Charlie prefer to avoid the publicity that would emanate from it? It remained in use for many years on the station, the decking being replaced several times. The wheelrims and pull hooks finally became a feature of a gate and fence in front of the house of a future generation.

Regretfully, better times did not benefit the esteemed Charlie for long. Just three years after the settlement with the McKenzies, and again back at Goulburn, Charlie unexpectedly died of pneumonia, having contracted a chill at the Wagga Wagga show. It was only 20 years since he set off on the epic journey to cross the continent.

Newspapers ran obituaries, in which glowing tributes were paid to him: 'The utmost regret has been expressed throughout the West Kimberley district at the death of one who belonged to the best class of Australian pioneer settlers'. And, 'There was probably no-one up there held in greater esteem, and whose loss could be more felt.' *Western Mail, Saturday 21 November 1903*

The family vault in Goulburn confirms this accolade. The citation reads:

> *This wreath is designed as a tribute of respect and affection to Charles MacDonald*
> *From his fellow pioneers in West Kimberley, North West WA.*

Did Charlie have a premonition of his early demise? Did his acute bouts of malaria engender the desire to have his affairs in order? Was he conscious that he had achieved what his father had desired for the family, and wanted his siblings also to benefit from the now Fossil Downs prosperity?

His will made provision for £1,000 to be paid to each of his two sisters, Catherine and Annie, and £750 to his brother John. His property on the Goulburn River in NSW was left in equal shares to his brothers Duncan and Donald. His household property in Derby was left to Willie, as was all his money after payment of his debts and legacies. With Fossil Downs, a half-share was left to Willie, the other half-share being divided between brothers Duncan and Donald. *The Daily News 19 December 1903*

The terms of this will indicate that, up until his death, Charlie was the sole owner of Fossil Downs. Was that because of the pecking order of the siblings? Was it to obviate any possible dissension between all the brothers? There was probably no need of demarcation between Charlie and Willie as they established the property—the atrocious problems encountered on the trek would have brought any niggles to light. So, Charlie bequeathed half the station to Willie, and a quarter each to Duncan and Donald (Dan). That implies Charlie alone bought out the McKenzies. And it also seems that despite Willie putting in as much blood, sweat, and tears, literally, in achieving their Fossil Downs objective, the lease was only in Charlie's name until his death.

The milking cow died in 1903 shortly after the death of Charlie. She was probably the oldest cow in Western Australia at the time, and was the last of the original herd that walked 3500 miles across the continent from Goulburn, NSW, to Fossil Downs, Fitzroy Crossing, WA.

Willie Marries Ida

Was Willie conscious of the aloneness both he and Charlie suffered from when the other was away from the station? Now that Fossil Downs was prospering, he and Charlie had been taking it in turns to have a long break back with their family and friends in Goulburn. On Wednesday 30 April 1902 Willie, back on his break, married Ida Lillian Oliver. The setting was the Goldsmith Street Methodist Church. Ida was a teacher at Raeburn school, and the pupils, all dressed in white, romantically strew the path with rose petals and confetti as Willie and Ida left the church. All the presents, and who gave them, were listed in the local paper, as was the custom at the time. Much of it was silverware.

Had this romance started and blossomed during his previous leave from the station? Or had they known each other prior to Willie commencing the trek to Kimberley, from school days even? Had Ida promised to wait for him?

This quote from JMA's poem, when the trek commenced, highlights Willie's reputation:

Yet, of the twain, the youngest son the lasses most regret,
For Willie was so full of fun and quite the ladies' pet.

Maintaining communication between Fitzroy Crossing and Goulburn could only be by telegram, not a particularly ideal method of maintaining a love affair, sharing sweet nothings, or conducive to planning life together. Even letters could take months to arrive. But what solace it would be to Willie to receive a letter, albeit several weeks old, knowing that someone was thinking and caring about him and waiting for when he returned to Goulburn.

After visiting Tasmania, the newlyweds made their home at Ingleside, Knox Street, Derby. Does this indicate that Fossil Downs was now being run from Derby, 160 miles away? It would be more family friendly to live in an established town such as it was, where some freight, stores, company and communication were available most of the year now. Was Ida unable to cope with the isolation of Fossil Downs, especially since their son, Charles Kimberley, was born the following year? Sadly he was not robust, and it was thought that he would be unable to take on the rough and tumble life of a cattleman in the Kimberley. If medical help were needed for him, Ida would want to access that help quickly. Did she ever visit Fossil?

Willie was either back at the station, or in Derby, when Charlie died. How did this affect him? After the intolerable experiences they'd endured together on the trek to the Kimberley, the brothers must have had an extremely close bond. In fact, it was Willie's devotion to Charlie's instructions that impressed 'Long Michael' Durack, when he'd caught up with him on the trek back in Northern Territory. Willie must have been devastated when he received the news of Charlie's death. There is no doubt that he would miss Charlie dreadfully, both his company, direction and very dry wit.

Now that Willie owned half the property of over a million acres—the size had increased with the uptake of the Cowendyne and Yurabi leases—in combination with two of his brothers, naturally it needed to be grazed to a level appropriate to the state of its development to be financially viable.

Ida had returned to Goulburn with their son, Charles Kimberley, and with only their manager, and occasional visitors calling in, Willie's loneliness at Fossil Downs would be very intense. His social disposition was well known in Goulburn. He must have wondered what was the point in carrying on this isolated and stressful existence? Were the financial returns going to be worth the anguish of living this lonely life?

Nevertheless, he continued with the development plans he and Charlie had agreed on, and he purchased Red Poll bulls from New

South Wales to cross with their original Shorthorn herd. This was designed to improve the colour of the Shorthorns and the milking ability of the cows to better nourish their calves.

The better returns for beef, which had accrued since the discovery of gold in Kalgoorlie, meant that Willie could now employ a manager. Jack McDonnell who'd been with them for many years, had moved on, so in 1907 he appointed Gary Nicholson to run the station. Fortunately, he was still employed there until 1911.

In 1910, just seven years after the death of Charlie, Willie offered Fossil Downs to the firm of Connor, Doherty & Durack, his old friends, for £25,000. The offer was accepted, subject to M. P. Durack's approval.

(Dame) Mary Durack wrote that apparently Willie was in Perth when he made the offer. She felt his reason for wanting out was summed up in one word—loneliness. Also, Willie, along with his son, was not in real good health, and he wanted to be with Ida and Charles Kimberley back at Goulburn. Even with an employed manager to cope with the day-to-day running of the property, he must have felt it was not worth all the stress and pressure that was required to keep the still isolated place functioning and developing.

'M.P.' congratulated his partners on the remarkably good deal they had struck. This would give Connor, Doherty & Durack a strategic base in West Kimberley to argue with the ruling interests there, often in conflict with East Kimberley issues. This general state of satisfaction for the firm was short-lived, however, as a further communication advised that Willie, still in Perth, had died at the Waverley Hospital on 16 July 1910, and brothers Duncan and Donald disputed Willie's authority to sell without their consent. The question then could become a legal one. The Duracks decided to discuss it with their solicitor when he returned from grouse shooting in Scotland.

Meanwhile one of the Durack brothers wrote from the country, saying if the MacDonald family didn't want them to have the place, then let them keep it. 'Haven't we got enough problems on our plate already,' he wrote.

This line of thought must have prevailed, as there was no further correspondence in the Durack files, and nothing to suggest whether they were disappointed or relieved. It could have been the latter, as in *True North: the story of Mary & Elizabeth Durack*, by Beverley Niall, it's revealed that the company fortunes of Connor, Doherty & Durack were always fluctuating. *Also: Sons in the Saddle, by (Dame) Mary Durack: pp 243/4.)*

The news of Willie's death was received with the deepest regret in the North West station world. The accolades accorded him were equal to those conferred on Charlie. They described him as one of the genuine pioneers of the northern cattle industry. He was a notable figure in the rapidly diminishing ranks of the old brigade. The Kimberley was only partially explored and practically *terra incognito* when the brothers arrived. Willie was a fine bushman, possessed a magnificent physique, and was fearless, unassuming, and hospitable, the obituary acknowledged. *The West Australian, 18 July 1910*

Written in the custom of the times, the following commentary appeared in the Goulburn Evening Penny Post, on Tuesday, 2 August 1910:

'The remains of the late Mr. W. N. MacDonald were brought from Perth by the steamship *Koombana*, and the embalmed body was conveyed to Mr. Craig's mortuary chambers in Goulburn. It was enclosed in a leaden casket, which was within a beautifully polished coffin of jarrah, the famous Western Australian hardwood. The coffin was heavily mounted with brass fittings.' Going on to give further intimate details, it stated: 'a glass plate had been inserted and through this friends of the deceased had an opportunity of viewing the features. The plate was afterwards sealed in the usual fashion. At 2.45 pm on Tuesday a short service was held at Mrs. Oliver's. At 3 o'clock the funeral cortege left for the Presbyterian cemetery, where the remains were laid in the family vault of the late Mr. Donald MacDonald, alongside the coffin of his late brother, Charles MacDonald. There were a large number of friends and relatives at the funeral. The surviving brothers and sisters of the deceased are Messrs. John N., Donald, Duncan, and the two Misses MacDonald, of Goulburn.'

Subsequently, the granting of probate revealed that Willie's pecuniary estate was £13,651, along with his real estate of the Derby residence and ½-share in Fossil Downs. Ida, and Charles Kimberley, was to receive the income therefrom. *Geraldton Guardian, 24 December 1910.*

Their fellow settlers in the Kimberley held Charles and William in such esteem that a plaque was erected to them both in the family vault in the old cemetery at Goulburn. They were both outstanding bushmen and were held in the highest regard and respected by all who knew them.

In 1929, the Centenary Year of Western Australia, their accomplishment was recognized in a series of features in the Perth *Sunday Times*, acknowledging those who had played their part in the development of the State. The achievements in 1885 and 1886 of both the MacDonald and the Durack Brothers were noted and it was mentioned that their names were still associated with the country they pioneered.

It went on to say, 'the feat of the MacDonald Bros. is a record in that it penetrated the furthest west. For three years every morning at early dawn, the heads of the bovines were pointed west for something like 3500 miles, and when the distant goal towards the setting sun was eventually reached it was with the original herd much reduced in number.' *Sunday Times (Perth) 14 July 1929*

Charles died aged 50, William at 46. Four years later, Duncan died aged 54. Their older brother, John, who didn't participate in any part of the marathon trek and never visited Fossil Downs, died at age 90 at Crookwell, NSW. Dan, the youngest, was 77 when he died at Goulburn.

Achievements of Donald (snr), Charlie & Willie:

15 May, 1882: Mr. D. MacDonald paid rent on four Kimberley Leases, Nos. K705—708
1883   Establishment of first cattle station in West Kimberley
1886   Completion of the world's longest droving trip
1886   Completed the first crossing of the Australian continent with a four-wheeled vehicle
1901   Charlie was appointed a Justice of the Peace for the Kimberley District, WA
1905   Introduced polled cattle to Kimberley from Bundure, NSW

Duncan and Donald Jnr. (Dan) (1910)

Duncan and Dan were now the joint owners of Fossil Downs, and continued grazing the abundant grassy plains. Cattle numbers had increased dramatically, and some profitable returns accrued. Always mindful of the enormous costs of transporting the cattle to any market, they agreed to continue breeding the best possible animals. 'After all, freight and handling costs are the same whether the animal is top-class, mediocre, or poor', they agreed. To reduce the amount of bruising while cattle were being transported they continued purchasing top-quality polled bulls.

Fossil Downs was the first station to consign a cattle shipment to Perth utilising the newly established State Shipping Service. This was a WA State Government transport initiative, created in 1912 to provide a reliable transport service to and from the northern ports of the State. Selling agents in Perth always advertised the sale of their cattle, with notices appended such as, 'We can with every confidence recommend buyers of store cattle to attend the sale. Reports advise that they are an exceptionally nice line of young bullocks.'
The West Australian 1 August 1911

In 1914, Duncan and Dan indicated their support for the proposed Wyndham Meat Works, which would be a much closer market. This establishment was opened in 1919. By 1915, the station was exporting 1500 live head annually to Java, ex-Derby. This achieved one of the goals of Donald, their father. It had taken thirty years to accomplish.

Duncan was frequently not well having contracted rheumatic fever which, like his brothers before him, left him vulnerable to contracting malaria. This happened on two of his trips to Fossil Downs. He died just four years after Willie. A comment in his obituary in *The West Australian* noted, 'the deceased was much esteemed by those who knew him intimately. He was of a most unassuming disposition. Wearing a long beard and having the appearance of a typical pioneer, fellow travellers on steamers made desperate efforts to obtain snapshots of him, but he was invariably successful in eluding the efforts of the kodakers'. *The West Australian 16 June 1914*

Achievements of Duncan and Dan:

1912   First consignment of cattle per State Shipping Service
1913   Began annually consigning live cattle to Java, Indonesia
1914   Support of Wyndham Meat Works

So, in 1915 Donald (Dan) MacDonald, known in the family as the 'black sheep', was the sole owner of Fossil Downs. As the youngest child of Donald Snr. and Ann's family of eight, did he acquire an overly ambitious trait? Was he over-indulged and spoiled by his older brothers and sisters, considering his mother died when he was an infant? Did his aunts pamper him? Dan was an entrepreneur, not afraid to try new things, and capable of divergent thinking. He loved travelling. In 1881 he had his Christmas dinner at the Negri River, south of Wyndham, where he was prospecting for gold. He had, therefore, been the first MacDonald to visit the Kimberley. No wonder his father had asked him to investigate Alexander Forest's discovery of 'millions of acres of green grassy plains'. He knew the area intimately.

A month after Duncan's death, a special stock sale in Perth reported having achieved a record average price for a consignment of prime bullocks from Fossil Downs, that average price being £14.11s.6d. *Western Mail, 31 July 1914*

As the seasons had been good, more fat cattle were sent to Perth while continuing the annual shipment of 1500 to Java. In 1919, the stock agents W. H. Fielding Ltd sold to the Western Australian

Government on his behalf, 1500 fat bullocks to be shipped from Derby to Wyndham, and treated in the works there. This was the first sale of fat cattle for processing in the Wyndham Meat Works.

In the 1920s, another first was created when Dan, on board a ship in mid-ocean with cattle bound for Java, clinched the world's first cattle deal by wireless with the buyers on shore, when he used the ship's radio to accept an offer for 1500 head. And, unlike his brothers who avoided publicity, Dan was frequently in the headlines:

'Mr. Donald MacDonald, of Fossil Downs station, who gave evidence on Thursday before the Royal Commission investigating the operation of the Stock Diseases Act, was reported in yesterday's issue of *The West Australian* to have said that following a case of pleuro-pneumonia on his station this year he was restricted from exporting cattle to Java. Mr. MacDonald said yesterday that there had never been a case of pleuro on his station, although one beast infected at Midland Junction was wrongly alleged to have come from his Station.' *The West Australian 12 November 1931*

And he continued the family trait of generosity, frequently donating a beast: 'C. H. Fielding. Ltd. sold under instructions from Mr. D. MacDonald, Fossil Downs Station, Derby, one fat bullock, proceeds of which are to be divided between the Children's Hospital and the Waifs' Home.' *Sunday Times Perth, 30 July 1916*

Mail Service

Communication was coming...to the stations! Telegrams, usually referred to as wires, had been the only form of contacting the outside world from Fitzroy Crossing for thirty years. In 1920 the Commonwealth Government announced that a tender had been accepted for the monthly conveyance of mails by packhorse from Halls Creek to Fitzroy Crossing, via Moola Bulla, Taylor's Camp, Lamby, Margaret, Louisa and Fossil Downs. *Sunday Times 21 March 1920.*

Dan contracted Jim Lahey to manage Fossil, as Gary Nicholson had moved on, and Dan didn't want to be bogged down running the station. Was this because Edith, his wife, considered he should share more of his time with her? Their son Archie was born in 1905, Bill in 1910, and daughter Jean in 1915. Was he leaving her in Goulburn to single-handedly raise their children, while he pursued ever-inventive ways to breed and market Fossil Downs beef? His entrepreneurial nature called him to pursue all avenues of beef production and marketing. Did he consider the Kimberley, at that time, not a place to raise a family? Even though transport had improved, the Kimberley was a long way from Goulburn—it still took at least two weeks to traverse by train, ship and vehicle. Health and education facilities were non-existent at Fitzroy Crossing.

In 1916 all records in the local cattle market were broken at a special sale of cattle at Copley's Siding Perth. Unfortunately 49 bullocks were lost on the voyage south so the supply was very short. Dan's cattle were sold first and competition was animated from the outset with bullocks bringing £26 and cows £22.12.6. *Sunday Times 14 May 1916.*

Sale to Kidman

Had the Station become a good cash cow? In 1918, (Sir) Sydney Kidman, the Cattle King, who had many other interests in the area, acquired a half-share in Fossil Downs for £85,000. Was it necessary to sell part, so that Duncan's legacies could be paid out? Was it just a good time, with such spectacular returns, to divest some of the capital gain, and invest elsewhere, particularly a nice home and a sheep property in the Goulburn area? Or was the money needed for some other reason? The selling agents advertised that they had negotiated this half-share sale of the Fossil, Yurabi and Cowendyne leases, comprising 870,000 acres of Crown lands, along with 25,000 head of cattle and 140 horses. *The Sydney Stock and Station Journal, Friday 6 December 1918*

It was then widely reported in 1919 that because of the intense drought in eastern Australia, livestock were being driven overland to Western Australia where there was plenty of good pasture. A mob of 300 horses, were slowly overlanded to Fossil Downs from Kapunda in South Australia. Was this a mob belonging to Kidman? Kapunda was his headquarters then.

Public Auction

The MacDonald/Kidman partnership continued for ten years. But on 13 March 1928, Fossil Downs was advertised for public auction in Sydney, under instructions from Messrs. MacDonald and Kidman, owing to the termination of their partnership:

'Fossil Downs, a famous West Australian cattle station, situated in the rich Kimberley district with an average rainfall of about 23in. will be sold by auction at the Royal Exchange, Sydney, on March 13, without reserve. The area comprises 1,064,633 acres—three adjoining stations worked as one holding—held under pastoral leases, which have till 31 December 1948 to run. Stock consists of about 22,800 cattle, 200 horses, and 60 donkeys, with working plant, etc. The present annual rent is £633.' *Sunday Times 12 February 1928*

Enter Bill MacDonald!

Second Generation: 1928—1963

Bill & Maxine MacDonald

'Fossil's been advertised for sale.' Uncle John MacDonald divulged this news to his nephew, Bill, in Goulburn where they met regularly on Friday mornings. 'What?' Bill exploded! 'How d'ya know?' Uncle John grimaced; 'It's in the Sydney papers.' Bill fumed. 'After all my uncles went through to establish that station, why's my father going to sell it? I knew when he sold a share to that cattle-king Kidman it would bring us grief.'

It was 1928. Bill MacDonald was eighteen, and brought up in the Goulburn area on his father's sheep property. He'd inherited the MacDonald male physique, was good-looking and multi-talented—an acclaimed baritone singer, violin player, actor and a victorious athlete. He'd been educated at the Goulburn High School and the prestigious King's College. Architecture was a spare time study. Designing the impressive grandstand at the Goulburn showgrounds was a very successful accomplishment—100 years later it was still in use. He enjoyed the civilised amenities and recreations of regional life in a prosperous town.

Stories of his uncles' historic achievements in overlanding cattle from Goulburn to Fitzroy Crossing were legendary in the family. His uncles Charlie and Willie were his unsung heroes—he was born the year uncle Willie died. Bill's tirade was prolonged, 'How's it come to this? Are all my uncles' unbelievable efforts to establish a family stronghold coming to nought?'

Dan, his father, had assumed total ownership of Fossil Downs in 1915 after his brothers Charlie, Willie, and then Duncan had died. Fortunes had ebbed and flowed—good years when seasons and prices were favourable followed by those when disease and drought ravaged the herd. And always, the financial costs of running a station in such a remote area, with so little infrastructure, diminished the returns. Freight charges on everything were astronomical. Sending the cattle either to Perth markets or to the Wyndham Meat Works, plus cartage costs on inward supplies and every item of equipment, shrank the proceeds. Trips by ships and trains halfway round Australia were an extra outlay. Additionally, to allow him to keep tabs on his Goulburn sheep farm, Dan preferred to employ a manager at Fossil. Plus, the up-and-down nature of the cattle markets created uncertainties. It was only the immense size of Fossil Downs, now over 1 million acres, providing economy of scale, which enabled any profits.

The deficiency of even basic amenities always added an extra financial burden, as well as everything taking months to arrive. The £85,000 paid in 1918 by (Sir) Sidney Kidman for a half-share in Fossil Downs, no doubt was welcome finance at the time. During the tenure of the partnership, though, big mobs of cattle were sold off the property.

How well did this partnership work: smoothly, or with acrimony? Did the partnership have an agreed termination of ten years? In 1928 Kidman offered his half-share to Bill's brother Archie, so the station could be kept in the MacDonald family, but that option didn't proceed. Instead Dan negotiated an arrangement with Kidman that he re-buy Kidman's share, but the worldwide economic depression then meant he couldn't raise the funds to buy him out, or even to maintain the agreed payments. The spectacular beef prices of ten years previously had taken a monumental tumble. Kidman's finances, at that time, probably needed bolstering too as the depression affected all primary pursuits.

The spirit of his pioneer forbears had a profound effect on Bill. When his uncle Duncan had died in 1915, Bill inherited a legacy from him. 'My uncle made that money on Fossil Downs' he declared, still frowning. 'I will buy the cattle-king out and maintain the station in the MacDonald family'. That decision made, did he loan this money to his father to save on conveyancing fees, or could these leasehold properties only be registered in a person's name who was considered an adult at that time, i.e. twenty-one or older? Or was it to save face? It was widely reported by the agents that Dan, alone, had re-purchased the Kidman share: 'Sir Sidney Kidman's half-interest in Fossil Downs Station, comprising 1,064,000 acres pastoral leases and plant together with 22,800 cattle, 200 horses and 50 donkeys, has been sold to Donald MacDonald of Goulburn. He is an unassuming man, and his home is at Goulburn, New South Wales, where he is affectionately known as 'Dan'. And plain 'Dan' is a millionaire in acres.' *Goulburn Evening Penny Post, 14 March 1928, Geraldton Guardian, 17 April 1928*

> Fifty years later there were occasional donkey shoots on Fossil Downs, as donkeys were declared vermin by then. With the advent of mechanical transport, teamsters who had provided great freight carriage to isolated areas had let their donkeys go free, which led to the unexpected explosion of numbers.

In 1929, news that the *Southern Cross* plane was missing reached Goulburn. Dan sent an urgent telegram to Fossil giving instructions that all of the station hands and blacks [sic] should commence searching for the missing fliers immediately. The station was little more than 100 miles from the Port George Mission where the *Southern Cross* was eventually located. Dan knew that country intimately and realised the difficulties the airmen would have to contend with. He set out immediately by train and boat to travel there to help with the search.

Then nine years later....

Dan Dies

It was reported that Donald (Dan) MacDonald, owner of Fossil Downs station, Derby, and for many years a very prominent cattleman, died at Goulburn, NSW, aged 77 years. Bill, his son, now controls Fossil Downs. In 1929, aged 19 he was taken into partnership with his father who retired to Goulburn where he controlled a fine property. He used to re-visit WA frequently where he had many friends. *Sunday Times 4 March 1937*

Dan had built a substantial home in Goulburn, which he named Yurabi, replicating the indigenous name of the land around the Fossil Downs homestead.

Bill is Manager

Each generation of the MacDonald family has stamped its unique footprint on Fossil Downs. Each has brought a different vision, skillset, and competence. If the first generation made history with their calamitous but world-breaking trek across the continent, along with innovation in marketing and originality in infusing superior blood lines into their cattle, Bill of the next generation inherited his father's visionary traits. He was also noted for his ability to bring publicity to a cause and to accomplish whatever he set his mind to, sometimes against formidable odds. Having sole management of the property meant there was no need to consult with any family members or company directors and shareholders. He was able to tell it like it was!

He wasted no time in going into print in many newspapers. In a long article in *The West Australian* newspaper on 21 September 1933, he pointed out the changes that were required to allow profitable grazing in the Kimberley. He stressed there were millions of acres of well grassed plains there, growing excellent beef and wool, but the infrastructure for the local beef trade and shipping to Perth was woefully lacking. Facilities badly needed an upgrade to prevent unnecessary bruising of cattle. He detailed everything that needed attention from the Derby wharf to and including the saleyards at Copley's Siding and Robb's Jetty in Perth. He questioned the State Government's intention of imposing restrictions that limited supplying Kimberley beef to only the metropolitan area in Perth. Why not other areas? The previously good trade of cattle to Java and Singapore, initiated by his Uncle Duncan, had been lost through the slump in rubber and sugar prices there. Was this Bill's first publicity on these subjects? It most certainly wasn't his last.

Not born to the outback, and with limited experience of outback living, possibly had advantages. Bill wasn't used to putting up with things. He didn't agree with the oft-spoken attitude 'good enough for the bush'! Having enjoyed the civilised amenities and recreations of a regional city life, he would bring them to his new cattle station. So, Bill came to an area that needed an infusion of energy, imagination, ingenuity and style. He had plenty of those attributes.

In 1929, there was little infrastructure beyond the towns of Broome, Derby, and Wyndham. Tracks to Fitzroy Crossing and Halls Creek and up to Wyndham had been graded into earthen roads with gravel applied to muddy patches, and some stone causeways had been created over a few rivers and creeks. But bridges over those rivers—some were 80 metres wide—and telephone communication to all cattle stations, was still fifty years away. Government investigations took place and reports prepared on various projects, and carefully filed away. The reality was there were so few station owners permanently occupying the area—Bill always had plenty to say about that too—and governments didn't have the funds to develop the Kimberley in league with the rest of the country. World War I, along with the overwhelming great depression in the first thirty-five years of the twentieth century had syphoned off the riches that might have accrued from the country's various gold discoveries in the last half of the nineteenth century.

Homestead

Bill's dream was to create a model cattle station. The first Fossil Downs homestead at Old Station, 9 miles northeast of the present homestead, naturally only had the bare basics. It was built in 1886 with the materials carried on the trek. Charlie was not married, and eventually acquired a dwelling in Derby. Although Willie married in 1903, his first 17 years at Fossil was as a single male. Originally, the station homestead was four rooms with a passage down the middle to allow a breeze to drift through, surrounded by a veranda. This was suitable for their initial needs. But by the time Bill was in possession of Fossil Downs, the foundations of this old homestead had provided good fodder for termites.

He bided his time and observed the requirements for families tolerating both the dry and wet season climate in the tropical North. With his architectural training he soon grasped what was required for a comfortable and accommodating homestead. It needed to be strong to withstand the extreme heat and weather in the wet season, which included cyclones and ferocious thunderstorms. Good airflow was needed to keep the place cool, and it needed to face correctly for the scorching sun to not overheat it in the humid wet season, but also keep it warm in winter. The average wet season daily temperature was 115°F. Air-conditioning was not an option then. He became acquainted with the materials available on the property. There were several species of timber, plus stones, flagstones, and sand in the rivers, that were suitable and could be used in the construction. And he was well aware of the need for a barrier between timber and termites—concrete would be used for the downstairs floors. He started drawing up plans. This would not be just an idle home, but a stylish, comfortable, accommodating, working cattle-station homestead. Did he also have in mind it being a memorial to his uncles' record pioneering venture across Australia?

Project Manager would be an apt description of Bill today, along with visionary and entrepreneur, when he set his mind to achieving a plan. He couldn't devote all his time to this project, however, as he still had to keep the station functioning to accumulate the necessary cash flow to achieve his dream. Plus, he was buying the half-share he didn't own from his father's estate. But, his vision of a homestead and headquarters set-up was never far from his mind. He was determined that it would happen.

Jean MacDonald Visits

Bill's brother Archie didn't visit Fossil Downs but sister Jean did in 1937. Travelling to Kimberley from Goulburn took nearly two weeks. She and Bill first caught the train from Goulburn to Sydney, then the interstate train from Sydney to Perth via Broken Hill, Adelaide, Port Pirie, and Port Augusta in South Australia, across the redoubtable Nullarbor Plain to Kalgoorlie and on to Perth in Western Australia. This east-west journey then entailed changing trains four times, because of the different-sized gauges of railway track laid by each state. The standard gauge railway between Sydney and Perth was introduced in 1970.

With no social media, few phone connections, and scant forms of other communication, everything was noted in the local papers: 'Mr. Bill McDonald accompanied by his sister, Miss Jean McDonald, of Goulburn NSW, will leave during the week for his station property, Fossil Downs, in the Kimberley.' *Sunday Times (Perth) 2 May 1937.*

From Perth they boarded a coastal vessel for the 1800 miles to Derby, and finally they motored by truck the 230 miles inland. Ten months later, when Jean returned by air to Sydney, it took four days, a distance that took her ancestors three and a quarter years to traverse with the cattle. That commercial flight today takes approximately 4 hours.

Living in the somewhat primitive conditions at the old homestead didn't faze Jean. She was the first MacDonald woman to visit Fossil Downs—the spirit of adventure ran deep in their family veins. On her return to Goulburn, newspapers sought interviews with her and organisations eagerly asked her to speak about her time in the Kimberley, an area still unknown by most Australians.

Jean was so enthused by her adventure that one newspaper commented she'd discovered a new fascination—'Kimberley scenery and contented Kimberley life'. She described watching the sunrise over the blacksoil plains onto steep escarpments whose minerals glowed red and yellow, and changed to purple as the shadow of the day fell on them. She likened the sides of the gorges to 'clean-cut pieces of fruitcake', and was fascinated with the prolific white eucalypts, the Leichhardt pine with its bright lemon-yellow timber, the red-flowering Bauhinia, and the quaint bottletrees *(Adansonia gregorii)*. Fast-forward fifty years, and the Kimberley is one of Australia's leading tourist destinations. Maybe Jean also stumbled on a first!

Did she suggest to Bill some necessary inclusions in the proposed new homestead? She recounts using the unscreened open shower on the veranda, and whistling loud when she heard someone coming. However, establishing a new homestead and headquarters was not the only thing on Bill's mind.

Still managing to keep up with the latest inventions from the City, Bill had a camera that used colour film. In 1938, and back in Goulburn, he showed these colour films to his mother's friends at her house. The Kimberley scenery, and scale of cattle production in the northern states of Australia, was still generally an unknown and unfamiliar activity then, even for the Australian population.

> Michael Kerr, from Mornington Station, which abounds the northern portion of Fossil Downs, commented once on how hard it is to get those beyond the Kimberley, Northern Territory and Northern Queensland to understand the scale of the cattle industry there. He had in-laws in New Zealand where the dairy, sheep and beef industries are extremely intensive and productive, but even people in those industries there still found it hard to understand the scale of Kimberley operations. The general population really struggled. 'My wife and I go there every two years,' Michael said, 'so I thought I'd give it one more go at trying to explain to her rellies what Kimberley cattle production is all about.' Thinking ahead, he'd taken his

video camera and shot some great footage when mustering was underway back in the season. There were choppers overhead guiding huge cattle mobs several kilometres toward the stockyards and drafting pens. Several mounted ringers were cutting out and drafting the stock in the yards, and there was dust, dogs, horses, cattle and 53 metre-long road-trains everywhere. Michael's plane was nestled nearby. 'That'll give 'em some idea now,' he assured himself, rather pleased with his idea and his photography. The first group he showed it to seemed to undertstand, he thought, until eventually someone asked, 'Where d'ya send ya milk for processing?'

Bill Marries Maxine

Bill had been travelling between Goulburn and Fitzroy Crossing for seven years—sometimes he travelled from Sydney to Perth by ship. On one of these journeys, though, he'd decided to drive, but gave up at Adelaide thinking it would be quicker by ship rather than tackling the track over the lonely Nullarbor. He left his car with relatives in Adelaide and embarked on the first ship that came. Was it fate? He met Maxine Darrow on board, daughter of the late Judge Darrow of Point Piper in Sydney, and Mrs. H. J. Carr. She'd seen him arrive. Attractively blonde and lissome, Maxine was a popular traveler. Bill sought her company at every opportunity. Ever the debonair male, he entered the ship's talent quest one night. Many years later Maxine divulged that she hated people making a public spectacle, and was in trepidation before the concert. When it was Bill's turn to perform she was flabbergasted. He could really sing! In his rich baritone voice, he sang her a love song. She was smitten. Soon afterwards their engagement was announced in numerous newspapers and magazines:

> 'The engagement of Maxine Claire Darrow of Sydney, only daughter of Mrs. H. J. Carr, and the late Mr. R. J. Darrow, of Tararua, Thames, New Zealand, is announced to William Neil MacDonald, of Fossil Downs, West Kimberley, West Australia, second son of Mr. and Mrs. Dan MacDonald, of Yurabi, Goulburn, New South Wales'. *Australian Women's Weekly Saturday 20 March 1937*

Then the wedding announcement:

'Maxine's fiancé is the owner of Fossil Downs, a cattle station which measures just the mere 2,000,000 acres. It was partly owned by Sir Sidney Kidman, but William bought him out. The bride has had no country experience, and can't ride, but is full of enthusiasm for her home. The house has been built of concrete blocks perforated with a large hole through which runs iron piping from ceiling to floor to keep the place cool. The wedding will take place at St. Stephen's Church on March 21.' *Australian Women's Weekly 5 March 1938*

Inaccuracy of facts needn't spoil a good story!

The wedding, celebrated in Sydney on 21 March 1938, was a society affair. Much was made of Bill being sole controller of the largest family-owned cattle station in Australia, and Maxine never having visited the country, let alone the outback in far away northern Western Australia.

Attired in the fashion of the time, her satin-backed lamé gown was of the same handsome fabric as the Duchess of Kent's wedding dress. Embossed with silver and embroidered with seed pearls, the long sleeves finished to a point at the middle knuckle of the hand, and were also edged with seed pearls. Four bridesmaids added to the glamour. The reception was at her home in Longworth Avenue, Point Piper, appropriately decorated with cream roses, cyclamen, and blue flowers to tone with the bridesmaid's gowns. Two days later Bill and Maxine departed Sydney on the ship Kanimbla to visit relatives in Adelaide, then Perth.

Popular in Perth

Still being trailed by *Australian Womens Weekly*, on 23 April 1938 the following paragraph appeared:

'Mrs. Bill MacDonald is being much admired in Perth. With her husband, Mrs. MacDonald—before her recent marriage Maxine Darrow, of Sydney—is being taken everywhere and meeting all Bill's friends before making off to Fossil Downs station in the interior. The bride has a fine new residence waiting for her, and Bill's sister, when she visited the West recently, made it as homelike as possible in readiness for the new occupant.'

More inaccuracies! The Press was infatuated with Bill and Maxine—it was the era before media celebrities. And although they both were amenable to speaking to the media, it was always with the objective of promoting infrastructure for the Kimberley.

The announcement that Bill was appointed a Justice of the Peace for the West Kimberley magisterial district was made in *The West Australian* on 14 May 1938.

Maxine arrives at Fossil

Ever the sophisticated young city woman, Maxine had no idea of where she was heading as she left Perth society behind, she related later. She didn't even know where Fossil Downs was. On initial appearances, she would be the least likely person to make her home on an isolated cattle station with minimal facilities. Flying was still in its infancy, although Western Australia was always at the forefront of commercial flight. Rolling her eyes, she recalled, 'in those days you caught the plane at Guildford, and flew all day to reach Carnarvon. Then you would keep flying and flying until you reached Port Hedland. The next day you got to Broome.'

Bill's Buick sedan was parked there. When, after a week of travel from Perth, they did eventually arrive near the station, she commented on the white eucalypt trees, which she'd never seen before. Bill, tongue-in-cheek, explained that the aborigines were so excited about her arrival, they'd whitewashed the trees in her honour—and she believed it! Arriving at the Margaret river crossing, they were surprised to find the water still running, too deep and swift to drive through. With no vehicle on the other side they had to wade across—Maxine in her stockings and high-heeled shoes—then walk the two miles up to the homestead and station sheds.

The now dilapidated old homestead, at Old Station, was a depressing site. Charlie and Willie built it on the black soil plains so that they had clear sight of anyone approaching. Now it was in the wrong place, as motor vehicles had become the preferred mode of transport—no longer was it horses, or bullocks and wagons—and the fear of attack had abated. Rain turns those notorious but highly productive plains into a quagmire, the sucking, slurpy, gluey mud sticking to everything, so in the wet season vehicles had to be left in a dry, sandy area near the Margaret river, some inconvenient distance from the homestead. Where was the supposed new homestead mentioned in the press?

What did this young, slim and fair soignée to the last degree, who might have stepped out of the pages of *Vogue*, think of the property she had come to? Amenities? There were none. Maxine came from a well provisioned home in Sydney. When she arrived at Fossil there was no plumbing, no inside toilet, no electric lights, no fridges—just a wood stove to cook on. Without any experience of cooking, one day Maxine decided to try and cook a batch of scones. In jest Bill nailed them to the kitchen wall! 'At first I only had a Coolgardie safe to keep things cool,' Maxine recalled. 'The food is put in a box covered by a wet hessian sack and stood in a breezeway. If the wind was blowing from the right direction in the dry season, it was just about possible to set a jelly!'

Later, when asked how she had coped with so few facilities, she'd reply, 'I was so in love, it didn't matter.' She drew on the strength of Bill's arms around her at night, but when lying awake, listening to the unfamiliar distant sounds of native singing, cattle bellowing, night-birds calling, and dingoes howling, along with the weeks of travel it had taken to get to Fossil Downs, Maxine realized how far away she was from her Sydney family home. Sometimes a penetrating silence in the night was unreal, and she would reflect on what she would do should something happen to Bill. Was this a premonition?

Thinking still further back, 'When I arrived here, I didn't know whether I'd love it or hate it. The land is very rough and tough, and it still inspires both emotions. My strongest recollection from those first days was the incredible beauty of the land.' Maxine chose to embrace it, and brought her own touches of sophistication to the uncultivated Fitzroy Crossing area like never seen before.

Venturing out with Bill to check on the cattle grazing on the lush, green Mitchell or Flinders grasses, she loved discovering yet another gorge. Native water lilies threaded their stems, sometimes 50 feet from the floor of the gorge up to the water line, there to display their beautiful blue-mauve blooms. The untouched landscape of those white eucalypts around the fringes of the billabongs and waterholes, reflecting the cloudless blue sky, were captivating. Further up the run, past Lerida Gorge in the foothills of the King Leopold ranges, she found the red ragged rocky outcrops intriguing, loving the sun-seared splendour of it all. Here aboriginal paintings nestled under protective overhangs. How long had they been there? Do they tell a story? Who or what do the figures represent—man or myth? And she never went without taking a fishing line to try her hand in the waterholes where fish were plentiful. With 100 miles to the top boundary of Fossil Downs from the old homestead, there were always plenty of new areas to explore.

Was this Maxine, the Sydney socialite and sometimes fashion model? In her wildest dreams, did it ever occur to her that she, the blonde city sophisticate, in just 25 years would be managing and running this massive, magnificent, million-plus acre cattle station, employing up to twenty white and sixty aboriginal staff? Although her looks were always emphasised by the ever-present press, Maxine was a trained and extremely competent comptometrist. This skill was to prove extremely useful. (The comptometer was a prelude to battery and electronic calculators and today's computers.)

When he went to Sydney for the wedding, Bill had left instructions with a builder for the construction of a house for Maxine and him to live in temporarily. It was to be at the new location for the homestead, beside the Geikie range. When they returned the only room with a roof was their bedroom! So, of necessity, she and Bill's plans were amended—they would live in makeshift quarters for a year while they built their intended homestead. Fortunately Maxine had fallen in love with the land, as well as Bill, because circumstances then dictated the carefully planned new homestead would not be finished for eleven and a half years.

Margaret River Runs

Eager to begin constructing their dream home, Bill and Maxine pegged out the foundations on New Year's Day 1939. Bill had consulted with the local aborigines regarding the siting of the homestead. A large area was needed to accommodate all the buildings which would eventually comprise the station homestead—cookhouse, stores and machinery sheds, stables, garages and generator sheds, as well as houses for married couples and mens quarters, along with an adjacent area for the aboriginal camp and its amenities. To be nicely aligned and spaced out, he knew it would cover several acres. The area selected beside the Geikie range was away from the notorious, sticky when wet, blacksoil plains and the aborigines assured Bill that this area had never flooded, as the Fitzroy River was some distance away on the far side of that range, and the Margaret had never spread its waters up to that area.

Coolness and strength, Bill had concluded, was needed in a homestead to cope with Kimberley climatic conditions. Therefore the house he designed was half-hexagon shaped, two-storied, one room wide with louvred windows on each side of each room for ventilation, concrete floors, and with the stone-flagged veranda creating access to each room.

Everything to build the homestead had to be constructed by hand—there were no bulk concrete trucks, with rotating mixing drums, to call on. No scaffolding, no cranes, no power tools or nail-guns. Bill estimated it would require 10,000 cement blocks for the walls. They would start by producing these down in the Margaret River.

They built a huge bough shed in the middle of the 80-yard wide dry riverbed, with a spinifex grass roof, on a 9' x 9' concrete slab. Although January can be a hot and very humid time of the year in the North, there's no cattle mustering, branding, or droving happening on the station then—it all shuts down for the wet season.

Thus they commenced mixing the cement and sand by hand on the concrete slab—not even using an unpowered concrete mixer. This mix was ladled into moulds to set, then placed in a nearby water hole in the river to cure. If the blocks dried too quickly in the intense wet-season heat they would be fragile.

They toiled, with all station hands helping. By starting at 4.00 or 5.00 a.m., when it was a few degrees cooler, they could all have the customary siesta after lunch, the hottest time of the day, then complete another two or three hours work before dark. It took many, many weeks. Eventually the day came when Bill estimated that the required number had been made and stacked in the waterhole. He and Maxine decided to go and celebrate this achievement with their friends, Bill and Grace Henwood at Noonkanbah station, approximately thirty miles down the Fitzroy River from the Crossing, towards Derby. They got dressed up and took off in the Buick. Most of the aborigines, who had been helping, decamped over to Geikie gorge for their customary annual walkabout.

The Crossing Inn was their first destination, to collect anything left there for them or Henwoods. The publican, Dick Fallon, asked where they were going. They explained they'd finished making the blocks for their home and were going to visit the Henwoods to celebrate. 'I bet you're not,' Dick argued, pulling a £5 note out of his pocket and placing it on the open-air bar. Mystified, they asked what he meant, so Dick pulled another piece of crumpled paper out of his pocket. MMA pilots, who'd been flying along the river, had dropped it saying the Margaret river was running a banker and a wall of water was flowing down. Although there'd been no rain near Fossil or Fitzroy Crossing, not even any lightning, apparently many miles further upstream the wet season summer rains had begun. The pilots had circled around at Fossil and could see there was no one there, so they dropped the note in Fitzroy Crossing hoping someone would receive the message and warn Bill or Maxine. It seems everyone knew the blocks for the new homestead were stacked in the riverbed.

Hurriedly Bill and Maxine sped back over the rough track, barely avoiding the bull-dust holes, back over the Margaret river crossing to their quarters, changed out of their finery into their working gear, then cajoled and hijacked every able-bodied white and aboriginal man, woman and child that called Fossil Downs home, and drove them to the river. A vehicle was dispatched to collect all those over at Geikie gorge. Work commenced with a vengeance. Those heavy concrete blocks had to be manhandled up the 7' high steep bank—there was no motorised elevator! They worked all that day and night until 8.00 next morning. Everyone's hands were rubbed raw. They were all sobbing with exhaustion, but the blocks were safely up on the bank.

Even though they were all in a state of collapse, when Bill suggested they go and see whereabouts this river water was, all the helpers piled on the back of the truck. Sure enough, a short distance up the river, the muddy water was swirling down in a yard-high frothy wall, laced with sticks, dirt and debris. They tore back to the brick-making camp just in time to see the bough-shed collapse like a pack of cards when this torrent hit. The last thing they saw was the huge 9 foot-square concrete slab going end over end, across their river access and down stream. Three months later when the wet season had abated and the river had subsided, they went poking around with crowbars in the sandy river bed for a couple of miles to try and find the slab, but it was never located. This was the only time that Maxine saw the Margaret river commence flowing in this aggressive manner. Usually it trickled down—gently.

The surveyor, Alexander Forrest, in his original report of his expedition in 1879, suggested that the rivers in the Kimberley ran throughout the year. Observing the lush vegetation at the end of the wet season, that impression was understandable. However, Maxine said, in fifty years she only witnessed that happening once. Rain falling at regular intervals, while good for cattle fodder and water supply, also had downsides. There were no shelters on the run for stock camps. If rain fell during the dry season it created miserable, damp, soggy sites, with wet, muddy sleeping gear, and the cooking fire used for meals being sluiced out. Swags would become moist, humid and steamy. It's not warmly embraced.

With no bridges or suitable boat and a limited river crossing, it wasn't possible to exit the property after the river started running. It could be too dangerous to cross the river so it was better that serious accidents not occur then! In one period of six months Maxine didn't encounter another white woman, since they couldn't leave and no one could visit. Later, when more finance and amenities were available, a vehicle would be left on the far side of the Margaret river, and a tinny boat moored to row across, enabling access to Fitzroy Crossing from the station. Although, even then, it could be dangerous so you had to pick your time, and there could be even more complications when you reached the Fitzroy river.

'Once my mother sent me a new frock,' Maxine recalled, 'so I got all dressed up to go into Fitzroy. We got to the river and it wasn't running deeply. Not wanting to untie the boat and row across. Bill decided to carry me to save me undoing my stockings. In the middle he stumbled into a hole and dropped me. My beautiful new frock began to shrink immediately. I arrived at the Crossing not looking quite as glamorous as I'd imagined I would.'

Fitzroy Crossing Township

'Dry and dusty, hot as Hades, imminently forgettable', were many people's reactions to Fitzroy Crossing township. Still are. Although shown on maps since 1903, the town wasn't gazetted until 1975, when surveyed streets, with kerbs and channeling, were incorporated. To avoid the very regular flooding in the wet season the town site then was shifted to higher ground approximately a mile to the south of the original old crossing. The Post Office, however, was officially opened as a telegraph office on 1 September 1892. What a convenience that would have made for the early settlers, being able to access telegraph and other services there, instead of a three weeks ride away in Derby. Premises were erected at Fitzroy Crossing and a 'wayside house license' was issued on July 5 1897 for a hotel.

Old River Crossing

A crossing of the Fitzroy River had been created just below its junction with the Margaret River. In 1886, hordes of prospectors travelled from Derby and along the track beside the Fitzroy River, then followed the Margaret to the Halls Creek gold rush. A makeshift store was opened at this crossing but when the short-lived gold rush ended the storekeeper followed the disillusioned prospectors back to await the next rush somewhere. Then, in 1897, Charlie Blythe established the Crossing Inn, a homestead-shanty-cum-hotel, which later included a store and the Telegraph Station. Did he realise that in so doing he had founded the original town site of Fitzroy Crossing? As further sheep and cattle stations were established on the Lower Fitzroy more activity occurred. The township is 374 feet above sea level and surrounded by the flat flood plains of the Fitzroy River. The local soil type is a mix of red-brown clay, plus the productive blacksoil. 'Pindan' is the name given to the red-soil country of southwestern Kimberley, and in places it's very red. The term comes from a local language and applies both to the soil and the vegetation associated with it. Fitzroy's average annual rainfall of 27½ inches mostly falls between December and March. The average maximum temperature then is 97°F. so it's frequently much higher. Average minimum temperature is 68°F. Pastoralism, tourism, mining and aboriginal enterprises, are the major industries in the area today.

The Fitzroy River is one of the longest in Australia with a catchment of 34,750 square miles. Just north of the townsite the tributaries of the Leopold and Margaret/Mary rivers join the Fitzroy before it turns west to empty into King Sound near Derby. During the wet season the swirling muddy waters can rise 80 feet over the old concrete low-level crossing in town with a massive estimated flow rate of 30,000 cubic yards per second.

Fitzroy Crossing today with its paved and kerbed streets, information centre, shops, business services, and other amenities, is a totally different place, even from the 1960s. The street names honour the early settlers and identities.

Up until 1938, Fitzroy Crossing, as its name implies, was simply a place where travellers going from Broome and Derby to Halls Creek and beyond could cross the Fitzroy River. If there'd been massive rainfall up in the high catchment areas the river could rise up to 30 feet, or more above its usual height making it impossible to cross. Although the settlement was small it served everyone on the surrounding sheep and cattle stations where accidents frequently occurred. Naturally the locals wanted a hospital, but their hopes were dashed first by World War I and the Great Depression in the late 1920s, then by the government establishing a flying doctor base at Wyndham. Bureaucracy considered that was sufficient for the region. Had any of those decision-makers ever tried to drive the local roads (read tracks)? In 1939, reluctantly the Australian Inland Mission Board agreed to establish a hospital at the insistence of Dr. Alan Vickers, one of the early flying doctors, who believed it was vital for the area. After construction it also became one of the social centres of the town.

Beryl Scott (nee Gilkes) recalls her time nursing at Fitzroy Crossing with fond memories:

> 'The hospital was run by three nurses, along with the Itinerant Nurse doing station clinics. We would take it in turns to look after the outpatients, inpatients and cooking on a weekly rotation. The person on outpatients usually did any night work that was necessary. I had never worked in a hospital where the nurses all went to bed at night and the patient came and woke you up if they needed you. There was no choice though, as we had no one else to do it.

We had an occasional day off, but that was onerous as you knew the others had to do all your work.

I learned to suture while there. Although I had worked in theatre previously, I had never been shown how to do it. I could not manage knots with the forceps—so I tied them by hand. I also had to take x-rays. I had two days instruction with the radiographer in Perth on my way to Fitzroy Crossing and then I had to show the others how to do it. I think the only good x-ray I did was when I x-rayed the sealed packet containing my engagement ring that my fiancé had asked his mother to buy, and send up from Victoria!

I guess the nursing itself was not hard, but with our limited experience it could be very stressful. We had all worked in large public hospitals with every facility available and with many others to turn to. All of a sudden we were IT, in a situation that was totally different to any other in our experience.'

Sports

The Police Station had a jail—a never locked lock-up. Windy, one of the Fossil natives had committed a misdemeanour and received a 3-month sentence. He was a very competent stockman, so during his incarceration he borrowed some horses and taught the policeman's children how to ride them. At times he had the company of other miscreants and after a while they'd crave a good feed of 'roo', so they'd prevail on the police sergeant to loan them the police Land Rover and a rifle, so they could go bush and get their preferred food for dinner. This was an excellent supplement to the food provided by HM The Queen, although apparently not appreciated in all quarters. Windy was one of the few aborigines at that time who knew his birth date and this occurred while he was in jail. He informed the policeman's wife, who was responsible for feeding the prisoners, that it was his birthday, 'So I baked him a cake,' she said. Prisoners did not mind being in jail. They were rarely locked up.

For Saturday afternoon sport some of the locals had hacked out a golf course of sorts in the area in front of Crossing Inn. Was this the only golf course in Australia that had piped music? The jukebox on the Inn's veranda was constantly fed 20c coins by the local indigenous people, and golf was played accompanied by the melodic tones of Slim Dusty's country singing. There was a gully on one side of the course, and the fairways consisted of dry grass which was tractor slashed at the beginning of the season, while the "greens" were made of sand. During the week, Gogo's cattle would graze there, stirring up the greens, so on Friday nights at the Crossing Inn, certain aborigines would be apprehended, spend the night in detention, and be fed a good greasy breakfast next morning. For their punishment they'd be given the police Land Rover and a set of pipe scrapes, and sent down to the golf course to smooth out the greens, ready for the afternoon golf. The police sergeant, of course, was the president of the golf club.

While today this may be considered a demeaning practice, in those times it was acceptable procedure and bothered no one in Fitzroy Crossing, including the so-called offenders. They deemed it fun, driving around the course and down through Brooking Creek in the Police Land Rover. When the authorities in Perth eventually learned of this arrangement a directive was issued that the practice had to cease, along with the prisoners being allowed to go hunting with police property. How could bureaucracy over 1,800 miles away in Perth know what were suitable activities and behaviour in Fitzroy Crossing then, which not only provided a food source but occupied the prisoners actively and productively?

My only ever claim to golf prowess occurred at this Fitzroy Crossing course in 1970. Club championships were staged and, using Mrs. Mac's clubs, I played in a threesome with a nurse from the AIM Hospital and a teacher from the Mission school. On the first hole, the nurse drove her tee shot well down the fairway but at the last it shanked into the adjacent gully. It took 18 strokes for her to extricate the ball from this overgrown and unkempt trap, but involuntarily she counted only 17. Not wanting to make her feel worse, I didn't protest—and the teacher hadn't bothered to count her strokes at all. After that beginning and no doubt getting her bearings the nurse played brilliantly while the teacher and I played our usual very ordinary games. The final tally revealed the nurse won the Women's Championship, beating me by 1 stroke!

The other sport played then was tennis. There was a court at the AIM Hospital and when it wasn't too hot it was played on Sunday afternoons. Tom the Cheap, a cut-price grocery chain in Perth, donated floodlights and sent them up to the hospital so that tennis could be played in the cooler evenings. The hold-up was finding an electrician who could install them along with someone who would erect the appropriate poles. Eventually they were installed.

A shared tea at the hospital frequently followed our games, or sometimes it was a barbecue at Geikie Gorge. No fancy gas appliances were there then—just scrounge some bark and sticks, ignite with a cigarette lighter, wait until the logs burn into coals, plonk a piece of chequer-plate steel over the top, and throw the meat on until it sizzled. Sitting around the fire yarning was relaxing especially for those who worked mainly by themselves during the week like fencing contractors, water drillers, and windmill mechanics. When the fire looked like dying out someone would grab a chainsaw out of the back of a ute, lop down a dead branch, saw it into pieces and stoke the fire. For entertainment one night the suggestion was made that we play two-up—an illegal, but fun game. This put the two policemen in a quandary: being illegal, how could they allow it? The dilemma was overcome with the police running the game.

Geikie Gorge was always a popular destination as the breeze cooled over the water and provided welcome respite from the searing temperatures over the land. It was the western boundary of Fossil Downs then before it was declared a National Park in the 1980s. This magnificently scenic 30 yard deep gorge, with its unique savage beauty, contrasted sharply with the surrounding landscape. The Fitzroy River has carved a gorge into the remains of an ancient Devonian Reef limestone barrier and when it floods in the wet season the water rises over 150 feet up its limestone walls. The continuous rise and fall of water, over innumerable years, has left the lower portion of the walls bleached white, thus becoming photographer's heaven. Once it was possible to get mirror-image perfection of the cliffs reflecting in the water but since the advent of tours up and down the gorge that can be difficult. Many tourists fail to realize how close it is to Fitzroy Crossing, and miss seeing this iconic feature.

Drifting down the gorge in a tinnie boat during a full moon, with no motor to pierce the silence is an unforgettable experience. The white limestone walls and every leaf, rock and feature of the gorge is brilliantly illuminated without the hindrance of electric light pollution—a truly romantic experience. 'The moonlight evenings still repay the perspiration of the day' is a frequently quoted local saying.

Rev. John Flynn

The name Reverend John Flynn is synonymous with the Australian outback. He was known for driving over every road and track, made and unmade, in his sturdy Buick, laden to the hilt with useful items, even strapping extra bits and pieces onto the outside of the doors. He was always thinking of the needs of those in isolated communities. In September 1910 Flynn published *The Bushman's Companion*, an extremely useful reference book, which was distributed freely throughout inland Australia. By 1912, after writing a report for his Presbyterian Church superiors on the difficulties of ministering to such a widely scattered population, Flynn was made the first superintendent of the Australian Inland Mission. As well as attending to spiritual matters, he quickly established the need of medical care for residents of the vast outback. The Presbyterian Church, via donations, built a number of bush hospitals, one being at Fitzroy Crossing. A Mantle of Safety was part of his vision.

Even during World War I, Flynn was considering using new technology, such as radio and aircraft, for the establishment of The Flying Doctor Service. The Service had a doctor, a pilot, and John Flynn—the man with the vision—but lacked the communication technology to deliver services efficiently. A South Australian, Alfred Traeger, invented a pedal-operated generator to power a radio receiver. The pedal-radio, as it was known, became an outback icon as residents rotated the pedals, like a bicycle, to power it. By 1929 people living in isolation could use it to call the Flying Doctor to assist them in an emergency. Maxine claimed the service as an absolute godsend. The knowledge that help was available particularly after the children arrived, was precious.

Each station, and portable radio, had its own unique call sign on this network. Fossil Downs was VC. When it was first set up and allocated, though, it was VD! Naturally this drew Bill's wrath and he immediately demanded a change. 'My wife is not going to shout that into the radio,' he bellowed.

Transistorised receivers later replaced pedal radios making it possible for doctors to give radio consultations. It also meant neighbours, families and friends, scattered over thousands of kilometres, could exchange news and gossip after normal transmission hours. This time became known as the galah session, aptly named after the noisy, chattering pink and grey bird.

Eventually School of the Air was established, whereby children on isolated properties could 'attend' school each day, having direct radio contact with their teachers and other isolated students. Likewise meetings of organizations could be held via this radio invention. The Country Womens Association, the well-known and respected voice of women in the country, held their meetings monthly on a Sunday morning in the Kimberley. When a vote was required it was intriguing to hear the President say, 'All those in favour stay silent. Against, say 'no'. Of course, everyone could listen in. Bill MacDonald reckoned this meeting was the best entertainment available in the Kimberley! When it was scheduled he'd sit comfortably in his chair with a whisky in his hand, pipe in his mouth, feet up on the desk, and laugh uproariously for its duration.

Various Christian denominations would visit Fossil Downs Maxine saying all were welcome to come. The Bible Society Australia would fly in occasionally often bringing a pastor to visit. Their plane's registration always raised some outback humour—with the Australian aeronautical prefix of VH, and its rego being ELL, it became VH-ELL!

Roads

The following clipping from the Northern Times 30 June 1949 illustrates the prevailing conditions at the time:

Road Conditions

For the information of overlanders and travellers, the low level cement crossing over the Fitzroy River at Fitzroy Crossing which has been closed owing to floods and deposited river silt in the crossing cutting since May 23, has now been cleared sufficiently to allow light vehicles to cross with ease but heavily laden transport trucks have a difficult pull out on the Gogo side because only a narrow strip was cleared in the cutting and the high sides are now falling in on the cement as it dries out.

The road from Derby to Hall's Creek, Wyndham and Darwin is now open again and since the over-landing season opened on April 22, twenty-one vehicles other than those owned by surrounding stations have crossed to Halls Creek and other destinations. Twenty vehicles have come down the road and crossed the river going to Fitzroy. Now that petrol is available in southern areas a very large amount of round Australia traffic is bound to occur.

By the 1970s drovers taking big mobs of cattle to the ports at Wyndham or Broome, or the Derby abattoirs, had been replaced by the new road trains. These consisted of a prime mover plus two trailers—called 'dogs'—which could shift 103 three-year-old beasts, but road infrastructure hadn't kept up with mechanical inventions and technology. 'Remember how the road trains used to rumble over the old crossing?' recalled Arthur, a local who'd lived in Fitzroy Crossing for many years. 'The driver would sound his air-horn constantly for two miles before the river crossing to make sure everyone was out of the way, all the time keeping up his revs, so he could hurtle down the bank on one side, across the causeway, hoping he had enough momentum to get up the bank on the other side.'

Naturally there were many losses, fortunately no people. Once a terrible accident involving Fossil's cattle occurred in attempting to cross the river this way, and the cattle that remained alive escaped onto Gogo Station. John Henwood, at that time, was managing Ellendale Station, and Mrs. MacDonald spoke to him on the UHF radio, advising that 63 Fossil cattle were on Gogo and asking if he could come and help round them up. The voice of Gogo's manager, Vic Jones, with its distinctive pitch, butted in saying, 'there's only 62'. Today there's a bridge.

The Races

The annual race meeting, on the Fitzroy Crossing course adjacent to the town, was an eagerly awaited event. All around the stations, horses were chosen and trained in anticipation of being the next winner of the Crossing Gold Cup. The young ringers studied mail-order catalogues, and telegrams were despatched ordering the latest in western shirts, jeans, hats and boots. The women assembled the outfits they'd need for two days of racing, plus one day of horse sports, and an evening gown for the Saturday night ball. Swags were rolled up and tightly belted. Each station had its preferred sleeping area somewhere around the township. The Crossing Inn ordered vast quantities of food for feeding the expected influx of visitors. It was all stowed in the dining room freezers and cold room behind the bar when it arrived, along with the copious amount of extra beer.

The postmaster and mistress were the race-day's secretaries, who ordered in the trophies that were sponsored by each station. They seemed to have it all in hand, but it took all available local station personnel to actually run the events. Thursday and Saturday were race days; Friday was horse sports day.

Running the tote, along with an AIM nurse, was my job. Not being in the least familiar with this we were given basic instructions and the rest we made up as we went along. We were making a tidy profit for a while, even with the favourites winning, but patrons didn't like being paid a 95c dividend when they'd placed a $1 bet and their horse had won! The Secretary of the Derby Racing Club came to us and kindly explained that we had to pay out a minimum of $1.05 in that situation—it was the law of the Totaliser Agency Board. That reduced our profits somewhat.

Church

In the 1930s, the town of Fitzroy Crossing was a very colourful place. Many of the locals gravitated there to avoid having to live with the constraints imposed in regular society. At the time it was also the base of Rev. Andrew Barber, the patrol organizer for the Australian Inland Mission. Additionally he assessed the medical and other needs of the area.

The Crossing had not had a church service for many years. Nothing had been organised that remotely resembled a religious service—except the solemn rite of the two-up and poker schools! Rev. Barber approached the hotelkeeper who felt sure he could close down the poker school for a church service, but he was doubtful about the two-up—'It's a national pastime and must not be interrupted lightly,' he reasoned. However the earnest clergyman courageously contended that nothing at all should interfere with the deliverance of God's word, so went ahead and arranged a service to be held outside the back of the pub, under a spinifex roof shelter. Twenty-five bushmen attended the short observance, but not without some disgruntled murmurings. When it was over, though, there were diffident whispers about the 'c'lection'. The padre ignored that undercurrent—he was not going to sneakily deprive them of their cash. After several services in the now enthusiastic community, however, he agreed that a collection be taken up, and the hotelkeeper provided a saucer for the receipt of the gifts. This met with a storm of abuse, and an outraged poker player, turned church fanatic, kicked the saucer from the padre's hand. The clergyman was bidden to get hence to hotter climes and get something that would hold a real collection.

He returned with a soup plate. Two men—one to collect and the other to see fair play—proceeded to pass the plate around. The first worshipper they approached met them with two shillings in an outstretched hand. 'You ...' yelled the first collector, 'you haven't been to church for 30 years and you haven't even coughed up a penny a year'. Vainly did this parishioner protest that his money was 'in me other strides'. His trousers were found, and willing hands extracted a 10-shilling note from a bulging pocket. It was placed on the soup-collection-plate amid roars of approval from the assembled worshippers.

And so the Church of Fitzroy Crossing celebrated its first collection using methods unique in the annals of Bush Church history.

Mail

The police played a major part in Fossil Downs personnel collecting their papers and mail in the wet season. Just prior to the Margaret River commencing to run, the station would position a vehicle on the Fitzroy side of that river. In 1970 it was the newly acquired German Haflinger. To head into Fitzroy after the Margaret started flowing, the staff would take a gun with them, drive the two miles to the 80-yard wide Margaret River, untie the boat and row to the far side if it was too deep to wade through. Then start the Haflinger and slip/slide the twenty-six miles, often bush-bashing a new track to avoid getting bogged in muddy sludge. At the 100-yard wide Fitzroy River they'd fire a shot into the air. This would bring the police to the other side. They would untie their boat and motor across the river, collect and take them across and up to the Police Station. There they borrowed the police Landrover and visited the post office, Crossing Inn, and other establishments in town to transact their business. To return the procedure was reversed. It was a tiring all-day undertaking in the extreme heat and humidity.

World War II

Having transported the concrete blocks up to the site, block laying was commenced and the Fossil Downs homestead began to take on its two-storey, half-hexagon shape.

The concrete-block walls were up and the roof on, but no verandas, when World War II came to the Kimberley. As the bombs fell first on Darwin, then Wyndham, Derby, and Broome, Lionel Wright, the contracted builder, decided Perth was a more appealing place and decamped there. The Army decided to occupy the unfinished homestead as their headquarters. Along with the Army, Bill and Maxine, Merrilee and baby Annette, lived in the house sans windows, doors or finished verandas.

Bren guns were mounted on the flat roofs above the kitchen/dining area, and above the ground-floor bedroom/office. Most women north of the 26th parallel were evacuated south but Maxine stayed, as by then she'd learned to code and decode over the radio for the military. This competent comptometrist had also learned to assemble and dismantle the Bren guns.

General Gordon Bennett arrived in a Hudson Bomber one day, and remarked that the homestead, 'will be a very nice home if it escapes the Japanese!' He was firmly convinced the Japanese would invade—which may have happened if not for the constant sorties the allies (United States and Australia) flew out of Corunna Downs, the hidden airfield near Marble Bar in the WA Pilbara. Military intelligence indicated huge forces of Japanese were marching down through the islands to the north. But the Japanese never discovered this airfield and heavy losses were inflicted on their troops. *(Corunna Downs, The Invisible WW2 Airfield, by Antonio Gafarella)*

Maxine, and Thelma Mitchell, Bill's second-cousin who'd come to stay with Maxine for company, were at home alone with the children the day after the Japanese had bombed Broome and another Japanese plane had been sighted. Bill was away with the military. They heard a strange plane swoop low over the roof so took shelter in the (to be) billiard room, the best protected room of the house. Then they heard the plane land. What was happening? They were trembling with fear. Presently friendly airmen arrived at the house—to find themselves staring down the barrel of a revolver! Maxine suggested that in future it would be more circumspect to circle low over the house a couple more times before landing to ensure a less hostile welcome!

Although they didn't come inland, the Japanese bombed the Kimberley coastal towns after bombing Darwin in 1942. Broome experienced the second worst air raid on Australian soil on 3rd of March 1942. Activities in Northern Australia were severely disrupted. Much of this was caused by the almost total lack of information about the state of the war and the extent to which the Kimberley was under the threat of invasion. Communication equipment there was still minimal. The area around Fitzroy Crossing had no real community plan or method of organizing resistance and knowing if/when people should evacuate. Taking charge, Bill structured the West Kimberley Volunteer Defence Corps, and travelled around arranging guerrilla bands and planning hideouts in the hills for supplies of food and fuel. With aboriginal help, he identified and illustrated bush tucker to teach to the troops and some of the locals. If they found it necessary to go bush and live off the land they would know which plants were safely edible.

The work he undertook had an unusually long-term effect. Bill had carefully identified the bush tucker suitable for eating by first photographing it, then sketching and colouring it on paper for troops to follow if necessary. Additionally he drew maps of the whole of the Kimberley, as there were no accurate ones available. This would help the authorities if aircraft were shot down or locals had to search for man or plane. He was amazed to find that twenty years later his maps were still being used by MMA, the local airline.

Perhaps overstepping the mark one day, Bill strode into the AIM hospital in Fitzroy Crossing and demanded the nurses hand their radio over to him, their means of communication. Knowing their radio was only for medical emergency purposes they refused and stood their ground. The intervention of the local constable eventually defused the situation.

Bill recalled an interesting feature concerning the WA coastal ship Koolinda. In 1932 it participated in rescue work following a pearling disaster off Broome. It rescued a number of Japanese from the calamity and afterwards it received the Order of the Chrysanthemum and the Japanese Emperor's blessing. 'It may have been an unusual coincidence', Bill said, 'but this ship was not threatened once by the Japanese forces ten years later during the war'.

The demand for beef then became insatiable, as it was required to feed the Australian and United States troops who were defending the country. Prices were excellent and helped the Fossil Downs' finances stabilize. This made a nice change, Bill said, from the times when prices were so low they had to send a cheque to cover the cost of the transport and selling charges.

There was another bright side for Bill and Maxine. After Broome had been bombed, the army personnel who were still stationed at Fossil, were despatched to go and salvage a billiard table from a saloon there which had suffered a direct hit. In true army fashion, they returned with a beautiful full-sized table with elaborate carved legs, the huge overhead lights, sundry cues, scoreboard, balls, and all the necessary accessories. The cost? £28. It was just what was needed to furnish the billiard room that had been incorporated in the original homestead design as a social centre adjacent to the hall. That billiard table is still there and has been played on by hundreds of family, friends and staff members—although it has also suffered yet more significant disasters.

Building the Homestead

In 1946 with World War II over, attention could again be focused on continuing to build the two-storey homestead, but a shortage of materials was now the holdup. The manufacturing requirements for the war meant many factories had to fabricate components other than their normal inventory items—their regular stock wasn't replenished yet. Telegrams, still the only method of communication, would be sent via the Royal Flying Doctor Service network to suppliers in Perth, only for replies to come, eventually, stating how long the waiting time would be. Even when items were dispatched, sometimes they were incorrect. With telegrams still being mainly hand-written, confusion over sizing could be caused by the receiver's interpretation of the script. The beautiful jarrah timber staircase for the two-storied hall arrived with one stair too many. At least that could be sawn down to the correct size. Often ingenuity was required by the builder to make an item suitable for its intended function after it arrived.

The style of the hall, incorporating the staircase, was art deco. The balustrades, on the staircase between the upright timbers, was 1 inch wide flat steel, in horizontal layers, painted off-white, with the narrow sides picked out in red. It was all built with imagination and style, incorporating a polished cement floor of large red and white squares. Under the dark timber staircase was a discreet bar. Three pairs of leadlight doors, with ornate brass handles, accessed the front enclosed veranda, the lounge, and the back veranda.

This centrepiece of the homestead, along with the green room lounge, was designed to showcase the historic water bag and gramophone, two of the items that travelled with Charlie and Willie MacDonald on their epic trek from New South Wales. The smooth-bore musket, with bayonet attached and displayed in the lounge room, came with the MacDonald family from the Isle of Skye and was last used in the days of Bonny Prince Charlie, they said, although Bill thought it had been used either in clan skirmishes, or against the English in Scotland. The old-fashioned rimfire derringer, a .40-calibre cartridge pistol, was carried in the sleeve of a gambler in the American West before it was brought to the Kimberley, someone claimed. The pair of buffalo horns over the fireplace had come from an old rogue bull that had apparently become an outcast from the Northern Territory herds and drifted all the way into the Fitzroy River district. Prior thought had been given, and appropriate places designed, for all these artefacts to be beautifully displayed so they did not overwhelm the decor.

In deference to the climate, ease of cleaning, and termites, concrete floors were utilised on the ground floor. Upstairs floors were constructed of locally milled Leichhardt pine and fig. When cut, this pine is a vivid orange colour with a pungent pine smell—the fig is a soft timber. The framework of the wide downstairs access veranda was created from beams of a very hard local timber known as black heart. All this timber was felled along the Fitzroy River and hauled around the end of the Geikie Range to the homestead site by donkey wagon teams and milled at the Fossil sawmill. In places the wheel ruts from where the donkey wagons hauled the timber are still visible.

Flagstones from the banks of nearby Boab Creek paved the verandas and front lobby where fossils, for which the station is named, are embedded. The concrete Grecian pillars used to hold up the roof were cast on site using handmade moulds.

The original construction was of the main bedroom and bathroom upstairs on one side of the stairs, and two bedrooms and a bathroom on the other side. Downstairs was the green room lounge, hall, and billiard room, all beneath the bedrooms, and to the front was a large insect-screened lobby stretching right across the breadth of the house with an entrance way to the front again with the MacDonald Coat of Arms featuring on the outside.

At the back—where one generally approached the homestead—one wing encompassed the kitchen and dining room, whilst the other wing housed the large main bathroom/first-aid dispensary, small bedroom and the office. As guests began arriving the bedroom arrangements were at a premium so Maxine suggested that perhaps they could build dormitory style rooms above the two V-wings. 'No, that's not possible', Bill responded. As staying visitors mainly came in the dry season, it was possible to sleep on the verandas or outside on the lawn anyway. But during the wet season it was different. Then one day Bill got a good idea—they could build rooms above the two V-wings! And so that happened, and it became a very large 14-room homestead.

After driving through the MacDonald gates, approaching the homestead is impressive. Like modern townships, the street ahead is divided with a median strip now planted with bottle trees, frangipani and oleanders and incorporating a flagpole with the Australian flag. To reduce dust and give a broader green cooling effect this street is grassed now. Perfectly lined-up on the left-side as you approach the Big House, as the homestead is always called, are a huge machinery shed—ex-Noonkanbah shearing shed—the old stables and new stalls then the picturesque stone men's quarters, a 2-storey married couple's house, followed by the cookhouse which has the cook's flat on top, then the main storehouse. On the right-hand side of the street was another machinery shed then two Nissen huts one of which housed the saddleshed and the other the native store. A garage with a pit for servicing and repairing the vehicles was next. The huge vegetable garden preceded the Court House, which is Annette and John Henwood the manager's house.

Presiding over this street, at the apex, is the Big House homestead with its arms out wide embracing everything. Bill sincerely believed that if you were going to spend your life in the Kimberley, you should build as beautiful and comfortable as possible.

Although it took eleven and a half years, the building gradually became very congenial and convenient for the extreme weather conditions as furnishings were acquired and landscaping added. When the front gate and fence around the compound, also built of concrete blocks and featuring the MacDonald Coat of Arms was finished, it truly became the stately home of the Kimberley. It nestled alongside the rocky limestone Geikie Range both for aesthetics and protection from hostile weather in the wet season. Of course, some locals on other properties were detractors, with many asking, 'what does Bill MacDonald think he's building—the Taj Mahal?' saying the house was too flash for the Kimberley. Was that envy, or had they been brainwashed with the 'good enough for the bush mentality?'

Maxine's Touches

It now became Maxine's mission to add the feminine touches a homestead needs to transform a shell into a home with a comfortable ambience, a place that's convenient and says, 'Welcome'. Quality items to befit their intended style of living were purchased—sets of crystal glasses, etched with the grapevine pattern, which would be used every day. The silver sweet dishes from her mother's tearooms, 'Cheppywood', in the NSW Blue Mountains with the word 'Cheppys' engraved on the base, were acquired when they were no longer needed there. Large silver salvers and a sizeable silver meat cover arrived to protect the enormous roasts from insect contamination—and much more. Not for Maxine were things to be put away and only used on special occasions. Initially, however, when the Japanese threatened to invade, she buried the silverware but then dug it up again, saying she'd prefer to live 'civilised'. She was brought up using nice things—this was how it would continue at Fossil Downs in the then rough and tough Kimberley.

Although Maxine's beginnings at the homestead stove were humble, she had quickly developed culinary skills and her hospitality charm and warm welcome became legendary. People loved to visit and stay. And while she welcomed everyone and enjoyed the company it always created more work. Additionally, she dedicated herself to improving working conditions and medical facilities for the aborigines and staff on the station at the same time running the homestead and raising Merrilee and Annette. It had become a very hectic life.

Shipping containers had yet to be invented. All freight and supplies were dispatched from Perth to Derby by sea—where the 36' high tide meant that ships sat on the seabed twice a day. This caused unloading problems. Maxine's lovely Beale pianola had been sent from Sydney to grace the entrance hall in the Big House. Whilst being unloaded, it slipped out of the crane's sling and squished into the slushy mangrove seabed mud where it stuck fast. Later it was inundated by the swift incoming tide of salty water. Eventually it was retrieved but after its arrival at the station, with Maxine away, the enthusiastic native women set to scrubbing it down with hand-made sand soap. Thus its beautiful French polish took on a dull matte finish. A piano tuner, on his annual tour of the area, did manage to get it tuned, eventually. Fifty years later, after yet more disasters, the pianola was replaced.

The Western Australian media loved to focus on how Maxine had been a Sydney social-life trend-setter, and how she left it all to marry handsome, debonair Bill and live in the remote Kimberley with minimal facilities. It was still the era of women being 'the wife of' rather than being accorded their own name in the press.

But all comments Maxine made were with the intention of promoting what was good for the Kimberley. 'Lack of available stockmen is a problem,' she related. 'All northern cattle stations are similarly placed and could use as much labour as they can get. We would like to see more young men come to the North to learn cattle work,' she added. 'But with the present lack of amenities, there's little encouragement for them to do so.' Bill had been coaching her to utilize all opportunities to mention the lack of infrastructure and amenities for the, then, seemingly forgotten Kimberley.

By the 1950s, roads had been partially upgraded and some river crossings constructed. Air services into Broome and Derby were operating, sometimes. Australia's economy was forging ahead. Thus a stream of visitors began to arrive. There was much catering and housekeeping to do. Bill's cousin, (Dame) Roma Mitchell, observed that a dinner party for twenty guests was just par for the course for Maxine.

'Firsts' came in the DNA of the MacDonald/Mitchell family. Dame Roma herself later had a most impressive list of 'first' achievements, particularly as a woman in the judiciary in South Australia, the University of South Australia, along with her appointment as Governor of South Australia, amongst many other accolades. The biography of her life, written by Susan Magarey and Kerrie Round is entitled 'Roma The First'.

Dame Roma provided a wonderful answer to Annette's conundrum. As a youngster Annette felt she must have been adopted as she and sister Merrilee looked nothing alike—Merrilee fair and blue-eyed; Annette dark and brown-eyed. 'I can't possibly belong to this family' she would fret. After Dame Roma's visit at last Annette knew she really did belong—their resemblance was remarkable.

Fossil Downs gradually become a port of call for most dignitaries visiting the area, and Bill and Maxine welcomed everyone warmly, speaking enthusiastically of the place that Fossil Downs filled in the history of Australian settlement and relating the stories that the mementos in the hall and 'green room' had in that history—the waterbag and gramophone atop the stairs, and the musket above the fireplace plus the derringer, were always pointed out. The visitors' book, kept on the hall table to be signed by everyone who came, made fascinating reading. The days of not seeing another white woman for a six-month stint were long since gone.

Keeping this establishment ticking meant killing a bullock once or twice per week to provide meat for guests, family and staff including the 60+ natives. Fifty pounds of flour was baked into bread each day for all these people, and two native women helped the cook with that. A 72 lb. bag of sugar lasted a fortnight. Stores came three times per year from Perth, 2000 miles away, by ship to Derby then transported by cartage contractors. The cost of freight from Derby was £10 per ton. In the wet season, perishable fruit and vegetables were flown in, that freight cost being subsidised by the State Government. But there was a sharp cut-off date; the station's vegetable garden needed to be up and producing by then. Grapefruit and paw-paw trees surrounded the veggie garden providing an excellent organic supplement to the diet.

The office needed to be functioning well, too. Much like in 1882 back at *Clifford's Creek* before the trek began, long lists of grocery items, toiletries, first-aid, hardware and machinery requirements, five A4 pages long, were typed out. It could be awkward or embarrassing to omit something. If it was found an item had been overlooked, now at least a telegram could be sent to J. W. Bateman Pty. Ltd., Wholesale Agents in Perth, who attended to acquiring and dispatching the stores. But, depending on shipping schedules, items could still take months to arrive.

Now long gone from the socialite lifestyle in Sydney, except for visits there, Maxine had become very adept at keeping tabs on the many activities happening simultaneously in the homestead complex and out on the run. Later this ability became very handy.

Six indigenous women helped keep the fourteen-room homestead functioning. 'They are a great help', she contended. 'Cooks come and go, as cooks do, in a long procession from excellent, to good, to not good; it just depended on who was available,' she added.

No matter what project she tackled, or what housekeeping or cooking tasks Maxine undertook, she still managed to maintain a chic and well-presented appearance, that soignée attribute, even under the hottest and stickiest of humid conditions—a trait later inherited by both her daughters. Maxine always chose to look smartly attired with her hair coiffured as visitors might arrive at any time. People just arrived unannounced—there were still no phones to the stations.

Blue Mountain Lowries and Budgerigars

After the homestead was built, gradually birds were encouraged to frequent the area. Blue Mountain lowries became Annette's pets and were so tame they took sips of coffee from cups. Large flocks of beautiful green budgies were often seen, too, along with bustards, parrots and kingfishers, particularly as you drove along the tracks into Fitzroy Crossing. How long did it take for the early pioneers to establish that these birds, especially the budgies, could lead you to water?

Aborigines Inspect

In 1950, the homestead was inspected by a group of aborigines who still lived in the Gibson Desert. They had travelled to Fossil for a special ceremony—the tribal chief of the surrounding area lived there. The native head stockman came to Bill with a request: 'Could the tribesmen inspect the house?' Bill agreed, and the parade of 60 warriors in full corroboree dress followed. The Fossil aborigines were proud of the Big House as many of them had helped with the brick making and assisted with its construction. All the European people withdrew to allow an uninhibited visit. The Gibson Desert guests trooped through the downstairs rooms, then upstairs, onto the roofs, jabbering and chattering as they went. Proud native house girls demonstrated the refrigerator, electric light, stoves, hot and cold water, and gave them iced drinks and cakes.

What did it mean to them, in this new world? Their homes in the desert were little 'wurlies' made of sticks, bark, branches and leaves often built under a cliff ledge, their sparse water coming from small soaks or a billabong if there had been rain. They rubbed sticks together to light their fire. Goannas and lizards were their staple diet. An hour later the house was empty again—only the dusty pads of their bare feet remained. Despite so many people coming through at once, nothing was broken or shifted. If only the news reporters had been available to record this unprecedented and unique event.

Those who have visited the homestead complex, and know its history, marvel at the resoluteness of purpose that built this two-storey mansion and all the ancillary buildings, in this isolated, difficult, harsh country. Imagine today, attempting to construct a substantial number of buildings, with no mobile phones, no cranes or scaffolding, no electric or power tools and nail guns, and with the closest source for supply of materials being 2000 miles away and only accessible for seven or eight months of the year! Bill's nephew, Bob, maintains that Bill's achievement in designing and constructing this homestead and headquarters complex, in the wake of the tremendous disadvantages in the Kimberley area at that time, ranks alongside the achievements of his great-uncles Charlie and Willie in reaching the area with their cattle and plant.

Bill's other achievements were amazing, too. Never daunted by almost impossible odds, he forged ahead with every idea he dreamed of. They were numerous: he was first to establish a cattle stud in the north of Western Australia, the first to transport stud bulls by air, first to implement improving and irrigation of pastures, first to use aerial seeding of pasture, first to introduce mineral supplementation of the cattle, plus also writing and publishing a book on stud cattle breeding in the tropics. Many years later, Annette said, 'I think my father was a person with a touch of genius. No matter what he did it was visionary—before its time.' Closing her eyes she recalled, 'He was very artistic, he played the violin and sang beautifully, he was a champion snow skier, a good athlete, he drove racing cars and had some success as an amateur actor. He could have done so many things—yet this, cattle breeding in the isolated Kimberley, was what he chose to do.'

National Trust and Australian Heritage

Testament to his ability is the 'film-set township' he gradually created as the Fossil Downs headquarters. In 1999 the National Trust and Australian Heritage listed the homestead in recognition of Bill's architectural flair and courage to build on such a mammoth scale. Commenting on this, Annette said, 'Although this wasn't something that I pursued, in all honesty I think my father would have been both pleased and proud.'

Register of Heritage Places — Assessment Document, Page 9

This documentation states:

'The homestead could be described as of an Inter-War Functionalist style although this would simply classify the design by time (Inter-War c.1915 - c1940), and the material usage indicator (reinforced concrete and metal framed windows). The simplified style of the homestead is not entirely representative of Functionalist Style, and reflects the difficulty of procuring labour and materials in remote locations.' It continued, 'The overall effect of the main half-hipped roof to the east wing, the concrete sill and lintel blocks, the repetitive horizontal framing lines in the windows, and the unpretentious detailing is essentially modern—and of the 1930s design ethos.' Further on it contends, 'The somewhat curious geometry of the plan form is well conceived and resolved to form the courtyard and sheltering verandahs, and overall the spatial planning relationships are well sited to the living style of the Kimberley climate.'

The impression when you arrive at the homestead now is of style, comfort and permanence. It wasn't, and isn't always that way!

Perhaps mindful of his Uncle Willie's perceived loneliness after Uncle Charlie died, Bill continued to create a place in which to live that had the luxury and facilities suitable for a family to be raised happily and safely, and for guests to visit and stay comfortably. A haven in the area was his vision, albeit isolated. It was part of his Model Cattle Station dream.

Native Staff

Looking after this large homestead, along with other houses now forming the station homestead complex, required much assistance. Bill and Maxine believed that the aboriginal people, who lived in the area, were entitled to remain on the property. They were proud to say, 'we b'longa Fossil.' Many of them chose to work. The men were employed as stockmen and ringers, camp cooks, vegetable gardeners and yardmen, or assistants to the fencers, bore runners, or other contractors. At least ten women worked around the homestead buildings, men's quarters and the cookhouse, as housemaids, kitchen hands, and in the gardens watering the plants. The women usually worked for three or four hours each day, starting in the early morning before it became too hot. They were shown how to carry out their daily duties for the respective rooms and garden areas, which were their responsibility. For this they were paid a modest amount, plus received their keep. Housing, clothing and bedding were also provided, prior to minimum pay rate awards being introduced.

The station complex and gardens were run like a small township. Every morning a bevy of aboriginal women descended on the kitchen and all the various sleeping quarters and gardens to water, clean, tidy and generally maintain each place. 'It works best if this is done every day,' Maxine explained. 'Confusion is created if we try and do only some chores on various days, with the exception of washing and ironing.'

The housewomen had one method only of cleaning the floors of any dust and grime—put everything up on tables off the floor and bring in a hose and straw brooms. They loved paddling around in the water, sweeping. After completion the intense heat soon dried the floors.

Having learned an effective method of doing something thereafter it would always be done that way. A nurse from the Australian Inland Mission hospital in Fitzroy Crossing was at the station for a few days leave. She delighted in teaching some of the native women how to make the beds the hospital way with sheets pulled tight and mitred corners. Thereafter there was always a struggle to get into bed, as the sheets were pulled so tight!

The native people were always treated with dignity. 'Do you think you could get one of your 'gins' to do my washing?' a young professional man, who was working and staying for a few days, once asked of Maxine. The caustic reply was: 'my girls have their allocated tasks to do and will be busy all today.' She muttered later that the cattle buyer who stayed regularly never asked to have his washing done—he went to the laundry and did it himself.

Native Amenities

Always wanting to provide the best for his staff, in 1953 Bill put his architectural training into practice again to construct a block of buildings for the native camp. They were reported to be the first quarters of their kind erected on a private station in the Kimberley. The buildings were constructed of concrete blocks, like the homestead, but attractively faced with flat river stone and enclosed with insect-proof mesh. One building was 36ft long and included showers, water tubs for washing clothes, and a septic system. The floors were concrete. A second building contained an airy dining room, spacious kitchen and meat storage house. The third was a nicely appointed native hospital. Cottages were provided for all families. These upgraded amenities received much publicity at the time.

Additionally Maxine attended to the health of the aborigines, and was often called upon to provide a bandage for minor injuries, or some medicine for 'cold-sick', or 'guts-ache', a couple of their common disorders. In the case of serious illness, the Flying Doctor was consulted, and flown in, if necessary.

Having stood side by side with the aboriginal race for over fifty years, eventually Maxine was extremely knowledgeable of their culture and their manner of living, and maintained a good balance of caring for their needs, always remaining extremely competent. She commented once that academic people would come to interview the native people without realizing that the aboriginal person would say, 'yes' to a question if they thought that is what the interviewer wanted to hear even though it may not necessarily be factual. It was a totally different method of communication to the western style. Maxine was also very circumspect about how many times she would allow people onto the station to interview them, believing that these indigenous Australians also had their right to privacy.

Commenting one day about their health, she said, 'You know, they had such strong constitutions with lithe bodies, and strong bones, hair and nails, until they started eating western food. I'm not proud that our society has introduced them to biscuits and other overly sweetened and processed food'.

These comments were contained in an article in a Melbourne newspaper:

> 'I have written much about the neglect of the native in the North. Now it is both pleasant and satisfying to write about the way two people of vision, deep human sympathy, and understanding, are pointing the road to a new future for the native. I was impressed by the splendid healthiness, physique, and cheerfulness of Fossil's native population...Fossil Downs has many remarkable, many beautiful, many impressive features. But none is more remarkable, beautiful, or impressive than the great human effort of Bill and Maxine MacDonald for the aborigines that have come into their care. This, then, is a tribute to two fine people—and to two fine Australians who, having acquired their heritage, are not resting but discharging their responsibility fully to those who went before them and who will come after them.' *Argus (Melbourne) Saturday 6 August 1955, page 35*

This procedure continued with all the following generations of MacDonalds.

Diabetes 2 was unknown amongst the native people prior to 1970s. Sister Beryl Gilkes (now Scott) confirmed recently that this disease was not an issue at all in the late 1960s, or early 1970s, when she was stationed at the AIM Hospital at Fitzroy Crossing.

At that time, there was a law forbidding the supply of alcohol to indigenous Australians, unless they had their 'Citizens Rights'— i.e. the right to vote, and the right to drink alcohol. In an effort to bring equality to the races this law, preventing the sale of alcohol to aboriginal people, was repealed in 1967.

This Gooniyandi mob's way of traditional living was starkly different to that of Europeans. They always had to consider their own preservation. It may have been different in other tribes, but when you live totally off the land, every person of hunting age needs to fend for himself. Therefore they had to be conservationists, too. When a child was born the elders decreed that it must not eat, say, goanna, or bustard, or wild berries, or some other species of wildlife or vegetation. That decree operated for life as the elders were respected as the custodians of knowledge and lore. The nominated animal or plant would never be eaten by that person, ensuring there was sufficient for the tribe to be fed without exhausting the supply, and so that the species would not be hunted or over-consumed to extinction.

Also, their population must not increase—the balance between deaths and births needed to be maintained. If twins were born, one would be disposed of. That would also be the case if a child was born with a deformity, and would be unable to hunt when an adult. As offensive as that may be, that's how this tribe conserved its resources. It also ensured strong, healthy bodies.

It wasn't possible to operate the station, with the large numbers of cattle that had been bred to help feed and prosper the country, without the considerable labour input of the aboriginal people. Modern mustering methods, using aircraft and erecting smaller, more manageable paddocks, were yet to be introduced in the Kimberley. It was still mainly rangeland grazing. But in a relatively short time all that changed.

Modern Amenities

Now the station finances were in a somewhat better state, Bill looked at incorporating all the 'mod cons' he could into the homestead, not only to make the Kimberley more livable, but also to relieve some of the tedium of extra housework as guests were continuing to arrive. Each time he visited Goulburn or Sydney he delighted in ferreting out the latest innovations to assist the station run more efficiently.

He had a bore drilled near the homestead and high quality artesian water bubbled to the surface. A windmill drew the water up to the concrete tank sited on the steep little hill and gravity ensured a reasonable pressure down to the Big House. An electric pump was added to irrigate the gardens—secretary's task! Rainwater for rinsing your hair was a luxury that many town dwellers didn't have. Water slowly dripping off the roof of a bough shed, enabled by a pipe threaded through the netted thatched roof, provided welcome cooling when a breeze wafted around on the hot evenings. Sleep was possible then. Merrilee and Annette did their schoolwork there in the hot, humid weather.

Electricity could be produced with a generator powered by diesel, which was great for lighting, powering pumps, and miscellaneous activities. Now that bottled gas was available, gas refrigerators could be utilized which were first-rate, and for heating hot water services too. Gradually all these facilities were introduced. The bottled gas was so successful that Fossil Downs became the largest domestic user in Western Australia. Eventually it was installed in all seven residences there, plus the sheds where welding was performed. They'd come a long way from one Coolgardie safe in 1938!

Rev. John Flynn's pedal radio and Flying Doctor service had arrived. With the upgrading of an airstrip on Fossil to aeronautical standards regular airline schedules, if haphazard at times, made life more manageable. Then it was possible to leave the station in the wet season although planes could not always land and take off. It depended on the condition of the unsealed airstrip if there had been humungous rainfall overnight. Regular aircraft services, stopping at all the stations, were an exceptionally welcome initiative by the fledgling airline companies. Plus regular medical clinics for everyone could be conducted on the stations—a great step forward.

Much more infrastructure was needed, though, if families were to live on their stations with a relative degree of comfort and safety, having access to health and other services. Access to many Kimberley properties was still on tracks that turned to bulldust in the dry season and over unbridged river crossings that were impassable in the wet season. The wheels of progress turned very slowly in the Kimberley.

Visit of Princess Margaret

Eminent dignitaries continued to arrive. No doubt the most notable to visit were Princess Margaret and Lord Snowdon in 1972. Edna Quilty, from Lansdowne Station, recalls meeting them in her book, *Nothing Prepared Me*:

Princess Margaret and Lord Snowdon, staying at Gogo Station while visiting the Kimberley, will lunch at Fossil Downs today. Maxine has invited us to attend. Rod and I will be presented to Princess Margaret. Maxine, as gracious as she is beautiful, meets us. Her daughters, Merrilee Wells and Annette Henwood, are with her. Maxine, calm and relaxed, is used to entertaining famous and important people at her lovely station home.

Princess Margaret and Lord Snowdon arrive about half an hour after us. The Princess is tiny and slim. She is hatless with not a hair out of place. She has a lovely speaking voice and lots of charm.

Lord Snowdon, slim and elegant in his jeans, dark-blue shirt, white shoes, and ten-gallon hat is excited. Never has he seen anything like this. 'I say, old chap! So many cows, so much space, so much land where nobody lives. By Gad! Can one person really own all this, old boy?'

Princess Margaret, interested but less enthusiastic, would prefer to sit in the shade, I think. The heat and the dust must be very hard on her. Her lady-in-waiting sprained her ankle at Gogo last night and did not accompany her. The aide-de-camp carries her umbrella but never seems to be close when she needs it.

We go to the yards, where the stock boys will demonstrate getting a calf into a cradle and, after tipping it onto a tyre on the ground, branding it. Lord Snowdon stands close to the cradle. It is suggested that he should stand further back, but he doesn't move.

It's difficult for the boys to get the calf into the cradle with him so close but they manage it. They tip the cradle and it falls onto the tyre. The calf kicks up a mixture of manure and earth into Lord Snowdon's face. The royal pilot, standing next to me, says, 'I hope he had his mouth closed.'

Giving a demonstration of horse breaking that day was Allan Simpson, a tough Kimberley horse whisperer who worked at many stations around the area. He could handle the roughest horses and have them ready for the stock camp in record time, where they were known as 'half-day horses'. Invariably he worked in bare feet and shorts, but it had been suggested that for this occasion, perhaps he could 'tidy up'. So, he donned a pair of shoes! Just as he was about to display his methods, he spoke to Princess Margaret, saying 'Excuse me ma'am. I just can't work in these!' and kicked off the shoes. To say the Princess and Lord Snowdon were completely enthralled with the demonstration is an understatement!

Vlesio Zenelia

A noted visitor on a different mission was artist Vlesio Zenelia. Later he revealed he'd feared for his life while at Fossil! In 1950 he'd gone there to sight ancient native rock paintings. He planned to reproduce them. Had he heard about them from one of Bill's interviews or speaking engagements while in Sydney?

Having arrived at the station, in due course Bill took him up to the caves in the rugged ranges, where some of the paintings were under an overhanging ledge. He dropped him there, with his crayons, paints, and easel, along with his food and camping gear, and said he'd be back to collect him as requested. Mr. Zenelia proposed to camp alone for nine days, copying all the native symbolic paintings never before reproduced or seen by the public. When he realized he was camping in a native graveyard, he got the 'yips'! 'It was eerie', he said. 'The tribe whose area it had been were extinct, and it was rigidly avoided by other tribes.' He felt a strangely hostile atmosphere, which depressed him and he believed he would go mad. Deciding to leave, he realized he couldn't! There was no defined track back along the fifty-odd miles to the station homestead. He just had to wait it out, petrified, too scared to sleep much, until Bill returned to collect him, as arranged, later in the week. When restored to 'normalness', Vlesio Zenelia said he proposed to exhibit the pictures in Sydney, after they'd been referred to Sydney University anthropologist, Professor A. P. Mitin. He didn't request a repeat visit. *Barrier Miner, Broken Hill 15 February 1950*

Bill's Experiments & Publicity for the Kimberley

In 1936, Bill gave a long interview to the *Chronicle (Adelaide)* newspaper ranging over the many subjects that needed attention in the Kimberley. He pointed out the woefully inadequate infrastructure in this area, which was capable of producing huge amounts of beef and wool. He listed its natural attributes as being prolific rivers plus subartesian water at a shallow depth, fertile soil and native Mitchell and Flinders grasses. 'However, development is slow and under existing conditions the remote position from any large markets dooms closer settlement schemes to failure for many years to come,' he rued, shaking his head. He detailed how the Asian markets had been lost through imposed tariffs and how meat works in the area had been unprofitable. 'With Java on the gold standard, and Australia's present policy of protective tariff causing a reciprocal tariff by the Netherlands government of 24/- per head on all cattle landed in Java, a large market has been lost to northern cattlemen,' Bill affirmed. 'Singapore uses chilled beef, the Northern Territory has lost the Manila trade, and Vesty's £2,000,000 meat works proved unprofitable,' he regretted, running his hand through his hair in exasperation. 'Now the Government-owned Wyndham meat works, treating 30,000 cattle each season, and the absurdly small Perth market which absorbs only 600 head per week, are the sole outlets for Kimberley's extensive herds.'

Suggestions from the authorities of a railway through to East Kimberley for the improvement of cattle travelling to the Wyndham

Meat Works, and the establishment of a meat works at Derby, were the only possibilities of reducing the time and distance stock needed to be driven. 'The railway won't happen, though,' he laughed, 'as in the summer months the cyclonic rain would cause the line to be washed away, and repairs would take too long.'

Bill was no shrinking violet and worked tirelessly to bring attention to causes he thought were worthwhile, giving countless interviews to newspapers. He believed that publicity was the best way for improving and selling cattle in the Kimberley area, and Fossil Downs in particular. Did the daily papers seek him out when he was in Perth, Sydney or Adelaide? He was often quoted on diverse subjects related to the area, these interviews being syndicated throughout Australian newspapers. The Kimberley area was still remote and unknown by most of the population.

In the *Centralian Advocate* on 17 December 1954, he claimed, 'Roads are the lifelines of the Kimberley. Yet little effort is being made by governments to improve, or even maintain these lines of communication on which the economic future, and even the survival, of the Kimberley pastoral industry depends.' Explaining further, Bill said, 'The Broome meatworks provide the diesel roadtrains that transport cattle in loads of 103 head, over indescribable conditions that inflict bruising on the cattle and rejection of a too high proportion, even when travelling in low gear!'

The damage inflicted on the roads by the Redex Round Australia car trial that year, organised by the Australian Sporting Car Club, did not impress Bill. 'The roads were literally cut to pieces by 500 cars carrying officials and contestants and tourist followers.' Wound up, and shaking his head, he continued, 'Even before this devastating invasion, these roads were incapable of carrying the slow moving cattle transports or the station supplies to the settlers, without damage and loss.' Of course, the public living beyond the Kimberley loved the Redex Trial.

Change of Attitude

A change of attitude of the settlers was also needed, Bill believed. In 1949 he spoke out, saying that the trouble with (the residents of) the Kimberley is that for nearly 60 years people had regarded a sojourn there as something to be endured to give them a chance to live more comfortably down south. 'Few people ever tried to live well here—the mere idea was good for a guffaw,' he said. 'There's been a lot of money made here in the North but most of it has been spent elsewhere,' he claimed. 'If some of that cash had been spent here where it was made, life in the Kimberley could have been made much more pleasant for many people.' He sighed, 'This will always be a land of makeshifts as long as life here is just regarded as a passing phase.' *Western Mail (Perth) 8 September 1949*

Visits of newspaper personnel were grist to Bill's mill. After one such visit his thoughts on trading cattle with Indonesia were published widely. At the time it was argued in some quarters that Indonesia was eyeing off Australia's vast and largely unoccupied tracts of land. 'Development of a vigorous trade with the East, particularly in cattle, would remove a potential threat to Australia,' he contended. 'I cannot help but feel that Australia is missing the real importance of the North in not advancing greater trade with the Far East.' He shook his head. 'The best way to remove the threat of invasion is to realise these people do not want to leave their own lands. What they need, and need more and more, is food and if Australia can produce the food to supply their needs, and be a friendly neighbour with a recip-

rocal trade, a great measure of our danger will disappear,' he argued.
The Mercury (Hobart) 2 September 1953

Again, Bill was ahead of the pack, and continued, noting that, 'this area is very favourably situated in regard to world trade. Wyndham is four days nearer the Asian markets than Brisbane. One day I hope we'll be able to take advantage of that'.

Stud Cattle

In 1946 Bill registered his Kimberley Poll Shorthorn stud, the first cattle stud in the Kimberley or the Pilbara. He bought two bulls and five heifers from the then well-known stud of Gundibri Estate from Merriwa, NSW. One of the females was in calf to 'Gundibri Laddie 22' and her bull calf, 'Kimberley Laddie', subsequently became one of Fossil Downs' outstanding sires.

In 1947 three more stud heifers from NSW were added to the stud; then at the 1948 Perth Royal Show, Bill paid the top price and created a record for the Poll Shorthorn breed in Western Australia by purchasing the Champion Bull, 'Antrim Treasurer', for 400 guineas. (£420). These were the nucleus of the Kimberley Poll Shorthorn Stud. Returns from the commercial herd cattle had continued to be more profitable since the war, and were reinvested into breeding even more first-rate cattle.

Taking these southern bred cattle to the North was considered to be a courageous—some said foolish—experiment but it was successful, as good quality bulls were produced which were inured to Kimberley conditions and immune to bovine babesiosis, a tick-borne disease of cattle, also known as 'redwater'. These stud bulls elicited keen demand and were supplied to several stations in the Kimberley including Lissadell and Mt. House, and to Humbert River and Newcastle Waters in the Northern Territory.

Bull shipment makes history

History was made in 1951 when a draft of 100 herd bulls was supplied to Newcastle Waters station in The Territory. They were a particularly good selection, being a rich red and roan colour with excellent heads. They were clean polled animals without scurs and ranged from 18 months to three years old. These bulls were walked to Derby, shipped on the 'Koolinda' to Darwin, railed south to the end of the line at Pine Creek, then driven 120 miles overland to their new home.

Exporting beef bulls was a new role for Western Australia, which had usually been at the receiving end where interstate stock transfers were concerned. It was a feather in Bill's cap that Northern Territory cattlemen could now look to the West for herd improvement material. *Western Mail (Perth) Thursday 21 June 1951.*

Bulls Take Flight

At this time Fossil Downs was running 22,000 head of cattle, and shipping 2,000 per year off the station. Naturally this fluctuated with the seasons, and one year 4,000 head had been sent off the property. In 1970 there was a record branding of 6,843 calves, so three years later there would have been a big draft available for sale.

'Maxine', Bill enquired one day. 'If frozen beef can be airlifted, why not live cattle?' He was in entrepreneur mode again. 'Why not check it out', was Maxine's sage reply, wondering what next Bill would think of. Thus began another Fossil Downs innovation, another first.

Reports were carried in newspapers throughout Australia, as this groundbreaking way of transporting live stud bulls was undertaken. Under headlines reading 'Live Porterhouse Takes to the Air', 'Bulls Freighted by Air in WA', and 'Record Cattle Air Lift', the rest of the country learned about flying bulls. The initial airlift was of twenty herd bulls north to Mt. House station, and this was repeated the following year. Then a bull, and stud heifers, were purchased by Charlie Schultz from Humbert River station in Northern Territory, and were also transported by air. Bill had prearranged news photographers to be there to capture the event, and photos and reports were circulated in all cattle breeding circles.

The aircraft used was the Air Beef Ltd. Bristol Freighter, which had transported the chilled beef carcasses from Glenroy station to Wyndham. It would fly to Derby with a load of hides, collect and carry five tons of fuel to Fossil Downs, then pick up the bulls as backloading, at 30 shillings per head. Although Mt. House was only 80 miles away from Fossil, owing to the rugged terrain separating them it would have taken about three weeks to drove the cattle overland.

The first draft was part of 40 18-month old herd bulls purchased by Mt. House. Two days prior to the flight the bulls were halter-broken, which speaks volumes for the docility of the Poll Shorthorn. They were led into the freight compartment of the plane, turned around and placed five abreast. A crossbar was then fitted across the compartment and the halter ropes tied to it. Four rows of five were loaded in this manner and loading was completed in less than 40 minutes. The flight took 32 minutes.

How well did the bulls cope with air travel? Much better than three weeks droving on the tracks! They lost no condition, their feet were unaffected, and they were very quickly placed onto good feed and water at their destination, thus experiencing no setbacks.

It was claimed that this first flight of live beef cattle was a world record—that nowhere else before this had live cattle been flown. Western Australian authorities liked to bask in the achievements of pioneers at the forefront of commercial aviation. Many such firsts were created there. It was necessary to think outside the square because of the vast distances and appalling condition of the roads. Many of Australia's premier aviators found fame in Western Australia—Norman Brearley, Horrie Miller and Charles Kingsford-Smith to name a few—and they relished the challenges presented.

What would Charlie and Willie MacDonald think, to see that Bristol Freighter drop out of the sky onto the Fossil airstrip, and watch young stud bulls being guided up the ramp and tied to a crossbar, before taking off into the air again? It became the norm for them to be delivered up to 600 miles away to the Northern Territory before nightfall.

Air Beef Scheme

The Glenroy Air Beef Scheme, sited at Glenroy Station, part of the Mt. House lease to the north of Fossil, had commenced operations in 1949 and the second draft of cattle handled there were from Fossil Downs.

A consortium of two airlines, and the Blythe family, founded this Air Beef Scheme. A meat works, which included an abattoir, carcass freezing facilities, and an airport runway, was built on remote Glenroy. From 1949 to 1965 the scheme operated successfully. Cattle were brought in from Kimberley stations and were slaughtered, quartered, boned and chilled overnight, then flown the following day to Wyndham using the Bristol Freighter and/or Douglas DC-3 aircraft. The beef was frozen at Wyndham and then shipped to the United Kingdom. In 1959 the Derby Meat Co., DEMCO, was established and thereafter the air shipments were made to the closer destination of Derby. This scheme had been a great boon to the Kimberley stations. Between 1949 and 1962, 3000 return flights from Glenroy to Wyndham and Derby were made, uplifting 55,500 head of chilled cattle, while nearly 4,000 tonnes of cargo was back-loaded to Glenroy and other stations enroute.

As grants had eventually been made by the Commonwealth Government to upgrade the roads in the area—not before time according to Bill—to support the beef industry generally, it was realized that airfreighting of beef would therefore become uneconomic. In the Kimberley, the western section of the Gibb River road (track) was eventually upgraded. Road trains could then transport cattle more economically. Thus the Air Beef Scheme was closed in 1965. This enterprise was recognised in 2006 when the ruins of the abattoir and aerodrome were listed on the Western Australian State Heritage Register.

Bill had pioneered a new era of beef production using air transport. The East and West Kimberley, by developing its beef potential, at times were likened to a new Argentina. Production on the well-watered productive Mitchell-grass plains was still underdeveloped. More practical aid was merited from the Commonwealth and State Governments if this little-known corner of the continent was to become a major production hub. Bill was on his own in trying to bring attention to this cause—he was still the only family owner of a station living and working it—as most of the others were managed by employees, albeit good managers and cattlemen, for family or company interests.

Stock horses

Horses and mules with good staying ability to cope with the extremely hot and tough conditions on the station were needed. To achieve this, Bill focused on purchasing Percheron stallions with proven sustainability for breeding purposes. The station ran 300 mares plus young stock. Many bred on Fossil Downs were an attractive grey, with excellent general conformation and beautiful clean strong legs and feet. A particular grey stallion called 'Whyandi' was responsible for many of the foals. He had the same breeding as the 1890/92 Perth Cup winner called Wandering Willie.

This diary entry indicated some of Bill's intentions: 'bought three splendid-looking animals, which were shipped home. West Kimberley may be able to hold its own against the East Kimberley horses at the forthcoming races!' Did they? No outcome was listed.

Further Percheron bloodlines were introduced for their strength and quiet, gentle disposition. Although a strong horse, with a long free stride, the Percheron has an innate intelligence and boldness of character, being willing to perform well under all conditions. It has a large foot that stays sound with little maintenance, an attribute very welcome in the stock camp.

Walkabout Disease

Sometimes called Kimberley disease, horses on Kimberley stations could be disastrously and fatally distressed by this affliction. Horses so affected walk in a straight line, blundering into trees and rocks, until they die of exhaustion. While it seemed obvious that some plant must cause it, identifying the culprit proved difficult. Naturally losing working horses like this is a drastic and tragic loss to the stations, and heartbreaking to see.

Although it took many years, in 1958 Agriculture Department officers found that crotalaria retusa (sometimes referred to as 'rattlepod' after its seed pods) was the cause, a plant that reaches a height of about three feet. Mainly growing on the flats beside watercourses, which flood during the wet season, it carries clusters of pretty yellow pea-shaped flowers that horses eat readily when the plants are small. It seems that if they graze on it for two seasons, their central nervous system is affected and they walk themselves to death. This plant is still prevalent with the same debilitating effect.

As if that were not challenging enough, other horses at Fossil succumbed to diet differences, especially when fodder was brought to the station from other areas during droughts. WA's Chief Veterinary Surgeon conducted tests on three horses, and suggested it had caused colic, followed by founder. He said this occurred when horses unaccustomed to grain were fed too much wheat, barley or oats.

And yet a further dramatic horse disaster occurred in 1953 during the drought. Suddenly 90 of the Fossil horses were poisoned. It seems there could have been an unknown weed in oats fed to them. The first one died 2½ hours after eating the oats, a valuable stud Percheron, which had been imported from South Australia. A plane was chartered to fly the Chief Veterinary Surgeon and a stock inspector from Perth to Fossil to perform an autopsy. The brain, liver and stomach of a dead horse, along with the suspected oats, were flown to Perth for analysis. Bill was in a desperate position. There was very little native grass on the station, and he suspected the fodder, which had been bought in, was killing the horses. A botanist suggested it was the eating of wild radish. The cause of the deaths was never positively identified as the horse had been dead too long before the organs were removed.

Cattle musters were still carried out with horses—it was another twenty to thirty years before aerial mustering became the norm. Losses of horses to unknown causes created far-reaching consequences for the running of Kimberley stations.

Mules

Mating thoroughbred mares with a good type of jack donkey produced some magnificent mules. These animals were greatly in demand for both riding and pack-work in the North, as they were very long-lived and were not subject to walkabout disease. Bill had retained a well-bred grey colt mule and he was mated with the grey station mares to establish a very robust strain.

Pack mules were used to accompany the cattle being driven to Derby for shipment to Perth, or other destinations. One team consisted of 6 big, upstanding chestnut coloured animals, all perfectly matched. This proved to be a walking advertisement for the Station——Bill never missed an opportunity to promote. What could be better than this example of 'show—not tell'!

Bill sold mules. The Kimberley police, who often had to trudge over tough terrain, were especially good customers. However, he wouldn't sell horses to anyone, as he believed that would bring bad luck!

Drought

In 1952 Australia's notorious paradoxical climatic conditions surfaced, and the first drought ever known by the Kimberley pastoralists slowly engulfed the area.

Fossil Downs size was estimated at about 1,000,000 acres, by the early 1950s as a result of amalgamating adjoining leases. Approximately two-thirds of it was grazable and could be mustered without too much drama. It was carrying 20,000 branded head of cattle, worked by 20 whitefellas and 40 native employees. It had come a long way since the first generation of MacDonalds had arrived in 1886 with their wagon loaded with what remained of their plundered equipment and drought-surviving head of cattle, bullocks and horses. The Kimberley was generally thought to be immune to drought as the monsoon rains and cyclones usually dumped plenty of rain in the Mueller Ranges, which eventually flowed down to the plains in the Fitzroy Valley. Not in 1952.

Virtually all feed was gone and even native trees started dying as a result of the intense heat and lack of water. As the year dragged into 1953 it was estimated that half the cattle in the Kimberley had died. Bores were sunk hurriedly and for the first time feed was bought in to keep stock alive. All local supplies were depleted. Ever dramatic at Fossil, the dire situation made headlines. Bill was desperate to save his Poll Shorthorn stud. He was quoted in the newspapers as saying 'we've counted every mouthful of fodder the cattle have eaten in the past few weeks, to try to make it last. We've cut and carted every blade of vegetation we could from our irrigation plots in the hope that the rains would come. Cloudless blue skies with hot drying winds are blowing the topsoil from the country that was once fertile grass plains, and at the moment rain looks further away than ever.' Trucks, ships and planes were mustered to bring feed from anywhere it could be found, from down south by ship, then truck, and from the Northern Territory by plane.

Again in Sydney and Goulburn, Bill was quoted in their daily newspapers:

'Starving stock is chewing out the fibrous trunks of the bottle (baobab) trees, hundreds of which have split and crumbled under the weight of their great bulk'. This particular tree species is unique to the Kimberley. Some trees had grown to a height of 45' with a circumference of approximately 60'. Bill explained that gallons of mucilage were stored in the unique bottle-shape trunk from which the tree derived its knickname. He said it was a common sight at Fossil Downs to see 20 or 30 cattle clustering around the shell of one of these trees. Inside the trunk, another two or three cattle might be feeding. They existed by eating the sodden pulp. Bill, ever alert to a promotion opportunity though, was also quick to point out that his adaptable Poll Shorthorn cattle had actually fattened on starvation grasses, and highlighted how the stud stock were surviving quite well on spinifex grass plus the leaves of mimosa and coolibah trees.

Sadly, as in all cases of drought, it was necessary for the stockmen to carry guns to shoot the cattle that became too weak to walk to water. Even though the water pumps at the bores were working at full pressure, some herd animals succumbed to the constant lack of nutrition on the stations. Pathetically, a baby calf would be standing helplessly beside the body of its perished mother, having drunk the last of her colostrum milk. It was reported that on the lawns of nearly every station homestead were scores of drought-orphaned calves with insatiable appetites being bottle-fed, which stockmen just hadn't had the heart to destroy.

The desperate situation continued. 1954 arrived with still no life-saving monsoonal rain. By then, the Kimberley had suffered 34 months of heart-breaking drought. Back at the Perth Royal Show in 1952, Bill had purchased two champion Poll Shorthorn bulls, but agisted them on a property near Perth because of the drought. In 1955 he felt confident enough that the weather would break, so shipped them to Derby, thinking to truck them the 200 miles to Fossil. Break the weather did! Suddenly the Fitzroy River was 7 miles wide in places, and the water many feet high over the causeways. Undaunted, Bill chartered the Douglas freighter again, and the bulls were delivered to the station by air. *The Land, 4 June 1954*

This was the first time the Fitzroy River had flooded in three years. During the last week of January the best rains for more than two years were recorded. Was this *deja vu* for the MacDonald family? Was Bill and Maxine's reaction to this rain similar to that of Uncles Charlie and Willie when the monsoon rain began in Queensland after their months of enforced camping at the Nine-mile Waterhole while they waited for the drought to break there? Did Bill and Maxine stand in it, their faces upturned, while those thudding drops fell, as Charlie and Willie had done at the Nine-mile? Did they welcome it by running around naked, allowing the precious droplets to soothe their hot, tired bodies? 'Prickly heat' is an unpleasant red blotchy, itchy, skin condition suffered by many in the tropics. The Derby doctors claimed the best cure for it was to run around naked when the first rain fell in the wet season! Whatever their reaction, Bill and Maxine would have felt the utmost relief that their cattle would soon be foraging on the resulting abundant pastures.

In a backhanded way, the drought had provided a blessing to many stations, hard though it is to see during a drought. Work was rushed ahead on new bores, and fences were erected to provide paddocks that could be spelled, giving pasture-control over grazing land, which in the past had always been open range. Capital was spent on Kimberley stations—money that in normal times may not have been. Had the people of the North been taught a lesson? The impossible had happened—the Kimberley had had a drought. It wasn't the last.

Bill at homestead entrance

Droughtmasters

Maxine's photo at Fitzroy River Lodge Fitzroy Crossing

Corroboree at Fossil Downs

Giekie Gorge, Fitzroy Crossing

Waterhole on Fossil Downs

Sandra and the author in 2014

Original wagon which made the first crossing of the continent of Australia by a four-wheeled vehicle
Sourced from State Library of W.A.

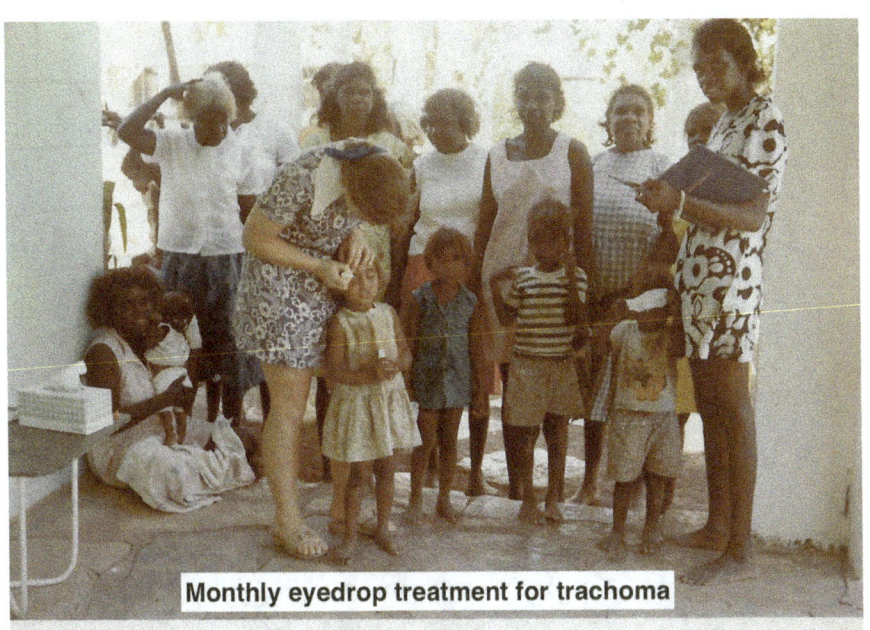
Monthly eyedrop treatment for trachoma

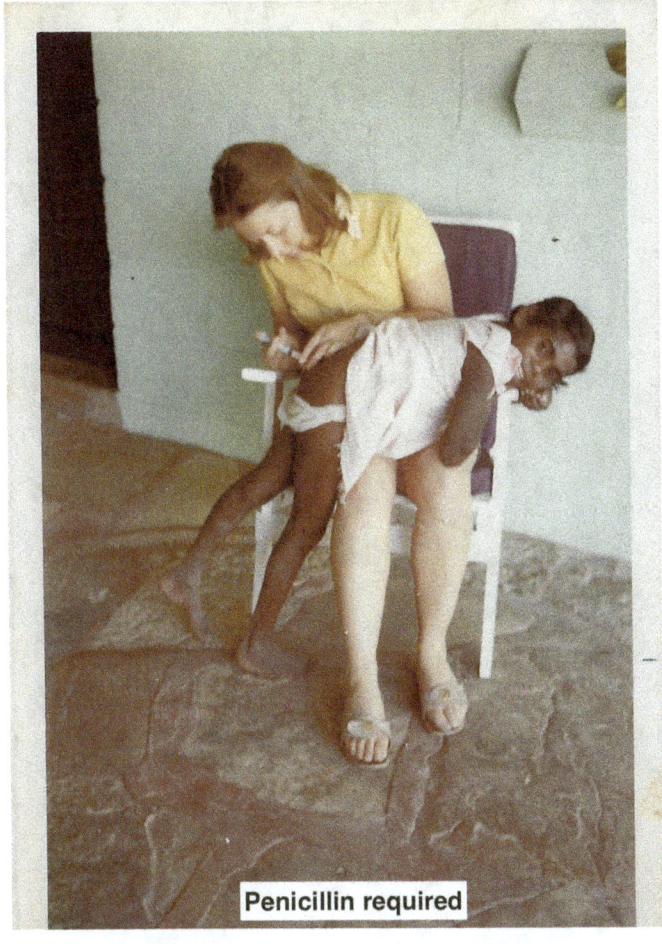
Penicillin required

Near Blythe's jumpup

Grassy plains

Lake Graham

Exasperation dam at Darriarrowah

Stock yards at Old Station

All steel yards replacing timber yards

Mustering droughtmasters

Old Crossing of Fitzroy River

Bridge installed in 1983

The author and Kathleen in 2014

Old Station, 9 miles from current homestead. First buildings erected in 1883. Sourced from State Library of W.A.

Maxine, Annette & Merrilee MacDonald
Sourced from State Library of W.A

Back veranda—the access to rooms downstairs

Pull hooks and wheel rims from first wagon which crossed Australia repurposed at the managers' home

Fitzroy River on Fossil Downs near Dimond Gorge

Spider Creek—Paddy's paddock

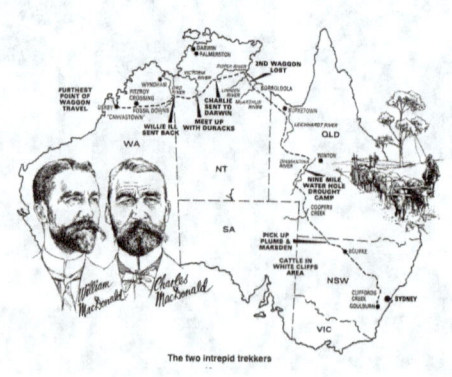
The two intrepid trekkers

The Green Room

The Hall—venue for evening drinks

Front verandah

Maxine using first model RFDS radio

Bill (WHM) MacDonald

Layout of homestead and works headquarters beside Giekie Range

Approach to homestead

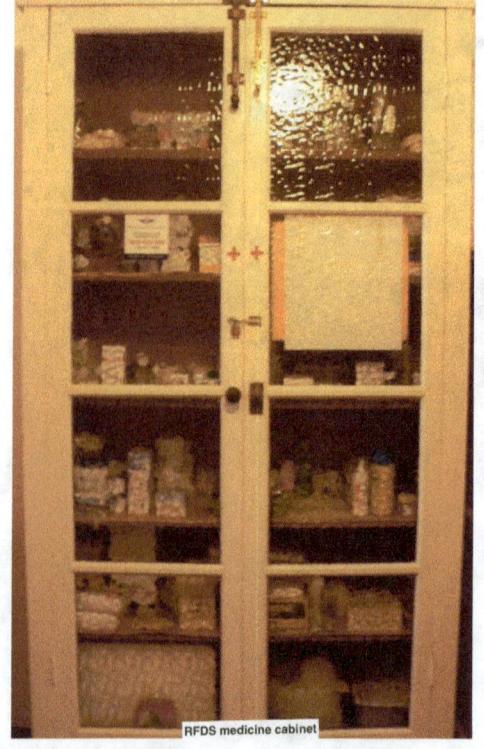
RFDS medicine cabinet

Annette & John Henwood

Main store, with mezzanine elevation to avoid flooding

Morning smoko in cookhouse

Fossil Downs cemetery

Ex Noonkanbah shearing shed housing some of the machinery required to run Fossil Downs station

Garage for making mechanical repairs

More necessary machinery

Margaret Gorge

Margaret River

THE WORLD'S LONGEST CATTLE DRIVES

UNITED STATES CATTLE DRIVES

AUSTRALIAN CATTLE DRIVES

Excellent Beef Yield

Abundant pasture now covered the stock-depleted runs. At Fossil, the cattle were only in fair store condition after the drought, but they quickly gained 2 lb. weight per day when back on their regular pasture. Bill, in entrepreneurial mode again, forged on with his theory that the Kimberley could produce earlier maturing cattle, especially with road trains becoming available to transport the animals.

At Alice Springs in 1934, the Army assembled the first road train. Kurt Johannsen, mechanic, inventor and dogged pioneer, continued making refinements to it. He designed a self-tracking trailer system that allowed a prime mover to pull several trailers at once. This was revolutionary. Now it was possible to transport a consignment of 103 three-year-old cattle by road.

Killing Cattle at Broome

As an experiment, in September 1955 Bill sent a consignment of 500 head of three-year-old cattle, by road-trains, to the Broome abattoirs. The results were excellent. Farming journals quoted Bill, saying that road transport was a boon to graziers in the Kimberley. He explained that it had taken three days to drove these cattle 30 miles to the trucking point at Fitzroy Crossing. There they were loaded onto the roadtrains and transported the 252 miles to Broome meat works in 15 hours. 'They arrived with glossy coats, in fresh condition and free from horn scurs, because they were hornless cattle,' Bill proudly claimed.

Killing sheets, which list the details of each beast slaughtered, later revealed the average dressed weight of the consignment was 647 lb. per head, with a grading of first and second quality for export of 91.31 per cent. For a comparatively young mob, this was notable. The rejection grading was 3.17 per cent, of which only eight quarters were eliminated for bruising, five for pleurisy and two for old and healed scurs. 'In the past,' Bill said grinning broadly, 'to get bullocks to the market in Perth, they had to be kept to the age of four or five to stand up to being driven 300 miles to the port, combined with a seven day voyage by ship.'

The following accolade came from James Farrell, a previous manager of the Wyndham Meatworks from 1932 to 1956, and who was a foundation member of the Australian Meat Board. The Wyndham meat works was said to be the largest in the Southern Hemisphere at the time. He had recently retired, and was at his family owned plant in Broome: 'This consignment of Fossil Downs cattle is the best I have seen outside of Queensland and certainly the best ever treated in a Northern meat works. Most of the carcasses,' he said, 'met the standard of choice quality chilled beef suitable for the United Kingdom market.'

Following that consignment, Bill transported some of Fossil's older Shorthorn bullocks by roadtrain to Broome. Although older Shorthorns had been marketed for many years, previously they had been offered to the wholesale trade on the hoof at the Robb's Jetty sale yards at Fremantle, Perth, and this was the first draft at Broome treated for export under certified weight and grading records. Pleasingly, 96 per cent of the four-year-olds were passed for export. The first-grade portion dressed out at 667.96 lbs. while the three-year-olds with 95 per cent acceptance for export, dressed out at 632.46 lb.

This experiment, and others undertaken by Bill, demonstrated by weights and grades that the Kimberley could produce beef to compare with any part of Australia, provided the problem of direct access to meat works was solved. Roads needed upgrading so that cattle could be transported without risk of bruising. 'Roads are the lifelines of the Kimberley,' Bill repeated, 'yet little effort is being made by governments to improve, or even to maintain these lines of communication. The economic future, and even the survival of the Kimberley pastoral industry, depends on them,' he emphasised. He applauded the Broome meat works for providing the diesel roadtrains to transport the cattle in loads of 103 head. 'But the roads are in an indescribably appalling condition' he added.

Beef Roads

Beef roads were eventually established in outback Australia in the 1960/70s for roadtrains to transport cattle to markets and abattoirs. Traditional droving methods had diminished as by trucking the cattle they arrived at the abattoirs much quicker and therefore in better condition. Did anyone then foresee the love affair Australian and overseas tourists would embrace with comfortable, air-conditioned four-wheel drive vehicles, now these tracks were drivable? An irresistible urge to see more and more of the outback was fostered amongst many city, urban and country dwellers considering they could travel there in relative comfort, even if not entirely without challenges and danger. It spawned a whole new industry.

Bill, having the attention of the press, said that taking into account the distances involved between the stations and the ports, consideration should be given to the establishment of inland meat works at key towns, notably Fitzroy Crossing. Stations within reasonable access could sell their bullocks at local abattoirs, thus creating more economical transport costs. It never happened. Most Kimberley cattle stations were forced to hold their bullocks for at least five, and up to seven years of age, before they were able to attain and hold sufficient condition to dress out at an average weight approaching 600 lb.

Confirming the upgrading and improvement in beef production, a representative from Dalgety's stock agents was quoted in their in-house journal as saying that Fossil Downs had pioneered a new era in beef production when Poll Shorthorn bulls were flown into the

Kimberley. 'Today they are producing earlier maturing and improved quality beef, and are eliminating the horns from the rising generations of calves, between 70 and 80 per cent of which were now being polled-bred.' He continued, adding 'hundreds of Poll Shorthorn bulls were now being air or road freighted to other beef stations throughout the Kimberley and the Territory to infuse blood of the modern beef type and to remove the horns that in the past had caused losses to beef breeders. Fossil Downs is doing a great national job. It is now up to Australia to take more interest in this remote forgotten land.'

And in a very back-handed compliment, the following item in *The West Australian* in September 1945, must have brought a wry smile to many faces:

Cattle Killing—A Kimberley Charge—Jury Acquits Accused

At the Quarter Sessions before Dr D. J. Oldmeadow and a jury of six yesterday, Alexander Brown Sadler (71), pastoralist, was charged with having on or about March 10, 1945, at Tablelands station killed a roan steer, the property of Walter O'Connor, with intent to steal the skin and carcass. Sadler is the proprietor of Tablelands station and O'Connor is the owner of Elgie Downs station, which adjoins Tablelands. Both are in the Kimberley. Evidence was given for the Crown that on March 10, 1945, while on muster on his own property Sadler, to provide meat for himself and his natives, directed one of his native stockmen to kill a roan steer with O'Connor's brands and to cut off and bury the brands and earmarks. Evidence of the alleged killing was given by three native stockmen employed by Sadler.

Sadler denied that he had given instructions as alleged or that any cattle belonging to O'Connor had been killed by him. He admitted that he had given instructions to kill a steer that belonged to Fossil Downs station. He said that this was the only animal fit for killing and that it was the custom in such circumstances to kill a 'killer' belonging to a friendly neighbour which statement was corroborated by several witnesses. After a retirement of ten minutes the jury acquitted the accused. Sadler was remanded until the next Quarter Sessions on two charges of a similar nature. *The West Australian, 21 September 1945*

Conducts Trials

Bill's analytical mind was always working. He loved to conduct trials and was good at keeping data and evaluating the results. After one such trial in 1952 he prepared a report and article, which appeared in several State publications:

'The Difference between Polled and Dehorned Cattle

In an effort to reduce bruising during the long trip our Shorthorns have by road and boat from the station to Fremantle (market place), I began dehorning steers and bull calves in 1935. I discontinued the practice in 1940 when I proved conclusively that surgical dehorning did not pay.

Although raised and fattened together, and separated only before being loaded on the ship in Derby, the dehorned bullocks failed to attain the same weight on maturity as the Shorthorns of the same age which had not been dehorned', Bill claimed. 'During the years 1935 to 1940 inclusive, 1782 horned bullocks were marketed in Perth, together with 1659 dehorned and the average price of the dehorned bullocks was 15/9 a head below the average of the horned bullocks.' Continuing, 'During the same period Fossil Downs began the task of breeding the horns off naturally and in 1946 the first consignment of natural polls were marketed. Once again the polled and horned bullocks were raised and fattened together and were only drafted off before yarding in Derby. On the boats and in the yards at Fremantle the bullocks were separate'. He said that it was some time before the butchers fully realized the gain represented by the reduced amount of bruising of the natural polls. 'In the four years 1946 to 1949, only 833 Poll Shorthorns were sold by Fossil Downs in the

Perth market against 1569 horned Shorthorns. The 833 Polls gained top average by 11/2s a head,' he concluded.

By 1950 the number of Poll Shorthorns marketed was 353 and these topped the average of the 895 horned Shorthorns by £1/9/6 a head. Bill enthused, 'the 1951 season just ended showed a further increase in the value of the Poll Shorthorns when 453 bettered the horned average by £1/10/6 a head throughout. Poll Shorthorns from Fossil Downs had thus, during the last seven years, added £1,649/2/10 profit on the sales, this figure representing over 20/- per head on each of the 1621 Poll Shorthorns sold in competition with 3383 horned Shorthorns.' *The Sydney Morning Herald 1 February 1952*

Faster Maturing Beef

Bill then set out to produce a faster maturing animal to enable the stock to be turned over more quickly. He shipped six steers aged 2, 3, 4, 5 and 8 years to Perth to prove the Kimberley could produce quality early age beef, and claimed the production in time-saving could be achieved by pasture control and management.

Misfortune overtook the experiment though. The ship arrived eight days late at Derby, so the stock missed the normal market and were sold at a poorly attended special sale and lost about 220 lb. a head through fretting—but the best-quality bullock, a three-year-old sold for £55 and dressed at 762lb. Before shipment, this three year-old steer, which had a girth measurement behind the withers of 85 inches and was 56 inches in length from withers to tailbutt, was estimated to weigh 1653 lb. Its dressed weight was estimated at 1000 lb. However, its actual dressed weight was 762lb., the second heaviest in the experimental consignment. Although this example was successful, it was frustrating to have no control over mitigating circumstances.

He continued comparing prices obtained for Poll Shorthorns and the horned bullocks he marketed. Early in the season, with the condition of the bullocks not then seriously affected by the prevailing drought, his first consignment consisted of 402 Shorthorns and 130 Poll Shorthorns. Competition was keen and the horned bullocks averaged £38/15/3 a head, beating the average price of £37/3/4 for the polled animals by £1/11/11 a head. In the August sale, with cattle in only medium condition, and the butchers seeking quality and lack of bruising, the polls reversed this position and brought a £3/0/0 higher average. *Western Mail (Perth) 13 November 1952*

Aerial Seeding

Always recognizing the potential of using aircraft, in 1948 Bill experimented with sowing grass seed to bolster the pastures, especially on the river flats where the cattle congregated. Whereas in later years fertilizer spreading and crop spraying from the air became commonplace elsewhere, notably New Zealand, this was said to be the first experiment of its kind attempted in Australia. An Anson plane, from MacRobertson Miller Airlines, was specially equipped to distribute the seed which was fed into a 15" funnel connected with a ½" pipe.

Approximately a quarter-ton of South Australian lucerne, Japanese millet, oats and wheat seed was dropped along a 40-mile stretch of the black soil flats along the Margaret River. All these varieties had previously grown successfully in the Kimberley district under cultivation. Culture, to inoculate the seed, was prepared by the Department of Agriculture and flown in the previous day. The seed was cast over a width of about 250 yards. The plane at first flew at a height of 500 feet but as the ground temperature of 108°F. caused the engine to overheat the remainder of the seed was dropped from 2,000 feet. The flight took 35 minutes. By contrast, men on horseback would take four days to sow the same area.

Fortuitously 12 points of rain fell shortly after the sowing. The seed germinated well and the grass was soon 6 inches high. The ground had not been cultivated in any way before the sowing and aircraft was chosen as the best method of ensuring a light and even distribution which would augment, but not supplant, the natural grasses of the country. The native herbage consisted of mitchel and flinders grasses and it was hoped that the introduction of leguminous varieties would shorten the period of fattening and result in more solidly fleshed animals.

Bill felt the experiment was a success and would prove of great value to the Kimberley district where deposits of silt after floods temporarily spoilt many miles of river-frontage pastures. The experiment offered a comparatively cheap method of improving marginal areas and speedily overcoming the effects of drought, soil erosion, fire and floods.

Maxine, always on the lookout to supplement the variety of fruit available for their tables, related how she used to give watermelon seeds to the ringers to scatter as they rode out on the run at mustering time. 'It would be a good idea,' she thought to herself, 'to sow some seeds from the air during the grass sowing experiment.' Undetected she added some of these seeds to the bulk grass seed. In the air when the chute was released to scatter the seed, these larger seeds clunked and chunked and made such a racket in the funnel and pipe, the pilot thought the plane had been sabotaged! Perhaps it had, sort of. She never said how many melons they harvested from her experiment—but cattle enjoy eating watermelon too!

Irrigated Lucerne

Other innovative programs and experiments were attempted. In 1951 on the blacksoil plains and alluvial flats adjacent to the Margaret River, Bill prepared two sites to irrigate stands of lucerne, which is exceptionally good cattle feed. One stand was to be irrigated from a bore next to the river, the other watered by the overflow from two 30,000 gallon tanks. This would be filled in the first place for cattle by a 20' windmill pumping from a 60' bore. 'These are small beginnings admittedly' he mused, 'but the example points the way to the practicability of bigger schemes'. Other pastoralists also did trials and considerable work to improve pastures and prevent erosion. The positive results were often shared and discussed at meetings and station field days.

In 2016 it was claimed that irrigating fodder crops had the potential to change the face of the Kimberley pastoral industry. At Fitzroy Crossing, Laurie Shaw, spokesman for the Gooniyandi people, said a partnership between his people and nearby Gogo Station to expand that property's irrigated agriculture operations would have big flow-on benefits in a region plagued by high unemployment. 'What we're trying to create here is a long-term thing; we want to create a clear path for our people to benefit through enterprise,' Laurie said. 'We no longer want to rely on governments, and this sort of thing gives us that opportunity.' Sixty-five years after Bill first tried it, maybe someone is taking notice.

Forward Thinking

Bill was a keen supporter of progressive moves anywhere in the Kimberley. 'If you can think it, you can do it,' could have been his motto. Damming the Ord River at the Carlton Reach would make a large area available for irrigation. He believed it would be a comparatively simple engineering feat to construct such a dam for approximately £3,000,000. In 1945 plans had been formed for this project. It would enable cattle to be fattened for the Wyndham Meatworks. Derby and Wyndham ports had not been utilized by shipping during World War II because of the danger of Japanese aerial attacks, and the Wyndham works were closed for a time. When they re-opened it was for a short killing season only. The normal cattle industry practices received many setbacks with the advent of World War II, the most serious loss being the curtailment of shipping for transport of cattle.

During a Japanese attack on the Wyndham aerodrome the flagship of the State Shipping Service, the Koolama, which had been bombed earlier at sea, sank at the jetty and was later towed out to sea and destroyed. Other transport ships, including the Centaur, were torpedoed off Brisbane, Queensland, early in the Pacific war. The Federal Government commandeered the ships Gorgan, Charon and Kybra for war purposes. Only the Koolinda was available for use on the WA coastal run.

The loss in trade brought about by the curtailment of shipping space was compensated, to some extent, by the military service's demand for beef to supply troops in the Northern Territory and Queensland. Expressing the hope that conditions would soon be back to normal, Bill contended that the herds had increased in size, but the quality had suffered because of war restrictions. In his opinion aerial transport was the coming thing, and it was bound to go ahead by leaps and bounds.

(The Kununurra Diversion Dam was finally completed in 1967, and Lake Argyle was built 25 miles south of the town, and opened in 1972. Just prior to this, the decision was made to remove the Durack homestead before Lake Argyle inundated it and to reassemble it on high ground to create a museum to preserve the Durack history. Significant graves were also relocated.)

Future Development of the Kimberley

It was explained that the 'North-West and Kimberley Development Association', formed at Whim Creek, was working for the future development of these somewhat unknown areas. 'We hope that if some requests from this association are acceded to by the State and Federal Governments, the area in the north of Western Australia will become taxation free for some years,' said Bill. 'This will, we hope, encourage the necessary workforce to come and work in the Kimberley.'

Did this push contribute to persuading the Chifley government to introduce taxation allowances? They were introduced in 1945 with the Commonwealth being divided into Zones A and B, each with a reduced percentage of taxation payable for those living and working in those areas.

The war had interrupted the search for oil, but it recommenced, and the authorities had great hopes of building up a big production in this regard. The beef trade had been greatly improved by the establishment of meat works at Broome, and now the future of certain iron ore deposits under the sea at Yampi Sound, near Cockatoo and Koolan Islands, had great potential. The Australian Iron and Steel Co. had resumed operations at these deposits, which were claimed to be among the richest and most accessible in the world.

Despite the still appalling tracks for vehicles Bill sometimes motored to Broome and surfed at Cable Beach, which he claimed to be one of the best in Australia. It was 'discovered' thirty years later by Lord McAlpine.

Most of what Bill foresaw as being necessary eventually came to the area—fifty years later. That was after Western Australia and the Commonwealth Government was receiving royalties from mining. Who could have foreseen that the eventual upgrading of the Great Northern Highway, giving everyone good road access to the Kimberley and the coastal towns right around Australia, which resulted from this mining wealth, would have catastrophic consequences for Fossil Downs?

Bruce Gray—Manager

Bruce Gray was raised in Queensland. Like so many young men in the 1950s he learned the elementary skills of working with and managing cattle on a property near his home. Working on the legendary big cattle runs of the Territory and Kimberley was always in the back of his mind though, summoning him like a siren. In 1960 his opportunity arose and he headed across to Kimberley where Bill employed Bruce on Fossil Downs. Merrilee, in her early twenties, was running the stock camp with George Solway then. Annette and her husband John Henwood were managing the other family property, Ellendale, on the Great Northern Highway, between Fitzroy Crossing and Derby.

When Bruce first arrived, Bill had not been well for some time—his breakdown after the war halted the ongoing expansion. Bruce felt the property, because of the restraints of World War II, was somewhat under-developed, and that a lot of fencing was required. One of his first jobs was to construct a 500acre bull paddock. Although good stud bulls had been purchased consistently, it was counter-productive that they couldn't be kept separate from the young breeding cows. This meant that frequently some heifers were in calf before they were mature enough. Bruce also constructed Torrens Yard several miles up the run so that the cattle could be mustered, drafted and trucked in that area without being walked all the way into the yards at the station homestead.

Later, in his eighties, Bruce had total recall of the activities at Fossil although he hadn't worked there since 1968. Bruce and Sandy had married, and had taken on the management of Anna Plains station, south of Broome. The story was often regaled how Sandy, the newly appointed Private Secretary, had flown into the station on the mail-plane. Bruce had been delegated to meet the plane, and light-auburn haired Sandy alighted cuddling a huge, oversized teddy bear. Bruce, ever the ocker stockman in this macho male world, could only think...'what have we got here'! Six months later they were married.

Sandy Gray

It was early 1969 when Sandy accepted the position of secretary. She arrived at Fossil Downs young, attractive and with the latest fashion knowledge from the city where mini-skirts were the go.

One day she suggested to Mrs. Mac that the hems of Mrs. Mac's dresses were too long for the current trend and she should consider wearing her skirts shorter. When she'd lived in Sydney Mrs. Mac was always the epitome of the latest fashions and she carried those styles with her in 1938 when she came to the Kimberley. She was hesitant about Sandy's suggestion, but agreed to let Sandy pin up her hem to see what it looked like. Next morning when Mrs. Mac emerged from her bedroom suite, she greeted Sandy with, 'I like that shorter look. Will you please shorten these—and handed her 28 dresses! Fortunately Sandy was an accomplished hand-sewer as there was no sewing machine on the station.

Thus Sandy earned the reputation as an excellent renovator of garments. Phyllis Male, Maxine's friend in Broome, would also contribute fashion advice. She suggested that the beautiful black guipure lace gown Maxine was wearing didn't suit her colouring, and it would be better not so close to her face. Phyllis hacked around the neck of this lavish creation with a pair of dressmaking shears. When challenged as to how Maxine could wear it now, in her dismissive way she waved her hand commenting, 'Sandy will be able to do something with it!'

Bill and the Bull ... by B. R. Morrow *The West Australian*
24 September 1948

From the summit of the sugar-loaf hill I gazed on the unending panorama of rugged beauty presented by some of the best cattle country in the West Kimberley. Behind me stretched the wild terrain over which we had travelled for six weeks. This was the one million acre Fossil Downs Station and we were on the last lap of the cattle muster. I caught up to the mob just as a horseman came towards us. Bill MacDonald, the boss, had been scouting ahead for cattle, and the rifle he carried, besides the .45 Colt holstered on the side of the saddle, was exclusively for the destruction of the old and sour-tempered clean-skin bulls that add to the hazards of a stockman's life.

"It's getting late," said Bill as he came up beside me. "You'd better head straight for camp. I'm going to ride over to the mustering." He cantered off, and it was then the white bull trotted over a rise. Bill saw it stop dead 150 yards away as it caught sight of the cattle and immediately Bill swung down from his horse and crouched on one knee to draw a bead, i.e. take aim, on it. Not until four rapidly fired bullets had whined over the beast's head did he realise that he had not adjusted his sights from long-distance shooting. He quickly lowered his aim for the fifth. It struck the bull high up on the shoulder, and with an enraged bellow it leapt straight into a gallop.

As the bull thundered madly down the slope and plunged out of sight in a deep gully 50 yards from its antagonist, Bill hastily filtered the sights and fired as it charged into view again. The firing pin clicked into an empty chamber. From where I sat on my horse, with the spellbound 'boys' watching behind me, and even the cattle standing motionless as though they, too, realised the crisis, I saw the look of horror on Bill's face as he dropped the rifle and leapt up and around in one movement to mount. Fortunately his horse was either too weary from the day's hard riding to shy, or was momentarily petrified as it saw the terrifying spectacle thundering towards it, for it didn't move as he bounded for the saddle with a suddenness that would normally cause the quietest of mounts to rear back.

Luck was with Bill that day. As his spur-goaded horse shot forward, the bull rushed by, one of its terrible horns actually combing the horse's flying tail. Desperately trying to gain speed on the rocky ground, the horse seemed to be straining every muscle in an unsteady gallop as the bull turned and charged again, each toss of its horns a foot nearer the flank of its fleeing enemy. Bill's hat flew off, and I saw him half turned in the saddle as he tugged at the flap of his revolver holster.

Unarmed and helpless, I was preparing to go to Bill's aid should he fall clear of the horse when I saw him jerk the revolver free and twist around, his right arm outflung. With its nose almost level with the horse's flank, the bull lunged forward and sideways with lowered head, and in that instant Bill fired. Bill admitted afterwards that he didn't aim at all, but fired point blank, knowing that if he missed, the bull's horns would have ripped into the body of the horse the next second. Both horse and rider were probably saved from a horrible death by a minute fraction of time. When a bull is galloping it tends to throw its hind legs outward after each bound. During the barely perceptible instant, it was in this position the revolver bullet smashed the maddened beast's shinbone.

Bill MacDonald Departs

Sadly, in 1963, at the relatively young age of 53, Bill suffered a series of strokes, which left him a semi-invalid. Always a particularly active, energetic, intelligent, and innovative man with a high profile, naturally he hated this condition. Annette was his secretary at that time. They had a very close relationship. 'He couldn't even sign his name', she recalled, her voice trembling with emotion, 'and his speech was quite slurred sometimes. So he wouldn't speak on the radio. He was becoming very insular. He'd been so used to calling the shots wherever he went'.

She urged her father to go to Perth for specialist treatment with his cardiologist. She had been taking his blood pressure every day, which was too high. 'No,' he insisted. 'I want to be here for your 21st birthday.' Really wanting him to go to Perth she insisted, 'that's not important, Dad. We can celebrate my 21st on any old day. Those specialists down there will be able to do a lot for your condition'—but she couldn't persuade him to go.

Sam and Phil Male, good friends from Broome, and their son Kim had travelled to Fossil for the 21st birthday party on Saturday night. The next day Maxine suggested Annette take Kim for a drive over to the spectacular and scenic Geikie Gorge, which he'd never seen. It was really hot, but reluctantly they went. On their return, Annette drove in and parked the jeep over the pit in the garage, and headed towards the kitchen in the big house. Bill was over near the manager's quarters, and called out to her, but she didn't catch what he said. 'I'll be there in a minute. I just want to grab a drink. I'm parched', she'd called back.

What Annette didn't know is that on the same day, 15 September 1963, Bill came down to Bruce's house, where Bruce was having a kip (sleep or rest) after lunch. Bill had said to him, 'If something happens to me, will you look after Maxine, Merrilee and Annette?' Somewhat mystified, Bruce had said, 'Sure. Of course I would'. Then Bill walked back towards the Big House. Bruce had only ever told Sandy of that conversation.

Maxine and the guests were all having a quiet siesta, reclining in the Green Room. Kim had joined them. Annette had run upstairs to her room. She heard a shot! Silence! Then a scream, 'Missus, missus—come quick!' Everyone rushed to find Bill lying on the ground, behind the office side of the Big House, with his Colt .45 pistol beside him. He was still alive. A stockman jumped into a vehicle and rushed the 26 miles over the rough bull-dusty track into the hospital at Fitzroy Crossing, where he rang the Flying Doctor in Derby with the request that the plane be sent to Fossil. A whistle call to VJB Derby was unlikely to be heard on a Sunday afternoon.

Waiting for the plane to arrive was agony for everyone. Annette stayed beside the UHF radio in the office—waiting—for an ETA. After an hour it was finally given. The plane was on its way. In readiness, they lifted Bill onto the back of a ute and drove out to the airstrip. When the plane arrived he was quickly loaded onto the gurney and into the plane, and no time was wasted taking off for the Derby hospital. The only thing Annette overheard on the radio, and which has dwelt in her mind ever since, was the doctor uttering 'I don't think we'll be able to save this man'. To Annette's everlasting sorrow, she never knew what her father had called out to her.

What brought on this implausible calamity? Was it the frustration of not achieving what could be accomplished with adequate government infrastructure? Was it the sheer magnitude of developing these million+ acres into its full potential? Did he feel he was letting his forbears down or the Kimberley? Did Bill feel he hadn't achieved his dream of a model cattle station? Or was it that he wasn't the man he used to be physically, which affected him mentally?

Not readily known, outside his close family and friends at Fossil Downs, was that Bill had suffered a breakdown after World War II. He had been heavily involved in so many different aspects of keeping the Kimberley safe for everyone from possible invasion, keeping it liveable, assisting in Broome after the bombing, all the while maintaining the station's beef production with minimal employed labour. Demand for beef was massive so prices were good then, and advantage needed to be taken. He was called for everywhere, and kept going and going. When the war ended, he collapsed.

So, Maxine had her first taste of Fossil's management just eight years after arriving there. That experience, while Bill was still there to guide her, would prove invaluable for the grieving widow.

Thirty years later Maxine was being interviewed by John Singleton for the TV program 'John Laws' World'. It was entitled 'The Lady of a Million Acres'. He commenced with 'G'day, Miz Mac, how'r'ya?' Continuing, he questioned, 'Bill had struggled through drought and flood to carve a piece of civilisation out of this harsh wilderness around you. You obviously shared his aspirations and hopes. When he had achieved so much, why would such a real example of an Australian take his own life?'

'Bill felt he was a burden on us all—Merrilee, Annette and me,' Maxine quivered. 'One stroke affected his speech so much he wouldn't talk on the radio for fear of it being thought he was drunk. It would be a great indignity for him not to be clearly understood'. Still struggling with emotion as she remembered the time, she continued, 'He said I was still a young woman and could marry again. There was the fear of even further physical disability from an even more severe stroke—and to a proud man it was too much to accept.'

Today there is advanced treatment, therapy and rehabilitation available for stroke and breakdown survivors, with faster communication and transport. In the Kimberley, in the 1960s, this was virtually non-existent. Despite Bill's efforts, distance and ready access to health support services had not yet been overcome. But in 1963, if he'd acted on Annette's urging and gone to Perth….

Maxine in Charge

Everyone, including the imperative bank manager, told Maxine she wouldn't cope by herself after Bill died. She was determined, insisting she could, so the bank gave her a year 'to make a go of it.' That year was the worst drought Fossil ever had, just eight years after the previous one had broken. 'I sold any and every beast I could,' she recalled, 'including some breeding stock, and at the end of the year had many fewer cattle—but a net profit! So the bank manager thought maybe I could manage all right.' Six years later, the station's highest calving occurred, so something was working. Guided by station managers Bruce Gray, then John and Annette Henwood, she continued unabated. New techniques started by Bill in mineral supplementation continued—and Fossil progressed.

Bill's dream of a model cattle station was pursued, but it took a while to settle into the pattern of different personnel in strategic roles, and how they perceived tasks should be undertaken. Had Maxine's twenty-five year apprenticeship been long enough for her to become competent in the overall management?

One million and sixty-four thousand acres extended over a lot of country! It's not possible to do a quick run-around, a sort of cattle beat, to see that all was in order. In places Fossil Downs was 100 rugged miles from boundary to boundary. Maxine was now a mixture of urban sophistication and rural practicality. She became adept at giving directions to station hands and staff when they appeared at the office screen door—the station manager, head stockman, stud stockman, fencing contractors, water-drillers, bore-runners, mechanics, even the cook sometimes, would form some of that procession. She was the hub around which everything revolved.

Bruce and Sandy Gray, looking to progress further, took up the management of Anna Plains station south of Broome in 1968, and John Henwood, Maxine's son-in-law, became Fossil's manager, a good move for Fossil. With his Kimberley environment and climate experience, and mechanical knowledge, plus Annette's prolific station knowledge, he began by looking seriously at the long-term strategies that would be needed to keep Fossil Downs a viable station. The government's introduced Pastoral Award would increase the payroll significantly. The tempo under which the station operated would have to change. Award wages, they knew, would be a challenge—there would be fewer aboriginal stockmen available to muster the cattle.

John became convinced that steel yards and mechanisation was the way to go for Fossil. Would a bulldozer to dig dams repay its cost? Better roads on the property would mean quicker access to strategic places, so therefore a grader to upgrade tracks into roads would be beneficial. If designated vehicles were acquired, and specifically equipped for a task, would that speed up time-consuming but vital tasks, like bore running? And would a plane justify its expense? Aerial mustering and reducing significant time away from the station attending a myriad of appointments in Perth, Broome and Derby would be beneficial. Checking windmills were working could become a breeze! Mustering contractors? Would that provide an answer? Everything was considered.

Maxine now was happy to relinquish much of the day-to-day running, but maintained the role as the 'voice' of Fossil Downs. Whenever she was in Perth, the media still sought her out. Accessing the station had become somewhat easier due to partially improved roads and transportation, so magazines still loved to run articles on this remote oasis in the heart of the Kimberley. Following Bill's example, Maxine endeavoured to keep the Kimberley in the public eye, continuing the belief that it was good for the cattle industry and therefore Fossil Downs.

Vic Jones

Vic Jones, the manager of adjacent Gogo station, and Bill had been arch-enemies. They frequently disagreed as both their nature and ideas were poles apart. The stockmen from Gogo were not beyond mustering Fossil's cattle into their mob when working along the Margaret River boundary. Generally stations were good at advising if some neighbouring cattle had inadvertently strayed onto their property. Normally that station would hold them, either to be returned or retrieved. Not so Gogo. The Gogo owner, and the manager, seemed quite happy to include Fossil cleanskins in their total. Bill often found this practice occurring so, really annoyed once that Gogo was not playing the game by the local rules, he mounted a court case against the perpetrators. It was held in Derby where the jury mainly consisted of employees of the Gogo holding company. Hence, the majority verdict went against Fossil Downs. Privately the judge told Bill that if he took the case to a higher level he would win—but Bill felt he had made his point. Sadly, succeeding managers at Gogo seemed to be imbued with a non-cooperative attitude, which was a lost opportunity for good relations for the district.

Debacle

Despite Vic Jones and Bill having differences, Vic always respected Mrs. Mac, describing her as 'a fine woman'. On an adjacent block of land to both Gogo and Fossil, was the Pastoral Research Scientific Reserve—known locally as Collins Yard. This was a small tract of land retained by the State Government.

The Department of Primary Industries was undertaking research on cattle grazing techniques on particular grass species there. The cattle for this were contributed by several of the adjacent Stations. One day a Fossil employee noticed all the cattle there were without water. After taking appropriate action to get water to them quickly, he promptly drove up to the homestead to report this to Mrs. Mac saying the cattle had been tonguing badly. Infuriated, Mrs. Mac went on the urgent telegram session at 7.00 next morning. This is when all the Kimberley is listening. Her telegram was addressed to the authorities in Perth, stating that the whole exercise was a debacle.

Vic, at Gogo, was listening very intently, as he did every morning, and took particular note of Maxine's message. A bit mystified by it, he consulted his wife, Lexie, asking her, 'what does "debacle" mean, Lex?' Continuing kneading the scones she was making for morning smoko, she replied 'I don't know, Vic'. Not being one to bother consulting a dictionary, in his hoarse voice Vic declared, 'I guess it just means bull-shit.' The project was discontinued.

It was general knowledge that Vic Jones fired a shot over the native camp every morning at daybreak to wake the camp so they'd get up and be ready to start work when he was ready to start. He drove the eight miles into Fitzroy Crossing daily either to deliver meat to the AIM hospital, or collect the mail, or find out the latest happenings down at the Crossing Inn. On a particular day in September 1971, he followed this usual procedure and was gloating down at the Inn in his rasping voice claiming, 'it's eight years to the day since old MacDonald couldn't contend with my superior competition anymore and did himself in!' Vic was getting older. His eyesight was failing, and he was to be replaced as manager at Gogo. The Company was making arrangements for him to be relocated to a smaller suitable property for his retirement. Proceeding home to Gogo, he pulled through the boundary gate, took a long look at the hundreds of acres of black soil plains he'd ruled for over thirty years, drove home, then picked up his gun, and executed himself.

In an ironic twist some years later, one of the nurses had moved on from the Fitzroy Crossing AIM Hospital and was then working in outback Queensland. She walked into a bush hospital, and stood there dumbstruck. Was she seeing a ghost? Hadn't she seen this vision before? Was this a female version?

'Yes', was the gruff acknowledgement from the Principal Nurse.

No words would come.

'Well … what do you want?' was the impatient question.

'I … I…' she managed to stammer.

'Speak up, woman, if you want something'.

Gathering her senses, she stuttered 'You remind me so much of someone I once knew'.

'Who?'

'The Manager of a cattle station at Fitzroy Crossing in the Kimberley—Vic Jones…'

'Brother'.

End of conversation!

Simon Maffey aka Lord Rugby

Many dignitaries including royalty, governors-general, and politicians have visited Fossil Downs, some staying as guests, but the only titled person who actually worked there was The Hon. Simon Maffey. When Simon talked on the UHF radio from another Kimberley station, Christmas Creek, his aristocratic English accent, articulation and distinctively enunciated utterances were like none other! This image suggested a tall, dignified, and ruggedly handsome person.

In 1958 a visit to Fossil Downs of the Governor-General, Sir William Slim, was imminent. Simon worked at Fossil then, and took great delight in choosing ten young native stockmen and, putting his Coldstream Guards military training to good use, trained them to form a guard of honour. Aborigines are great mimics, so they could easily copy exactly what Simon did on a horse—sit tall, head erect, shoulders back, knees bent at 90°. Saluting was strange to them, but they soon learned that! For the occasion the station gave them all a new outfit of trousers, shirt, hat and boots. On Fossil's similar grey horses, they were elegance personified.

When the VIP plane arrived they were lined up on the Fossil airstrip forming a guard of honour. After inspection and while the Governor and Lady Slim were being transported by car from the airstrip to the homestead via the road, these stockmen dashed through a short cut along a track, jumped the creek, and were lined up at the homestead when the official party arrived there. Had there ever been another such dignified welcome for a vice-regal party in the outback?

Simon was well known for various incidents on several Kimberley stations. How much target practice did his military training extend to? One of his claims to fame occurred when he attempted to shoot a snake, and shot his own toe off instead!

Another experience with Simon was not positive either. Mrs. Mac had only been in sole charge of the property a short time when she needed to visit Perth on business. She left Simon in charge with some very definite instructions, particularly with regard to the liquor cabinet, of which he could be very fond. His declared resolve not to touch it proved too hard for him to keep. He over-imbibed and chaos reigned. When she returned Mrs. Mac had to dismiss him, as her authority would have been undermined if she didn't, although she was very sad about having to do so.

In 1947, Simon's father had been raised to the peerage as Baron Rugby, of Rugby in the county of Warwick, United Kingdom. Simon's older brother Alan inherited the title in 1969, and then in 1990 it passed to his son. However, Kimberleyites are not overly particular about the finer details of UK inheritance. On Leopold Station there's a cattle watering hole named after Simon: *Lord Rugby's Bore!*

Peter Gray

Peter Gray, brother of Bruce, was head stockman at Fossil, and worked at the station in this capacity for 15 years. It is said of Peter that he was a bushman and a stockman without equal. He later became a well-respected station manager in the Kimberley.

When aboriginal labour was plentiful, the stockcamps would consist of a dozen or more male stockmen who rode horses to muster the cattle. Bronco branding was Australia's traditional method of classifying the cattle on big stations, and this unique method to identify stock was widely practiced. It involved the stockmen mustering the mob and holding them together on the 'camp', an open stretch of land. The head stockman, or an experienced ringer, would ride into the mob and rope a cleanskin, an unbranded calf, which would be hauled to the bronco ramp or a tree and leg roped. This cleanskin calf would mostly be a yearling 'mickey' bull or heifer. It would be earmarked, branded with a heated iron, and the males castrated and let up off the ground, the whole process taking less than one minute. This bronco method ensured cattle could be mustered and branded in one day, without having to be drafted—a time-consuming and stressful exercise. It obviated the cost of building large drafting yards or driving cattle long distances. It also meant that the stock remained in the area where they lived and mothering-up of cows and calves was a lot easier as the calf was released straight back to its mother.

The aboriginal stockmen thrived on this work. Weren't they just like John Wayne in the Western flicks? Peter, as head stockman, oversaw this procedure each day also keeping tally of how many young stock were branded. Traditionally the tally was kept in a notebook thus: ~~1111~~. That was the count for five. This number was necessary to know approximately how many animals would be available in three or four years time to send to the abattoirs or Perth stock sales. The station also used those numbers to estimate the number of stock on the property for official bookkeeping purposes: simply multiply the branding number by four!

Talking with Peter again 42 years later, the record branding number was mentioned. Without hesitation he quoted '6843 in 1970. That record still stands!' The Fossil Downs' brand was still ZV5, the brand that originally came overland with the MacDonald/McKenzie cattle in the 1880s.

Bronco branding was standard procedure on many cattle stations until the early 1970s. Then times changed. After the enactment of the Pastoral Award, stations employed fewer stockmen, so different mustering and branding procedures evolved. Steel drafting yards were built to confine the mobs. A calf cradle was invented, fixed-wing aircraft and helicopters were used, and contract teams of musterers were employed. Many stations purchased their own aircraft then, which had the additional advantage of seeing if anyone was duffing their cattle from a neighbouring property! Sadly, when the price of labour became too high, and the calf cradle came into being, this unique Australian system of bronco branding became obsolete—along with one of the exceptional skills of the Australian stockman.

Peter's role on the station eventually changed to bore runner, whereby the underground artesian bores were visited every second day to check that the windmills and pumps were working and providing sufficient drinking water for the cattle. A specially fitted-out flat-deck ute or truck was used for this, which had all the necessary equipment on board for making any repairs, including an aircompressor for blowing out clogged pipes. In the 40+F° heat, a 1000-head mob of cattle drinks a huge quantity of water. Fossil Downs still used windmills for pumping water to the troughs from the artesian source. Solar pumps, which are useful in many situations, were not yet suitable for big mobs of cattle in the extreme heat, as they couldn't pump a sufficient quantity of water quickly enough. Nowadays computer programs can be used to check on bores, pumps and troughs from the homestead office. And even more technical apps and aids are becoming available.

Peter moved on to Station Manager at Leopold Downs but sometimes returned to 'mind' Fossil while the owners/managers were away. After so many years there, he knew the million acres intimately, plus the Fossil Downs procedures. At times, though, he demonstrated skills other than those relating to cattle.

One stormy night 'Jarndi', Merrilee's old German shepherd dog who'd been sent to Fossil for his final duration, was frightened by thunder and crashed through one of the beautiful bevelled glass leadlight doors in the homestead hall. The dog was unharmed—not so the door. There were three pairs of these matching doors with elaborate brass handles. Peter offered to try repairing it. The individual glass pieces were measured and ordered from Perth. The lead casing was reusable. When the glass arrived, Peter started the job of restoring the door. It was the wet season, and the weather, of course, was very hot and steamy. He lost buckets of perspiration. After three days of painstaking persistence he finally got it all assembled and the door repaired, a testament to dogged perseverance!

During another wet, he was left a grocery list of jobs to do while John and Annette were away. One was to hack back and gain control of the rampant bougainvillea growing over the laundry, which grew several inches per day in the hot, steamy rain. He delegated his offsider, George, to cart the prickly prunings away with the tractor and trailer, and dump them somewhere well out of sight. Even in the 1980s the driving skills of the aborigines were still being honed.

George's driving skills were marginal and when he returned to Peter he confessed, 'I bin knockim' down gateway, boss'. He was referring to the impressive gate pillars displaying the MacDonald Coat of Arms that had pride of place at the front entrance to the homestead complex. So, an extra job was quickly added to Peter's list. 'I'd never done any bricklaying,' Peter confessed, 'but I needed to fix that gateway before any of the family returned. We managed to get a chain around the part of the fence knocked over, and used the PTO on the tractor to winch the concrete blocks up until they were roughly perpendicular. We thumped them into place with a post-hole rammer. I mixed up a slurry of cement, and slapped it on the cracks. I don't think anyone ever noticed.'

Healthy Soup

'Soup, soup, soup. I got sick of soup up there', a relative exclaimed. It was available for every meal. Perhaps, again, a MacDonald was ahead of time. Nowadays people have rediscovered the health benefits of bone broth which is what this soup was, utilising the bones of the beasts which found their way onto the dining tables. It is back in fashion now in the nutrition world. But it was not generally recognised then.

Chest Deep Freeze

Keeping up to date with the latest inventions and devices sometimes meant that an item would be ordered and be delivered without anyone really knowing how to use it to its optimum capability. This was the case with the 500-litre chest deep freeze, which arrived and was sited on the veranda conveniently outside the kitchen of the Big House.

It was primarily for frozen vegetables during the wet season when the station's vegetable garden was not functioning. So, a huge order had been placed for these vegetables. Did the mathematics confuse the orderer? Australia hadn't long changed from imperial to metric measurements. When the order arrived there was no way it could all fit in, so the overflow was despatched into the Crossing Inn and given to their cook.

> At Fitzroy Crossing others were experimenting on how to use freezers too. Nurse Beryl Gilkes (now Scott) commented in *Bough Sheds Boabs and Bandages. Stories of Nursing in the Kimberley (compiled by Anne Atkinson):*

> 'Cooking for the staff and patients was another issue. Being young, none of us had much experience in cooking so it was a steep learning curve. There was plenty of meat, with one of the stations bringing it in on the back of a ute covered in gum leaves. I'll never forget seeing that station manager walking into the kitchen with a leg of beef draped over his shoulder and dump it on the table. I had no idea how to cut it up and place it in the freezer. None of us had had any experience using freezers and no one thought to tell us a few basic principles. Thus, we used to cut the meat into big slabs and put

them on trays uncovered. When we wanted meat, we would take out a tray, partially thaw it, and cut off enough for the meal. The tray would then go back and the meat would be refrozen. We survived, but I understand now why the health inspector nearly had a fit.'

Lyn Arrives: 1969—1970

While still trying to absorb the palatial surroundings, as Jeanette drove us up to the cookhouse, a blond-haired immaculately groomed Mrs. MacDonald met me. Jeanette showed me to my room off the veranda—the office on one side and a huge bathroom on the other. I would be station secretary and *inter alia* I'd also be radio operator, station book-keeper, paymaster, starter of the power generator each day, waterer of the reticulated garden, first aid and beer ration dispenser, film projectionist for the fortnightly 16 mm films, and native store retailer on Friday nights. With the added pleasure of driving Mrs. MacDonald in the V8 Kingswood, there was plenty of variety.

Scrubbing out the chilling room once or twice a week after each beast had been killed, butchered and the meat placed inside on metal racks was another task. It mystified me how eucalyptus leaves appeared stuck to the meat. Next lesson—the butchering was carried out on a bed of fresh gum leaves, as that was the most hygienic way out in the paddock. I was unaware then that eucalyptus oil stimulated immunity and provided antioxidant protection. However, I was qualified for correspondence, pay-roll, accounts payable, wages compilation including Workers Compensation Levy, basic balance sheets, and ordering medicines, vehicle and other machinery parts as they were required. I loved composing and writing letters. The rest I would have to 'wing'. Another lesson to learn: the correct phonetic alphabet—A = Alpha; B = Bravo; C = Charlie, so that words in telegrams could be spelled to the operators of the two-way radio at VJB Derby if there was a lot of static or interference.

An important item was writing the station diary, keeping a record of what each employee did daily. 'If it's written regularly, and in ink,' Mrs. MacDonald explained as she handed it to me, 'it can become admissible evidence in a court of law. We had that experience once.' It was always a challenge to keep tabs on what all the staff did each day.

We'd arrived at midday, when the main meal of the day was served. 'It's easier for the cook that way,' Mrs. MacDonald explained seeing my surprised look. 'She can put a roast and veggies in the oven while it's still hot after she's baked the bread. That gets most of her work done in the morning giving her the whole afternoon off. The evening meal for the staff at the cookhouse is cold meat and salads—so there's no need to keep the wood stoves burning during the hottest time of the day.'

The chatelaine on the property for over thirty years then, Mrs. Mac had experienced most situations which could occur with a variety of cooks, gardeners, and house-keepers, along with the native staff, and knew what worked and what didn't. The Big House residents—at that time the managers, John and Annette Henwood (Mrs. MacDonald's daughter and son-in-law), Jeanette and myself and any guests—gathered each evening in the red and white flagged two-storied hall having showered off the day's accumulated grime and perspiration. The women changed into long gowns, men into a clean shirt and shorts or trousers, for drinks and then proceeded to the dining room for evening dinner, which frequently consisted of soup and a boiled or poached egg on toast.

Beryl, a sister at the Australian Mission Hospital in Fitzroy Crossing and who became a life-long friend, said that she was never actually at Fossil for an evening meal for which she was glad—she had nothing suitable to wear; neither her nursing uniform or shorts would cut it! It was a totally different style of living to which I was accustomed. Recently this had been in a share-house with single young women in Perth, and previously growing up just after World

War II in a very modest home and circumstances in the fruit-growing Yarra Valley in Victoria.

Having my room cleaned for me, and my laundry taken care of, was something I quickly became comfortable with. Each morning at 11.00 am, Mrs. Mac would bring me a freshly squeezed lemon or orange-squash in the office. But one day I brewed a pot of tea instead. In the wet season the heat, on the Fahrenheit scale, was 115ºF each day, day after day—it rarely altered. The humidity arrived sometime in October, and was known as the build up season. At 7.30 am my elbows would drip perspiration which splashed onto the flagstone veranda floor while I was attending to the medical requirements of the native women. But on this occasion the day didn't seem so hot. Checking the thermometer on the veranda I observed it was only 105ºF—hence brewing the pot of hot tea!

Siesta each day after lunch was in the green room lounge that opened off the two-storey hall. Two sofas, a chaise lounge, and large upholstered lounge chairs lent themselves to stretching out for a sleep. Extra sprung cushions could be dragged into a line on the floor. An air-conditioning unit in this room—was this another first?—plus the shady trees on the northern sunny side, cooled the room by several degrees. This was bliss. Everyone stayed there either reading or sleeping until about 3.30 pm, but the RFDS afternoon radio schedule came on at 3.15 and I needed to be in the office then with the UHF radio switched on, ready to hear the list of 'traffic' read out, or to send any telegrams we had. Staggering out of the green room onto the veranda to go to the office was just like hitting a brick wall as the heat engulfed you, rebounding off the flagstone floor and brick walls. After turning on the radio, I would sit at the desk for several minutes struggling to focus my eyes and trying to adjust my head to the searing temperature, while physically my body adjusted. Now there are air-conditioning units in all workrooms. How did the early settlers cope with these sweltering temperatures in their inappropriate clothing with no cooling comforts?

The high humidity during the wet season, October to March, made sleeping a challenge in the house. So in the early evenings the house girls would descend on the veranda and shift our light beds right out onto the lawns—even sleeping on the veranda could be too hot as the collected heat of the day radiated from the walls and flagstone floor. A vertical rod welded to the rear of these light metal bedframes was used to suspend a mosquito net. Securely tucked in, it also ensured that no snakes, centipedes or other 'bities' visited during the night. In the cooler months we slept either on the veranda or in our rooms.

Mrs. Mac was amused by all the articles I assembled prior to crawling under the net and on top of my bed—book, vacuum flask of cold water, torch, lozenges, pen and paper. Some nights were breathless—no breeze at all, and it was just too hot to go to sleep. In desperation I'd turn end for end with my head at the foot of the bed. Call it 'mind over matter', but it worked every time so I never abused the benefit of going to sleep in that direction.

Looking at the magnificent night sky in the clear Kimberley air, unpolluted by artificial lighting, was a special experience. Sometimes a visitor would teach us the names of various constellations—there were no apps on smart phones then. If giggling was heard behind the oleander bushes, we'd know a couple of the young aboriginal women would have something new to point out. After acknowledging them, they'd come into the compound and point out a new phenomenon in the sky—a star, planet or satellite. Their powers of observation were much keener than ours.

The oleanders thrived in the tough conditions of the Kimberley. Today they are trimmed down low to reveal the vista of the homestead from the entrance gates, but then they formed a barrier between the street and the lawn where we slept. One of the older women from the camp would sit down with a hose and water them every day—she'd constructed little moats to hold the water until it sunk into the very hard limestone soil.

That soil was not only hard, at the end of the dry season it was extremely hot. I made the mistake one Friday night of running barefoot down to the native store—after which the soles of my feet protested for several days!

Naturally, to cope with the tropical climate, the station started work early. The ringers and other men ate at the cookhouse, but our breakfast was eaten, ad hoc, on the wide V-shaped stone-flagged veranda. It always consisted of toast and cereal and pawpaw or grapefruit or mango—whatever fruit was in season—with a big pot of tea, all of which had been brought out on a big tray. Everyone just helped him or herself and headed off to commence whatever task needed attending to first. I was in the office for the first radio sked at 7.00 am, after which the native population dawdled down with any ailments they had prior to the 8.00 am medical radio schedule. Waking up early was easy—John, the manager, arose at 4.00 am, and walked briskly along the veranda in his flip-flopping thongs. No alarm clock was required!

Fossil had its own unique-flavoured paw-paws (*Carica papaya*). Whenever she could, Mrs. Mac would return home with seeds from paw-paws in other areas to hybridize with what was already in the garden. In 1969, the grapefruit trees had grown out of control and fruited well. At that time the 'grape-fruit diet', to lose weight, was fashionable so several of us decided to try it. Someone climbed up the tall ladder and sawed off the top branches, laden with fruit. It's funny, but the diet didn't work for anyone up there, after it receiving wonderful accolades in the women's magazines. Was that because Mrs. Mac laced all the grapefruit with sugar, maraschino cherries, and exotic liqueurs?

Under Mrs. Mac's supervision, and John's management, the station ran like a well-oiled machine, with only the occasional hiccupping cog. For example, there were two generators in the pump shed to supply power for all the houses and sheds. The smaller one had been replaced with a more powerful engine, but was kept serviced as a backup in case of a breakdown. The huge diesel supply tank was sited at the rear of this shed, adjacent to the Geikie Range. To keep everything running smoothly and in order, and especially to eliminate wastage, it was necessary to have rules. Here the rule was never to leave the pump shed while you were filling the overhead feeder tank with diesel to run the generator. It had a chain dropper on its side so you could tell how much fuel was in the tank, but it filled very slowly. Most days you just topped it up. But it could be a slow job if the generator had run excessively the previous day, and it was very tempting to skip off to attend to another chore while waiting for the tank to fill.

Mostly it was the Secretary's job to start the 240-volt generator each day, at approximately 10.00 a.m., to generate the electricity needed to powerup the appliances. Fans were especially needed by that time. The reticulation system for the gardens around the house was started then. As well as watering the gardens, the sprinkling water had a cooling effect on the atmosphere—for about five minutes. At night the generator was turned off from a switch on the veranda, when the last person went to bed.

Occasionally other people started the generator if electricity was needed for a task being undertaken, particularly in the machinery workshop. So it was when Irene ran to the office one morning, panting—'Lyn, diesel spilling down steps!' Oh no! Someone, who shall remain nameless, had left the fuel filling the tank intending to return from the sheds to turn it off. It was necessary then to spray detergent over the spilled fuel and scrub out the pump shed, including around the two generators, and the two wide concrete steps to make the access safe and to dissipate all the fumes and those wasted litres of diesel. No one was happy.

Bottled gas was another source of power. The six hot water services and ten refrigerators located in the cookhouse and the other houses were powered this way, as well as the gas that was required for welding in the workshop. Annually a technician would arrive to service these appliances. I'm not entirely sure what work he undertook, but he lay on the floor in front of the refrigerators and used a hypodermic syringe to do it. Annette arrived in the dining room as he was servicing the refrigerator once, and to tease her he waved the syringe around saying, 'I hope you don't mind, but I need a hit to keep me going!' She was horrified. In the late 1960s, as now, hard drugs and mainlining was not an accepted mode of behaviour anywhere. He apologised to her later and explained it was his joke.

At my previous employment in Perth, my wage had been almost double what I was paid at Fossil Downs—the remainder was made up with abundant supplies of toiletries, food, and occasionally using the station vehicles socially, which made up being totally 'found'. The only thing to buy was personal clothing—and most of it I sewed, having taken my sewing machine with me.

In keeping with the generally tidy and up-market appearance of everything, all the women wore dresses for work—no slacks, jeans and t-shirts then. Jeans and t-shirts had not generally reached the racks of the clothing stores in Australia, and knit fabrics weren't rolling out of the textile mills yet.

Having the laundry taken care of by the native staff enabled that spick-and-span look—our dresses were washed on Mondays, ironed on Tuesdays, and returned to our bedroom and hung in the wardrobe on Wednesdays. What luxury!

Third Generation: 1967–2015

John & Annette Henwood

Everything connected with Fossil Downs is BIG—the acreage, the rivers, the buildings, the stock numbers—everything. But most of all, the vision! If the first generation dreamed big, the second generation dreamed even bigger and created big buildings and big numbers of cattle, and the third generation implemented big ideas. Their motto could have been: 'Dream no small dreams, make no small plans; without vision we perish.' *(Proverbs 29:18)*. John and Annette Henwood both carried on with Bill MacDonald's mission statement and vision of creating a model cattle station.

Although it wasn't the original succession plan, Annette and John took over the managing of Fossil Downs in 1968. Annette commented in 1969, 'Fossil wasn't meant for us—it was meant for Merrilee.' Bill and Maxine's vivacious eldest daughter, Merrilee, had grown up on the property too, had run the stock camp at various times, was an excellent horsewoman, could speak the Gooniyandi language, and generally knew the station drill. Rodney, Merrilee's husband was a pilot. It's an extremely big step to take on the management of a million acre property, running 20,000+ head of cattle plus up to forty staff. Thus it was agreed that the Ellendale property, where John and Annette had been would be sold and Fossil Downs would facilitate the purchase of Frazier Downs Station, south of Broome, for Merrilee and Rodney. In due course 500 top breeding cows from Fossil were sent to help them upgrade their stock. Many years later Merrilee commented, 'Annette is the best custodian Fossil could have. She's the best at keeping everything licked and polished'. A fastidious perfectionist? Annette could be.

John was local having grown up on Noonkanbah and Calwynyardah. His father managed Noonkanbah when it was a sheep property. These stations were both situated on the Fitzroy River, between Fitzroy Crossing and Derby. The climate and conditions in the Fitzroy area were well known to him. He liked to tease Annette that his family ties with the Kimberley extended further back than hers. John's grandfather, George Rose, was a horse carer on the Alexander Forrest expedition of 1879, and he became a legendary Kimberley pioneer on Mt. Anderson and other sheep stations in West Kimberley.

With a small population in the area, most people were quite well known to each other. There was no secondary schooling so boarding school in Perth was the choice for most people. John was sent at the age of 7. Kimberley students were able to return home for Christmas holidays, but not always during the term breaks. When schooling was finished, the youth in the area frequently gathered together for social activities. This was when John started taking more notice of Annette. His first proposal to her was made at a noisy party at Fossil, which she thought was not serious enough. 'Come and ask me privately, so I can hear it again' she said. So they adjourned to where there were no others around, and John hastily thought up a better-sounding request. Then Annette agreed.

After this engagement was announced, old-timers said they'd be the first 'district-breds' to marry. 'It was like they were marrying off a couple of racehorses,' Annette recalls. 'Our wedding wasn't referred to as 'John and Annette's wedding' but as 'the' wedding. It was not very personal at all.'

John soon adjusted to the running of a cattle station as Mrs. Mac and Annette were there to consult, and the current manager, Bruce Gray, stayed on for a while. Peter Gray, Bruce's brother, was the extremely competent head stockman with plenty of experience in running stock camps.

Annette inherited her desire to see the property kept in an immaculate condition from her father, notwithstanding her mother's precise attention to detail. 'I'm happy here,' she'd insist, 'just working on keeping everything in good order. I really don't want to be anywhere else. People ask what I do on the property. Well, it's anything and everything from unblocking drains to unloading stores and always there's cleaning. I'm a good 'scrubber'.' That skill later became indispensable.

John's father taught him about machinery, and everything else on the property, by just telling him what to do—not by showing him. That meant he had to figure out how it should be done, and he became very adept at fixing machinery, and much more. It saved disagreements that John liked things done in the same meticulous way that Annette liked, particularly involving machinery. John taught the secretaries to wash under the bonnet of Mrs. Mac's Holden Kingswood to clean the engine—while Annette insisted that tins of food on the shelves of the station store and the native store should all be lined up neatly, and facing the front.

This except from Michael Gugeri's book *God Before Gugeri*, published in 2014, reiterates this point. Gugeri's, MacDonalds and Henwoods had all grown up in the Kimberley and knew each other well, having been friends for most of their lives:

> 'In March 1973, my visit to Fossil Downs was in a business capacity. It was my first trip as carrier after successfully tendering for the contract. The load consisted of general stores and fuel. I climbed down to a welcoming handshake from John (Henwood) who led me to the staff kitchen to partake in a hearty breakfast, after which, we started unloading. At the Feed Room we stacked wheat, oats and chaff on racks 'butts out and ears horizontal'.

Out at the aircraft hangar, fuel drums of avgas were unloaded with the help of the front-end loader, all perfectly lined up in the hanger with bungs horizontal. Inside the main store is nothing but orderliness. It was spotless. Towards the back of the store in the centre was a staircase leading to the mezzanine floor on which was stacked sugar bags: 'butts out and ears horizontal'.

Some may think I've over-emphasised about how John and Annette are so particular in the way things are done on Fossil. That is how it is! It really is a credit to them to uphold this standard, which must surely assist in the efficient running of the station. Occasionally devilment got the better of me. I would rotate a few tins of tomatoes or tinned dog just to torment Annette. On one occasion it had quite a reaction when she called the staff together and told them: 'Michael thinks he is being funny; just keep him on the truck and out of my store!'

Michael Gugeri continued with the stores delivery contract, even after the Great Northern Highway was upgraded and the supplies came by road to Derby, instead of by ship. When his big Leyland truck, dragging the 15' freight-laden trailer, arrived at Fossil, he would first unload a large stack of cartons at the native store, followed by the horse feed near the stables, then spare parts and equipment at the massive machinery workshop, the diesel fuel at the overhead tanks, then avgas 1 km out at the aircraft hangar.

The final off-load would be back at the mezzanine-floored stores building unloading the groceries. This was a huge, heavy job and required all hands on deck. Everyone, including all the young girls in the native camp, was commandeered to help unload. Michael would be up on the deck of the truck handing down the heavy cartons of tinned food to the girls. He admitted he enjoyed gazing at the sight offered by their nubile bodies as they leaned forward to take the boxes being handed down to them. What he didn't know was how the girls giggled up at the camp afterwards recalling what they had seen looking up Michael's shorts.

Everything was always constructed or repaired to a better standard than what existed previously. The contract fencing team was exasperated once in 1970—they were eager to return to Perth—that they had to pull down and reconstruct a mile of fencing as John did not like the angle they had created, and felt it would look untidy from the air. Was John also ahead of his time? Aerial mustering was not yet the norm and Fossil's aircraft was yet to be purchased.

Maxine, with the aid of Bruce Gray, had overseen the running of the station since Bill had died in 1963. When John took over, he felt that to sustain the cattle numbers needed to be a profitable station in the prevailing economy, and the proposed Pastoral Award, more mechanical innovations and the latest techniques in land management needed incorporating. Although Bill MacDonald had successfully established the Poll Shorthorn stud, and had sold and air freighted considerable numbers of stud and herd bulls within the Kimberley and Northern Territory, trends were changing and John was no longer convinced there would be a demand for their progeny. New breeds of cattle, notably the Brahman, Santa Gertrudis and Droughtmaster especially bred for tropical conditions, unlike the Poll Shorthorns, were becoming more popular. Trials and analysis results were showing these new breeds would perform better in the extreme dry and wet, hot and humid climate, than the traditional British breeds. To continue with the Poll Shorthorn stud, which required the services of a stud master for part of the year, could be counterproductive. The latest research, development and techniques were acquired, studied and considered.

The Pastoral Award

The Pastoral Award, which required fair wages for all staff, was instigated in 1971. Merry & Merry, the station's accountants in Perth, had devised a new bookkeeping system for the station, and the Kalamazoo system of payment of accounts was initiated. Computers were only in large industries and universities then.

To people without intimate knowledge of the social structure of the aborigines, and how they lived on the stations at that time, it seemed reasonable that they be paid the same money for comparable work. What was not generally realised were the social services the stations provided for these workers, although regretfully not in all situations. If you want to retain good staff of all races, you provide good conditions. At Fossil Downs the aborigines each had their own family dwelling, communal bathroom facilities, and they received their 'keep'—that is, bread and meat, tea and sugar, flour and baking powder, soap, rice, vegetables from the garden in season, and *baccy* (chewing tobacco)—not just for the worker but also for his extended family. Abundant surplus food from the kitchens was also made available to them.

A stockman may have his wife, numerous children, his parents, even uncles and aunties with him. This required the station baking more bread each day, butchering more beasts each week, and having on hand sufficient stores to accommodate this supply. Also needed were the buildings and suitable space to store these provisions—the stores order arrived only three times per year. A special chilling room had been erected to stockpile meat, fruit, vegetables, and other perishables. A stores shed, using pipes for shelving, kept the five tons of flour in the best condition as air needed to circulate around each sack to keep it devoid of weevils. Likewise, the three tons of sugar, in 50 lb. sacks, and numerous chests of tea took a large amount of space. That was all stacked in the station store. The native store was a large Nissen-hut shed, where the workers purchased extra needs. It had a large inventory of supplies, too, like tinned fruit, baked beans, spaghetti, soup and stew. Rolls of cotton fabric and other clothing items were also available there—this was all carried by the station.

Previously, when minimal wages were paid, twice per year the station supplied the stockmen with clothing—summer and winter shirts and trousers, boots, hats and blankets plus a new swag cover, along with medical items and treatment. It was completely foreign to the aborigine to handle money and budget to buy these items. An economy was not part of their culture. Wages were paid monthly, so at the native store there was a system of 'tick'—their money usually ran out before their likes and needs. Each payday whatever amount was owed on the book had to be deducted.

The native populations then did not have their own means of transport, unlike today where there is an abundance of Toyota Landcruisers. Station vehicles and drivers would take the children into school at Fitzroy Crossing and collect them at the beginning and end of term, plus a tractor and trailer would be loaned for them to go walkabout on Sundays. These items were not large in themselves but all became part of the total provision. With the enactment of the Pastoral Award, the inevitable happened as the law of unintended consequences materialised. Many of the stations, instead of employing a native man and keeping all his family, opted instead to employ a single white stockman. The resulting debacle was that many of the aborigines, although not Fossil's, were 'bushed' into Hall's Creek and Fitzroy Crossing, to sit down 'longa the reserve' where there were inadequate health and hygiene facilities, and insufficient infrastructure and activities to occupy the several hundred who gradually assembled there.

Most of the pastoralists, including those from Fossil, were well aware of this likely social dislocation, and tried to warn the authorities. They regretted the breakdown this would cause in European-Aboriginal relationships, and several in the Fitzroy Crossing district got together to try to work out how they could implement the projected Award slowly so that it would not cause the anticipated major upheaval. The authorities largely ignored these concerns. The Award was pushed through and sadly, in many cases, its application meant loss of country, loss of work plus loss of self-esteem and identity for the aborigine for many years. The Arbitration Commission visited all the stations and studied their wage books to check that they were abiding by the Pastoral Award.

Fossil retained as many native people as they could afford—many were lifelong friends. The older ones still say today that their station days are the happiest they remember. Long-time Kimberley resident, Frank Lacy from Mt. Elizabeth Station, in his book, *The Rivers of Home,* observes: 'There were big aboriginal populations on the well-run properties on the Fitzroy. All stock work was done using horses, and a large number of stockmen were essential. Contrary to the feeling that arose later in the uninformed public, the fact that aborigines were being employed as stockmen was an asset to aboriginal life and assisted their assimilation. Their family was together, and their children were going to school. The men were learning and employed in useful stock trades, and earning their living. They were well fed, I believe much better than they are today in town reserves', Frank contended. He went on: 'the aborigines then had no contact with alcohol whatsoever, a big contrast to present day aboriginal life. They were, on the whole, a happy lot.' [Page 93]

Jane de Pledge from Mandora Station related they had to cease employing aborigines when the Pastoral Award came in; 'you were feeding about thirty of them for five that could work. We couldn't afford to feed aunty, granny, and the rest then,' she explained sadly.

Joy Muir (later Motter) was the Itinerant Community Health nurse, and was based at Fitzroy Crossing in various roles from 1968 until 2003. Her health-service Land Rover was fitted out with everything needed for mobile nursing. She travelled to all the local stations, plus the town reserves, to educate aborigines in preventive medicine, particularly emphasizing immunisation. She also endeavoured to teach them the right European food to eat to maintain healthy bodies since they weren't eating their customary bush tucker and station-provided food any more—fat and salt-laden takeaways had become their preferred fare. Joy said the main nursing treatment she initially dispensed was for chest infections, diarrhoea, cuts, and minor ailments. After the advent of the Pastoral Award, and subsequently the aborigines receiving their Citizen Rights, she says this changed to injury based nursing—she'd be patching up broken bones and stitching wounds from fights and arguments. There was also more venereal disease. Later drugs and Type 2 diabetes escalated. Tourists wandering through the area, along with more mining and road camps, aggravated the breakdown of traditional aboriginal culture.

Many of the local identities described the Pastoral Award as a cultural catastrophe for the local indigenous people. Fifty years later, after the Native Title Act had awarded ownership of various tracts of land to the local indigenous people, ways are being sought to create employment by various agencies—but at least two generations have been without employment, and the example of presenting for work each day.

Efficient Equipment

The first mechanical purchase to commence implementing new land management policies in 1970 was a D6 bulldozer. A cheque for $39,000 was written, a sizeable sum then, although you only get a modest sedan for that nowadays. John was experienced at bulldozing and intended to propel four dams initially to allow the cattle closer access to water, then to bulldoze humps and hollows to manage and improve the natural water flow. To avoid soil erosion, John graded what were locally known as Henwood Humps, over the tracks. These were like wide speed humps that channeled the rainfall to areas where damage could not occur. These humps needed to be at 90° to the track so that vehicles and cattle transports could cross them easily. With suitable fencing, this would minimise erosion in prone areas. It wouldn't take long to recoup the cost of the 'dozer, John figured. It was still operating in 2015.

Also purchased was a Haflinger, an all-wheel-drive German-made light utility vehicle, similar to a Jeep without a roof. As well as for running around the complex, it was to be stationed on the far side of the Margaret River prior to that river commencing to run in the wet season, thus enabling access to Fitzroy Crossing and freeing up a station ute. Sid was the general handyman and found it very convenient to whizz around, doing repairs and maintenance to buildings, gates, and whatever needed it, loaded with the necessary tools. One day he and his wife, Pat, who was the station cook, were observed walking round and round the Haflinger looking at it quite intently. Sid wanted to obey the rules and check the fuel, oil, water and tyre pressures before heading out on a bore run—but he couldn't find the filling point for the fuel. Without a gauge on the dashboard, how did you know how much fuel it had? Feeling silly, he'd enlisted Pat's help, and when she couldn't find it, didn't feel quite so inept. Finally they came to the office to consult the Haflinger manual and discovered you tip the driver's seat forward, and the fuel tank and filling intake appears. Poking a stick into the fuel ascertained its level.

Looking ahead to the implementation of the Pastoral Award, John realised that in the future there would not be the same number of personnel to work on the property. Needing to speed up many of the regular chores like checking that windmills and bore pumps were working and water troughs filled, along with much faster excursions from the station when necessary, a Cessna 182 was purchased. John soon gained his pilot's licence. Primarily used for aerial mustering, it became a useful tool for checking whether stock camps on adjoining leases were duffing Fossil's cattle, too! And socially, on occasions, they were able to visit neighbours who were over a hundred miles away—for lunch.

A regular vehicle replacement policy was instigated. Reliable Toyota Landcruiser utilities, with flat decks, were acquired and equipped with what was needed for its intended function. This enabled any maintenance to be completed on the job without returning to the homestead for other specialised tools or equipment.

Without the native labour, everyone remaining on the station, both owners and employees would be required to do the work previously undertaken by two, three or more people. Efficient equipment was paramount. Bob MacDonald, Annette's cousin and Fossil's agronomist, maintains that the only way the station functioned efficiently, then, was because of John's substantial machinery plant. Even with this, all personnel were frequently running!

Future Farming at Fossil

After studying the latest research results, John and Annette decided to focus on soil health and native plant regrowth. In 1986 a Pasture Improvement Program was instigated. Annette's cousin, Bob, from MacDonald Agri-Services in Dubbo, NSW, became Fossil's agronomist and was contracted to design its curriculum. Special blocks were fenced off and experiments conducted to ascertain the best grasses for the various conditions—soil type, water availability, and dry season/wet season challenges.

'We want to improve total ground control and cover for rangeland protection,' John said, as he and Bob climbed into the Cessna to make an assessment flight. By making the best grass their objective, not only were they caring for the pastures, they would be producing healthier, more productive cattle. Thus, protecting and propagating vegetation, legumes, pastures and native plants became high priority.

'We decided to experiment by collecting native seeds and distributing them in specific areas where there didn't appear to be any,' John said. Native seeds to be analysed were also collected. He was particularly encouraged to do this from an old drover who knew the area well after hearing stories that lots of species had disappeared. 'In the beginning we didn't have much success. Sometimes the seeds would germinate and then disappear. But in the paddocks where we were regularly moving the cattle, we noticed that the native plants were beginning to thrive and spread,' John smiled. 'Called the 'stock effect', we were encouraged by this little breakthrough.'

'Also, during the dry periods when protein levels drop in the pasture, we were having difficulty maintaining the cattle's weight,'

John explained. 'Cousin Bob found three particular native species which were higher in protein and provided good all year round feed for our cattle. These were Blue Bush (*Chenopodium*), Ruby Saltbush (*Auroco-num*) and Mulla Mulla (*Ptilotus Exaltatus*). Collecting and spreading these seeds, along with rotating the cattle regularly to let the paddocks rest, meant the seeds were able to germinate twice per year sometimes.' This procedure contributed to the increase of bio-diversity and diet-diversity for the cattle. Mulla Mulla is of great benefit to both the environment and the cattle. Its extensive root system allows it to grow well in disturbed soil, and helps prevent further erosion. It has both a high protein and sulphur content which is good for cattle's digestion, particularly in the third stomach. They also benefited from nutritious native blue bush, and ruby bush because of its high salt content.

Unrestricted grazing had been destroying these species. Therefore a system of cell, or rotational, grazing of the cattle was introduced. The cattle being shifted into another paddock before the grass was totally eaten out allowed the just-grazed paddock to rest, recover and regenerate quickly. This eliminated over-grazing some areas, which can happen when the cattle are spread over much of the property, rangeland style, particularly near water. Nevertheless, it needed a good rainfall the following wet season for the seedlings to establish. 'It can still take several seasons before the benefits appear,' John lamented.

An unplanned for, but very welcome, outcome was the gradual return of birds and wildlife to the area. Night parrots and goannas and lizards became more plentiful as the areas of grass multiplied.

Droughtmasters

The red-coated Droughtmaster cattle, one of the breeds specifically developed for the climate in the north of Australia, aroused John's interest. Would they perform better in the hot, dry Kimberley conditions than the Poll Shorthorns? Was there another breed that would be better?

Droughtmasters appeared to John to tick all the boxes. It's a tropical breed developed in North Queensland from crossing Brahman and British breed cattle, principally the Shorthorn. The breed was conceived in response to the need in the Australian tropics for a breed of cattle that had good tick resistance and could utilise the environment and the native pastures to give higher weight gains and fertility. Over the years, selection had resulted in calving ease and parasite resistance that are characteristics needed on the big rangeland runs. Heat tolerance, the ability to adapt to the extreme climate, high fertility, and docility were also needed. The Droughtmaster breed was found to also have good walking and foraging abilities. Their red pigmentation helped protect them from eye cancer and sunburnt udders. The vast majority is polled, plus the meat quality is exceptionally good.

Continuing the policies previously practised on Fossil, top stud bulls were purchased from Queensland. Top quality breeding cows were already on the station, so gradually Droughtmasters replaced the Poll Shorthorns, which had replaced the Red Polls of earlier years.

Jim Scott, an officer with the Department of Agriculture and Food WA in 1969, said that the first time he visited Collins Yard— DAFWA research area—and saw the quality of the cattle in the surrounding area, he was stunned. These beasts were vastly superior to much of what he had seen in other districts of the Kimberley. This was an area on the Margaret River, the boundary between Fossil and Gogo stations. 'It didn't matter that the neighbour's cows and bulls sometimes go mixed up in the river,' he said with rakish humour. 'Both stations bought top quality bulls, so it didn't matter which bull served which cow, a top quality beast was still produced.'

BTEC

In 1970 Industry, State, Territory and the Australian Government united to form the national Brucellosis and Tuberculosis Eradication Campaign (BTEC). It ran for 27 years under nationally agreed guidelines with the national goal being the eradication of Mycobacterium bovis and Tuberculosis from Australia's cattle and water buffalo populations.

Herds went through a program of vaccination and blood tests, with the culling of positive reactors, until two clear tests at least 6 months apart were achieved. A massive amount of fencing and numbers of holding paddocks were required on rangeland properties for this to be achieved. Brucellosis and TB were tackled concurrently and recognition of the elimination of the diseases was granted in 1989 (Brucellosis) and 1997 (TB).

In addition to what was required for the BTEC program, Fossil began a new concept of strategic fencing. This gave better control over regeneration of pasture, helped with natural water flow, and controlled where the mobs grazed. Fencing along the rivers avoided overgrazing there. The benefits of pasture use and reduction of soil disturbance were obvious immediately.

It was easy to become enthusiastic about the results. With this improved land management, the cattle grew more quickly, increasing overall productivity and sustainability. John was so encouraged by the results he was eager to commence working with more grass species. 'So far we've focused on vegetation, legume, and native plants,' he said. 'As well as re-establishing some species, other unidentified grasses and trees have appeared where there were none or very few before. Who knows how many native plants exist here that we haven't detected yet?'

'We benefit a great deal by burning the spinifex,' Annette added. 'That's up in our top end country which is mostly rocky and rough. The cattle really love the spinifex when it's kept short and green—they do brilliantly when it's had a good burn. Other grasses are not burned. We can't afford to waste grass by burning it,' she maintained. 'Burning adversely affects the better perennial grasses. Mitchell and Flinders grasses take a long time to recover. Having said that, we're wondering if we're being over-protective of them,' she mused. 'When we've had heavy wet seasons, we get a big body of old, dry feed that nothing eats. We're wondering if it does need a burn, but we're cautious as we've always felt these grasses don't take kindly to it.'

The best one-third of the country on Fossil Downs is river frontage and black soil plains. This is where the Mitchell and Flinders grasses grow along with buffel, birdwood and native grasses. This isn't burnt. One-third of the station is more Pindan country, where new grasses such as veruna, seca and eurocloa have been introduced. It also has some good areas of spinifex, which is burned selectively. The last third is rugged, rocky country. Very dryly, cousin Bob commented that when they started to get grass to grow between the spinifex bushes, they'd be making real progress!

To increase soil health, further work was carried out for erosion control measures. Wide, flat, surface-graded roads were positioned for fire control and minimal water disbursement. New roads and humps were strategically located according to topography, water lines and gateways, to avoid erosion before it started. 'We found the native regrowth helped minimise erosion by reducing water run-off. With better vegetation, ground cover and healthier soils, more moisture and carbon is stored in the soil. This not only helps us improve the environment here, but it has helped boost productivity and the sustainability of our business,' John commented.

In a WA Government report looking at the health of the Margaret River, it found that the pools of water on the 35 miles of the Fossil Downs boundary were the healthiest of any part of the river. This occurred because most of the river frontage had been fenced off, keeping the cattle out and preventing overstocking.

An industry Range Land Report concluded that Fossil Downs had a potential of 16,923 cattle units. Since then new improved grazing regimes have been employed allowing for more cattle to be run sustainably. Now 26 paddocks are assisting the management and enhancing pasture sustainability and use. By focusing on these issues, Fossil has potential for increased cattle units, but John believes 17,000 is enough to handle with minimal staff.

Since 1992, many innovations have been introduced—new watering places, new paddocks and paddock realignments, and a new, modern, easy working steel yard facility located more centrally, as opposed to the original old timber yards beyond the front gates.

Approximately 1,000 replacement heifers are retained annually thus the herd is maintained with the oldest cows rarely exceeding 10 years of age. Fossil's annual sale cattle are eagerly sought each year for export, local consumption and breeding.

Philosophically John commented, 'Farmers not only provide safe, good quality food, we also provide the care and custody of remote vast areas of land. Annette and I care deeply for, and respect the land and our livestock,' he ventured. 'We're the caretakers at Fossil Downs, a property that's been in our family for three generations—and what's good for our property is good for the environment'.

Dung Beetles

'Dung beetles yours Friday. Bornemissza'. This strange telegram arrived one morning on the 7.00 am radio sked. What did it mean? The circumspect radio operator made no comment, of course, when it was read back to her, but you could sense the whole of the listening Kimberley wondering what was happening at Fossil Downs now. Mrs. Mac couldn't decipher its meaning, either. It was thought about, on and off, all day. Then over drinks at the evening gathering in the hall, John said, 'Oh, dung beetles. Yes. I remember something about them. I said we'd be in the experiment.'

In 1965, the CSIRO had commissioned the 'Australian Dung Beetle Project'. The introduction of large cattle numbers to Australia over time had caused a biological imbalance in pastures, brought about by too much cattle dung. CSIRO's Division of Entomology was charged with restoring this balance. In charge of this project was George Bornemissza who subsequently introduced into Australia twenty-three species of beetle from South Africa and Europe. By ingesting fresh cow dung, the dung beetle would bring about restoration of this pasture imbalance, it was hoped.

The packages of beetles duly arrived at Fossil on the mail plane, and were taken out on the run where the cattle were pastured and plenty of fresh dung was available. Presumably this arrangement occurred in all Australian cattle breeding areas. In the Kimberley the buffalo fly was the target. The appropriate follow-up action and checks were made and it's estimated that the quality and fertility of pastures right across Australia improved markedly with this importation.

As it happened, the Australian bush fly—the one that gives rise to the expression 'Aussie salute'—had exploded exponentially with the extra supplies of dung from all these cattle, and would continue to do so if allowed to breed unchecked throughout the country. The bonus outcome from this Dung Beetle project to rebalance pasture was a degree of control of the population of this iconic Australian bush fly. Most town and city people who visit country areas are far more impressed with the estimated 90 percent reduction in these persistent pesky pests, than they are with restoration of pasture balance or reduction of buffalo flies!

Corroboree

'Missus. Corroboree starting now!' A young man raced up to the Big House and announced this news. The native camp people had been getting ready for a corroboree, an occasional happening. Clacking clap sticks and sombre sounds of the didgeridoo and singing had been intoning the airwaves for a few days. Mrs. Mac grabbed the biscuits, drinks and other goodies she'd accumulated ready to go, and everyone piled into the car and drove down to the cleared site near the Margaret River. 'They never know when it will start', Mrs. Mac explained as we piled out of the car and headed over to the campfire. 'You just have to be ready for when they want you to come.' Fourteen young men, decoratively painted for the occasion, began performing dances to the rhythm of the clapping sticks. No aboriginal women were there.

Interacting with their dreamtime through dance, music and costume constitutes a corroboree—a word actually coined by the European settlers from the east coast aborigines word of 'caribberie'. The participants painted their bodies in different ways and wore various adornments, which are not used every day—rather like 'white-fellers' going to a ball. Songs and dances performed during these ceremonies passed on information about 'The Dreamtime'. Some songs and dances are sacred, like those taught in initiation ceremonies, but not all of them. 'Sometimes a corroboree will be held to make it rain,' Mrs. Mac said as she handed the cakes, biscuits and drinks around after the performance. They were eagerly accepted and shared.

River Runs

Did this corroboree cause the Margaret River to commence flowing in 1970? Louisa Downs, a station further up the Margaret River, sent a message that the water in the river had commenced flowing past their homestead. Everyone kept a watch for it arriving. Again a young native man ran up to the homestead with the message, 'Missus, river him bin comin'.' Everyone working around the homestead piled into vehicles and drove to the river to watch this natural, but unplanned, event. We gazed in awe at this water trickling down, and took photos of the aborigines dancing in the riverbed until the water flowed deeper. More amazing, some were spearing fish! How could that be?

Gradually the frothy, muddy, debris-laden water reached the Station's river crossing, and banked up until it eventually spilled over and headed down to connect with the Fitzroy River. On the other side of the Margaret was the Haflinger, hastily positioned ready to provide access to Fitzroy Crossing when it was safe enough to row the tinny boat across. The station tried to time its third delivery of stores for the year to arrive just prior to the river commencing to run. Diesel fuel, without which the station could not function, was topped up from Derby, at the last realistic delivery date. But for the next few months, generally, access to Fitzroy and the rest of the world, by road, was cut off—who knew for how long?

Amber & Norman

Old Norman had been one of the trained honour guards, and one day in 1974 there was a lot of mirth coming from the native camp. Norman, now retired from the stock camp, was astride a horse mimicking the riding style of an American visitor who'd been at the station that morning and who'd been taken by horseback to see some of the property and the cattle. The aborigines loved the Western films showed at the station each fortnight, and readily identified the different American style of riding of the cowboy to that of the Australian ringer.

Picture night was a lot of fun, and sometimes people from nearby stations would visit for this event. The screen was set up on the back lawn along with the white wooden chairs and the projector. The natives were happy to sit on the grass; you could hear them talking excitedly as they came down from their camp, anticipating the film. A passionate love film failed to impress them, likewise anything deep and meaningful, which were rarely ordered anyway, but cowboy films they could relate to were greeted with yells of whoopee!

John and Annette's daughter, Amber, recalls Norman. 'He used to come down to the homestead every day and saddle up the horse for me, and he'd lead me around and around for hours and hours and hours. I was 3 or 4.' If only Norman could know the accomplished horsewoman and camp draft competitor Amber became. Nowadays in New South Wales, she breeds stock horses suitable for mustering and camp drafting under the Fossil Downs Stock Horses banner, still with the ZV5 brand

My Name Now Is ...

In 1969, there were approximately 60 indigenous people in their camp just over a small hill, but in close proximity to the station buildings. Many of the men worked in the stock camp or around the various sheds, yards, or veggie garden while the women worked either in the cookhouse, in the gardens, or with specific duties in either the homestead, the manager's house or cleaning the mens' quarters. Most worked, but the elderly ones were retired and were recently enrolled in the Federal Government's Age Pension Scheme.

This new experience was a learning curve for me, as I began to understand some of the aboriginal culture and recognize their amazing skills of tracking animals and people, their knowledge of how to locate a water source, along with their ability to survive in harsh conditions. Their hearing and eyesight seemed so much sharper than mine. Had I just become lazy in using all my senses, depending on inventions to work? A few of the young women always came with me when driving into Fitzroy Crossing in the station ute. If something happened with the vehicle, or we got lost in the bush for some reason, I knew I would survive the hot, rugged conditions in their company.

In the station files, one day, I found the certificates of 18 and 16 year-old Irene and Ruth, both of whom had passed typing exams when they were at high school in Derby in the late 1960s. They were employed around the homestead, but Ruth did not always carry out her work with enthusiasm. I sympathised that, as a trained typist also, at that age I may not have been overjoyed being employed cleaning house. It was understandable that their father, Pluto, wanted them together as a family unit on the station where he worked, not living by themselves in Derby or Broome, the only places where they could be employed in offices to utilize these skills.

Irene loved putting flowers in the floating bowl on the table in the hall. At Christmas, she teamed the red poinciana flowers with those from the white boab tree, which harmonized beautifully with the red and white checked concrete floor, all following traditional Christmas colours.

Surplus dresses were given to these young native women. Irene, Ruth and Kathleen, particularly, with their slender hips and lithe manner of walking, always seemed to look more elegant in them than I did. It was their intense black skin, which contrasted better with the fabric colours than my pale white, I told myself.

Gradually I came to understand the language of the older women, who spoke in a mixture of pidgin and English. It was intriguing to guess some of the meanings—the longer it took to say a word meant how large the item being described was. There was a differing number of cattle if they spoke of *b-i-i-i-g mobs* compared with *b-i-i-i-i-i-i-i-g mobs*. 'Mobs' was used a lot—it related to quantity of anything. Some of their words crept into our everyday language—we'd speak of 'having a bogey', their expression for a shower.

The aforementioned Age Pension Scheme posed a conundrum at times. Cheques were mailed out from the government to all people receiving the Age Pension. These cheques had to be signed by the recipient, in front of someone so money could be exchanged for the cheque. As a service to the pensioner, shops, post offices and other places, where there were no banks, would do this and then deposit these cheques to their own account. At Fossil Downs, we had to ensure there was sufficient cash on hand for pension day. With forward planning that was not too great a problem—a far greater problem was the time taken in getting the recipient to sign the cheque. Generally, they could not sign their name. In the interests of efficiency, over the years the secretaries became very adept at making a wobbly cross, endorsed with 'his/her mark', and witnessed, after the cash had been dispensed. No fee was ever deducted by the station, nor was there ever any thought of it, for this service being provided despite it taking considerable office time for it to be administered. Social services were just part of the mosaic of living made up by various activities undertaken by everyone.

Kathleen came down to the office one Saturday morning, and said, 'Dicky bin comin' home today.' This was news. No telegram advising the station of this had been received. Dicky was Kathleen's husband, an older man, who'd been in the Derby leprosarium for four years. Sure enough, at midday a vehicle arrived at the front gate, containing Dicky. The aboriginal senses of sight, smell and hearing were still attuned to the environment and each other—and mental telepathy still worked for them.

Annette's aboriginal name was Jaira, John's was Coolalegoo, and their daughter Amber was Gunballi. Merrilee's name was Nanmerria. After they felt they knew you, the native people would choose their own name for you. Sandy, the secretary preceding me, was always called Chandra, utilizing the longer form of her name. It was a special time for me one morning when some of the older women came down to the lawn outside the office and bestowed me the name of Wandiga. When I asked what it meant, they just said, 'proper good name'.

Killing the Snake

Cattle, horses, sheep, even donkeys and goats I can cope with, after a fashion. Snakes? Nope. At my primary school in the Victorian Yarra Valley in the 1950s, we were taught how to kill them, and what to do if we were bitten. Antivenom had yet to be formulated. My solution if you saw a snake, was to run fast—in the opposite direction. Of course, in the Fossil Downs environment, tucked in beside the rocky Geikie Range, there were plenty of snakes, although not usually around the homestead. There was always too much activity and noise for snakes to hang out there. But one night there was a death adder in the grapevine strung along the veranda. I vanished until it had been 'disappeared' by someone.

Then one day, dear old Ruby, whose eyesight was deficient, was raking up leaves outside the office and called out. When I looked, there was a big black snake—and I couldn't see anyone else around. 'It's up to me,' I thought racing outside and grabbing a hoe that was leaning against a pergola pillar. 'I'll have to summon all my courage and dispose of it, somehow.' Ruby was in danger of being bitten, and I couldn't let everyone go on thinking I was just a useless wuss, even if the black snake was poisonous! 'This is my big moment—but what a pity there's no one to take a photo of me killing a snake. Who's going to believe that I actually did it?' was egotistically darting through my mind.

With the hoe raised in the air, I was ready to annihilate the offender by cracking its back, when a shrill voice behind me called out, 'No Lyn. I do it.' Irene was racing full-pelt down the hill from the camp. Wresting the hoe from me, she very gently twisted it on the snake's head. That left the rest of its body unbruised so it could be cooked for tea in the camp that night.

Rain Stones

The 'build-up season', also known as 'mango madness', could be all of October, November and December. The tropical regions in the north have high temperatures and high humidity—distinct wet and dry seasons. The wet can last for six months, between November and March, and is hotter than the dry, with daily temperatures mainly between 85 to 120 degrees Fahrenheit. During the build up, violent thunderstorms can occur. Huge cloud masses pile up in the afternoons and spectacular lightning shows can offer hours of entertainment, like great fireworks. This rain is localised, short-lived and heavy, often preceded by strong winds, which could be very refreshing.

These weather patterns change as the monsoonal season progresses. The small isolated storms can be replaced by big low-pressure systems that can dump incredible amounts of rain. If such a tropical low moves out into the ocean it can turn into a powerful cyclone. The Kimberley may experience weeks of sunny, hot and humid weather with only the occasional thunderstorm. Sometimes areas get hardly any rain. But then, when it rains it pours, and Fossil Downs becomes an island with boat or plane being the only way to exit.

The wet season in 1969 was very dry. Only 8 inches of rain fell for the whole year. The native women, particularly Whibella, were frustrated by this and found their rain stones. Six of these were set in Porgy's flat water container on the veranda outside the kitchen. When that hadn't produced rain in a week, the depth of water was increased and Whibella took to the stones with a scrubbing brush, after which there were some spasmodic storms.

The Rain Game

The first radio schedule for the day was at 7.00 a.m. when Jim or Norma Keisey, of VJB Derby, would come on air and announce the stations for which they had telegram traffic—all messages were by telegram. There were no telephones to the stations until the 1980s! Before reading out the telegrams in the wet season for everyone, the operators would ask for rainfall to be reported from each station. Everyone on air heard the conversation. Normally the Bureau of Meteorology in Australia measures rainfall at 9.00 am, but for the Kimberley stations it was reported at 7.00 am, as that was the radio schedule that most station personnel accessed. Vic Jones at Gogo station always waited until VC's rainfall total was reported before he reported theirs, and they always had more! Fossil Downs has been continuously officially reporting their rainfall for the Bureau since 1904.

A skeleton staff was all that remained at the station during the wet season, when no stock work could be accomplished. Most stockmen, fencers, builders, painters, electricians, mechanics, and water drillers generally decamped to cooler, less humid places down south or east until the next dry season. During my first wet, there were only 5 of us for morning smoko at the cookhouse. Being isolated with no mail or papers arriving, and the 7.00 p.m. ABC radio news being mainly blotted out with static, plus no one being able to negotiate the river to visit, we had very little input for our conversation—except to speculate on how much rain we'd receive that night. 'I bet we'll get an inch tonight,' Sid, the handyman, said one morning. 'I bet we don't,' countered John. And so the 'Rainfall Betting Game' was born. Every morning we'd each put in 20c and nominate our estimate for that night's rainfall. The person nearest the actual amount was winner, and winner took all. Old Leo, the water driller, thought he'd outsmart everyone, and bet zero rainfall for every night. Sid, who was 'keeper of records' then found it necessary to call a cabinet meeting at smoko, to make rules—and it was voted that if there was SOME rain, a person who bet NO rain could not be declared the winner. He only won on the occasions there was NO rain. Somehow, without the aid of social media, this competition leaked around the other stations, and there'd be radio calls during the 'galah' session, 'Wot's this game you're playing over there?'

1969 was an extremely dry wet season, with only one-third of the average rainfall. Frequently big, dark storm clouds would gather in the west, and roll and tumble ominously towards Fossil—but disappointing falls would result. On those occasions the Big House was blamed, intimating that the clouds hit it and were divided, one lot being sent up to Lansdowne, the other across to Gogo. Mrs. Mac said it wasn't fair to blame the Big House.

The other topic of conversation was 'How far away can thunder be heard?' John said 100 miles away. None of us believed that! How could he possibly hear it at that distance—he was half-deaf anyway—although perhaps it was just the enormous job of managing a million-acre-plus property with its myriad activities occurring simultaneously that his mind sometimes seemed to be elsewhere, ignoring the inane banter. Mrs. Mac laughed heartily at my letter to the Bureau of Meteorology seeking their opinion which was headed: 're: Thunder'. Typically from a government department, the reply neither agreed nor disagreed with the 100-mile suggestion—'given certain circumstances it could be possible', they acknowledged.

'Millsy'

As there were three regular radio telegram skeds per day plus the medical sked, the call signs, names and voices from the other stations became very familiar. The Royal Flying Doctor Service ran this vital communication system. Philanthropically, the Victorian Section of the RFDS adopted the Kimberley as its outback and raised the funds needed to support the sparsely populated Kimberley division.

Increasingly in the late 1960s mineral boom, mining exploration camps had portable transceivers linked to the RFDS for medical and other emergencies, and to transact their business by telegram. Stations also had portable transceivers used by their stock camps. The established stations could be a bit condescending to these portables that were getting on the airwaves and cluttering them up. A French couple, in their mining camp, must surely have extended Norma or Jim's composure when they ordered dinner sets and other exotic items in French! But the bone china dinner set eventually arrived at their isolated outback camp. That charming French couple were at a party at Mt. Hart some time later, where they'd arrived with a case of French champagne.

Another I heard regularly was BHP's exploration party, WGE, especially when their helicopter crashed and burned near Kalumburu. Three years later, 6000 miles away in New Zealand where I then lived, I was at a Murray Grey Cattle Breeder's conference talking with a younger couple. 'I think I've heard your voice before', I suggested to the male. 'I'm bloody sure I've heard yours,' was the swift reply. This exploration geologist had left his position with BHP in the Kimberley and returned with his wife to New Zealand to graze sheep and cattle on her family's property, and I had left Fossil and married John and we were farming there too. We were all breeding stud cattle. Through that Kimberley RFDS radio experience we became friends and have remained so. Millsy always retained his deep love of the unique Kimberley area and communicated it to his daughter who is now a well-known presenter on ABC radio in Broome, also known by the same moniker.

Mt. Hart

The aforementioned party at Mt. Hart was memorable. Peter Murray was the manager of this Theiss Bros. owned station, and as Mr. Cecil Theiss was coming for a visit, Peter thought it was a good chance for the community to have a get-together and all meet Mr. Theiss and each other. The Theiss company of five brothers was a major engineering and resource management company operating all over Australia. At that time, women's fashion was to wear long frocks at evening functions. We chose our gowns, packed up the Kingswood sedan and Nissan utility, and seven of us set out over 200 miles of rough, tough roads. We passed Leopold Downs and Fairfield stations, Tunnel Creek and Windjana Gorge, and turned onto the Gibb River track. It was only a track, unlike the graded and formed road of today.

Mt. Hart homestead was approximately 30 miles north off that track, with twenty-something creek crossings to negotiate. Peter had great organising ability. He'd driven into Derby for supplies, and 'kidnapped' the chef from the Boab Inn—his job at the party was chef of the BBQ meal. All the young men from the Mt. Hart stock camp were schooled in their role to look after the guests. They had to wear a clean shirt and trousers, and were lined up to meet the guests as they arrived, and show them to their overnight accommodation. The approximately 100 guests were feted with hospitality in all directions. Despite our long dresses, we were still able to clamber onto the raft and float around the lagoon adjacent to the homestead in the brilliant moonlight, a ubiquitous flagon of red wine accompanying this cruise.

Ken Warriner, an icon in the cattle industry today, was manager at Mt. House station on the Gibb River track, and had flown his party over in their 6-seater plane. Next morning he said he was going to fly back to Mt. House to check in with his stock camp and asked, 'Who wants to come for a fly?' I'm not sure why I volunteered—well, I did enjoy flying and observing the landscape from the air—and there were four others who enjoyed seeing the scenery from above who volunteered to go too. Flying to the camp was fine—but flying round and round and round while Ken communicated by walkie-talkie to the head stockman at the camp below, while the altimeter in the plane appeared to be registering zero, was something I only remember for the after-effects.

Back at Mt. Hart, Annette and Mr. Theiss had organised a tennis tournament. It was so hot with the sun radiating up from the rolled ant-bed surface of the court, that play was permitted for 6 minutes only before it was time to take a break in the shade.

A very tired group wended its way home to Fossil that afternoon. Next day Mrs. Mac, herself an impeccable hostess, commented on what a wonderful hostess Anne, Peter's wife, was. 'It was all beautifully organised,' she said. 'Anne was totally available to her guests. She didn't need to turn her hand to anything'.

Rowing the River

The Margaret river was running. Ros, one of the nurses, had called up on the UHF radio from the AIM hospital saying she needed to come out and see someone at the homestead. We agreed to meet at the river. It was about 3' deep, but not running swiftly. I untied the tinny, and proceeded to try and row it across the 80 yards of running water. I was making little progress. Ros, observing my pathetic rowing effort, called out, 'Turn around. You row backwards'. Duh! My useless rowing efforts were going in the wrong direction, but eventually I got the tinny to the other side. Another lesson? Wisdom then decreed it better to walk it back through the river, dragging it alongside us. Eventually Ros and I got to the Fossil side each with soaked clothes from having dropped into unseen holes in the riverbed. It hadn't been the smartest undertaking to try. John felt it wiser to return the tinny to safety in the garage!

Moonlight Magic

Changing the tyre on the ute was not successful either. The governess and I were driving home from Fitzroy Crossing one night, with eight native women on the back, when a tyre burst after hitting a bulldust hole. Now, this is something I can normally deal with easily. Years in Victorian Young Farmers, entering the women's tyre-changing competition, ensured plenty of experience. Except we didn't have any light other than the bright moon, so it was difficult to locate all the nuts and bolts under the tray of the ute to access the spare, jack and the tyre brace. After fiddling around for an hour, we gave up. The rest of the women said they'd stay with the ute—although that wasn't necessary. Caroline and I walked the 3 miles back to the homestead. That was not an exasperating experience though—it was magical. The moonlight was clear and bright in that unpolluted Kimberley atmosphere. We felt we could touch the stars, the planets, the Southern Cross and the Milky Way—every leaf and piece of foliage illuminated like daylight. Next morning, Syd and his helper retrieved the ute with all the women.

Personalised Plates?

Inches of either mud or dust, depending on the season, coated the tracks to properties. They were always studded with bull-dust holes. The locals still found a way to access the towns and other stations both for business and social occasions. In the still weather, you'd think you were catching up to another vehicle as the dust hung in the air—but that vehicle could have driven along the track 20-30 minutes previously, or more. The state of the roading was accepted as 'that's how it is here', although Bill had never lost an opportunity to publicise that Kimberley meat and wool producers were earning huge amounts of overseas income for Australia, but there was little infrastructure returned to the area.

Other than taking a swag, accommodation at social venues could be non-existent, so in 1958 Bill decided to convert a horse float into a 'sort-of' caravan to be taken to local races, rodeos and sporting events, and anywhere else where it would provide useful accommodation for up to four people. It was used on the property, too, if fencing, yards, or other work was being undertaken some distance from the homestead where returning each night was impractical. Remember it was 100 miles of bush-bashing, range-cresting country to the top boundary! Thus 'Miss Kimberley' was born. The last time I saw it, Annette was scrubbing it down so that she and John could utilise it while he was bulldozing some dams a few miles up the run, with the D6 bulldozer.

Vehicles, from the 'dozer to several 4WD flat deck utilities to the Cessna plane, all facilitated both work and play to give the station folk something of a social life, although paramount was the efficient functioning of the station.

Most of these vehicles required licensing, of course. In Western Australia this was done through local authorities. The number plate on a vehicle indicated the area it came from. When driving in that state, it was a variation of 'I spy' that travelers often played to see who could identify the most number plates of the other vehicles travelling too. The initials for small shires could be somewhat obscure.

Back in the 1950/60s, Bill MacDonald had had the numberplate KW1—Kimberley West (Shire) No.1. This was like a personalised number plate, before they were introduced and became commonplace. Was this another of Bill's firsts? But, Mrs. Mac's lovely V8 Holden Kingswood had a very insignificant number plate. It had been registered at 'central casting' in Perth. Mrs. Mac's friends had purchased it for her and driven it to the Kimberley. The KW1 numberplate still had pride of place on the wall in the main store adjacent to the carport, as it was a special station artefact. But I felt cheated I missed out on driving around sporting that iconic number-plate at that time—and being an insufferable smarty-pants.

It was great fun, though, driving that Kingswood into The Crossing when reaching the only strip of bitumen in the area. Outside the hospital, post office and police station, I could plant my foot and delight in the deep throaty growl emitted from the V8.

Penicillin Vaccinations

Medical skills? Beyond dispensing an aspro and band-aid, I had none. This created some challenges at 7.30 each morning when the aborigines would present outside the office at the end of the flagstone veranda with their various maladies, wanting remedies from the Royal Flying Doctor medicine chest. I had to try and be a knowledgeable and helpful 'nurse'. The medical instruments and dressings, along with the fifty-plus medications were set out in a tall cupboard in the bathroom with two red crosses painted on the outside, and numbered appropriately on the shelves. The doctors at Derby Hospital could be consulted, if necessary, on the 8.00 a.m. Flying Doctor radio sked—when their advice would go something like: 'Give two No. 25s twice per day for 3 days. Over.' If the patient didn't seem quite bad enough to consult the doctors, Mrs. Mac or Annette were a good source of information. Sometimes one of the nurses from the AIM hospital at Fitzroy would be at the station for some rest and recuperation (R&R) leave, and would be prevailed on for help and advice. Everyone's details were recorded on a card index system and could be consulted too—what were they given last time?

Dispensing 'rubbing medicine' and something for 'guts-ache', or 'cold sick', was relatively easy. Trachoma treatment was given in the form of eye drops to the indigenous women and children, for one week of each month. Popping drops into eyes was generally easy if you could get the recipient to look in the opposite direction to where you planned to plonk the ointment. Either Ruth or Irene, young women who assisted me in many ways, helped by marking off everyone each day to make sure all were accounted for, and a round-up would ensue if they weren't.

The nurses from the hospital taught me how to give penicillin injections—'mark out the buttock into four quarters with metho on cottonwool, and inject in the upper outer quarter'. I managed to avoid inflicting my inadequate jabbing skills on anyone for about 6 months. Then came the day there was no one around to help. Martin, a big strapping stockman required penicillin treatment. The penicillin was retrieved from the kitchen fridge and I assembled the needle and syringe, but still felt totally inadequate for the job ahead. In the bathroom dispensary, the place for treatment, Martin knew the drill and had dropped his trousers. He was leaning forward with his elbows on the bathroom cabinet, his back to me. 'I can't just leave him standing there,' shot through my mind, so I took a couple of deep breaths, stepped forward, marked out the buttock, and kap-pow! The needle sailed in very easily and the penicillin was administered.

Buoyed with confidence from that brief experience, I was quietly in control some time later when Tilley presented with the need for penicillin. This time the result was very different! The needle bounced off her extremely thick buttock—after all, she'd spent much of her 65 years sitting around on the ground, sans underwear!

The Flying Doctors would conduct monthly clinics on the airstrips of the stations, where they liked the stations to have a bough shed erected for some shade and privacy, to conduct their examinations. There was always chaos trying to find everyone, loading them on the back of a ute, and having them ready at the airstrip when the doctor plane arrived, along with the card index of previous treatments. It took most of the morning. One of the medicos was particularly interested in Tilley, as he diagnosed her with Type 2 diabetes, and believed she was the first aborigine in the Kimberley to be so afflicted.

Medico Madness

Dr. Lawson Holman was an iconic Kimberley medico. All Kimberleyites from the 1960/70s can relate anecdotes involving Doc Holman's inventiveness, courage and dedication to the medical wellbeing of everyone who lived in the Kimberley when he practised there. Once, over the radio, he asked me to dip my finger in and taste an unknown substance a little boy had swallowed and tell him what it tasted like, after I'd washed my mouth out. Ugh! I couldn't identify it, but if it was poisonous we both survived.

In the 1950s when he first arrived fresh out of a southern medical school, conditions in Derby were primitive—if they existed at all. One of his first efforts was to categorise the entire Derby town population into blood groups, so that if blood was needed in an emergency he knew which local to go to and extract it from—the procedure sometimes carried out on their front doorstep.

Surgery, as we know it today, was non-existent there then but Doc Holman was always willing to give things a go. It wasn't unusual for the hospital matron to be administering anaesthetic to a patient, while a nurse read out the 'as you go' operating instructions from a 'how to' book of surgery, while Doc Holman operated.

The story is told of a young aboriginal boy who was seen by himself way out on the Canning Stock Route, as he was unable to keep up with his mob because of a badly deformed leg. Somehow he'd picked up the dreaded leprosy, Hansen's disease, which was rife in the area. The young boy was choppered into Derby, perhaps the first such rescue from out there in the Great Sandy Desert, and Doc

Holman operated on his deformed leg. Was the foregoing surgery method used? Two years later another operation enabled the boy to eventually run and become a good hunter. That was satisfaction enough for the Doc, but this patient also went on to become a celebrated artist.

If ever you required treatment or a stay in the Derby hospital, there was no chance of lying on a bed having a rest or feeling sorry for yourself—you'd find yourself working in Medical Records or central dressings rolling up bandages. Dr. Holman found a job for everyone.

Leprosy had been introduced into the north of Australia by indentured Chinese and Malay labourers early in the 20th century. The first recorded case of leprosy in an aboriginal was in 1908. Like tuberculosis, it spread rapidly in the indigenous population who had no previous contact with mycobacteria. By 1966 the northern part of Australia had the highest prevalence of leprosy in the world.

Doc Holman dedicated so much of his life to helping these patients that he eventually succumbed to the condition himself, the neurological damage to his hands forcing him to give up surgery, so in the 1970s he was appointed Director of Health in Western Australia. He established that State's Community Health Services in an effort to improve the life of those living in the remote communities. He recognised that prevention was better than cure. 'More would be achieved' he believed, 'by appointing indigenous health workers to practise this way, rather than building more hospitals'.

In 1970, Dr. Holman and Dr. Anne Troop were visiting Fossil Downs for lunch. In my opinion, the table spread was even more splendid than usual, and the silver was polished even brighter in honour of this occasion. Dr. Holman was invited to carve the roast at the table—he'd had surgical training by then! The meal eventually over, it was my job to drive the doctors back to their plane waiting on the airstrip. While opening one of the gates on the way, Dr. Holman stabbed his hand on an errant piece of fencing wire which was sticking out unsecured from the gate's strainer post. Dr. Troop severely castigated me for not bringing a 'gate-opener', i.e. an aboriginal youth, who would ride standing up on the back of the ute and leap off to open and shut the gates. I was so unused to the luxury of those tasks being performed for me, it hadn't occurred to me to trek up to the native camp where everyone was having siesta, to cajole someone who'd come and perform that chore.

Several doctors stationed in the Kimberley had widened the boundaries of traditional methods and medicines in an effort to bring healing to those in what was then a remote area. The book, *Legend of the Kimberley*, compiled by his wife Janet, tells more of Dr. Holman's adventurous exploits, along with the, at times, miraculous airmanship in raging storms and cyclones displayed by pilots from the Royal Flying Doctor Service.

Adenoids Removal

A situation arose whereby one of the native babies, because of a stay in hospital, needed supplementary feeding on baby formula. His mother's milk had dried up. This created all sorts of problems that the domestic management team (Mrs. Mac, Annette and I) talked through. What feeding schedule should be employed? Should all the bottles be made up in the morning, and stored in a fridge? However, there was no working refrigeration up at the camp. And who would remember to come down from the camp to collect a bottle each feeding time? Conversely, who could take the bottles to the camp at the correct time? Who could be available to make up bottles during the day for 'on demand' feeding if it was decided that would be the best option? Could his two teenage sisters, who were quite good in the kitchen, be inveigled into service? We all agreed it was not their responsibility—plus they had their other work. Everyone had full work schedules.

A nursing sister from the AIM Hospital, Ginny, was having some R&R leave at Fossil so offered to make up all the bottles for the first couple of days. She seemed to be in the kitchen for hours attending to this task. After she departed, Mrs. Mac took over for a few days, grumbling about the time it took. Then she, too, departed the station to go to Perth. So, the secretary scored the chore.

Ginny had been adamant there were no shortcuts in mixing formula—40 flat tablespoonfuls of the powder had to be counted out, then mixed with the appropriate amount of water. I was far too busy with my office and other chores for that, so I carefully measured and found that four flat cups of milk powder was the equivalent to 40 flat tablespoonfuls, and could be made up much quicker. When Mrs. Mac returned I showed her. 'That's a good idea,' she said, but being the generous-to-a-fault person she was, proceded to dump four heaped cups of formula into the mixing bowl. 'If some is good, more is better' could easily have been her motto. No amount of suggestion on my part could persuade her to flatten off the cups of powder with a knife before mixing it with the required quantity of water. The child was fed on the resulting thick goo, which sometimes went sour when it was left in the sun. He survived and thrived.

Sometime later, this child was toddling down the path from the camp towards the machinery sheds, chewing the sharpened end of a pencil. He tripped on a jagged rock, which was sticking up, which resulted in the pencil being pushed up through the roof of his mouth near the back of his nose. This necessitated an emergency whistle call to the Derby hospital. Providentially, the RFDS doctor plane was in the vicinity, and deviated to Fossil's landing strip to collect him and his mother. Two days later he was returned to the station, apparently no worse for his experience. Next time Dr. Spargo came to Fossil to conduct a clinic, he reported that when the child had reached the Emergency Department, they just needed to clean the wound and stitch it up. This youngster had successfully removed his own adenoids!

24 Gallons of Curry

The barrage at Camballin, on the Fitzroy River flats southwest of Fitzroy Crossing, was an area where some American people had constructed a weir intending to irrigate the flats from it to grow cotton. The next wet season floods annihilated their efforts with most of the structure ending up in King Sound. In 2009 Sarah and Mary, native women, were there on a nostalgic visit having brought out an older resident from the Numbala Nunga Nursing Home in Derby to see the Fitzroy river again. In chatting with them, it transpired that I'd known Sarah's father at Fossil Downs. We reminisced about those times and Mary commented that she grew up on adjacent Gogo Station, but they loved sneaking over to Fossil for Native Christmas, which was usually held on the Saturday before Christmas Day.

In the 1950/60s, Native Christmas was a special time. Games were organised: high jump, sack race, anything in which the young ones could compete, have a fun time, and win prizes. Trestle tables were set up under a bough shed on the lawn and under the sweetly scented frangipani trees. The approximately sixty indigenous people on the station brought along their own plates and utensils. The popular menu was curry, ladled out of a big drum, and rice, washed down with soft drink, followed by fruit salad and icecream. So popular was the event that sentries had to be stationed at the front gate so 'hangers on' didn't arrive and ambush the event, leaving nothing for the Fossil natives. Their culture is to share—and they would have done that—but the Fossil management team wanted to reward their own natives and let them have first bite of the cherry, so to speak.

It required twenty-four gallons of curry to feed everyone. The native women, and anyone else available, accomplished this by sitting down the previous morning and chopping up meat, onions, carrots, and other vegetables from the veggie garden, making it into a big stew. Coconut milk, curry powder and spices were mixed up and added, and all put into a large oil drum, and left to simmer on an open fire which was periodically stoked throughout the day. The aroma was mouth-watering.

Next morning, everyone was horrified when the lid was lifted off and the curry was found to be 'bubbling'. Apparently the drum in which it was cooked still had slight residues of motor oil left in it when it was washed. That curry was tipped out. It was all hands on deck and another twenty-four gallons of curry was hastily prepared in super quick time to be ready for Christmas dinner.

Muludja

In 1984 the State authorities promised the aboriginal people their own community and individual houses. In a way, this was very appealing to them. Some were moving on from their traditional outdoors way of living, although many still felt claustrophobic in a building. The now unused reserve, which had been Collins Yard on the eastern side of the Margaret River from Fossil, was to be the site for Muludja, the name chosen by the Fossil aborigines for this new community. John and Annette pointed out to the government authorities how the area flooded massively after a cyclone or heavy rains up in the higher catchment area. So, soil was pushed up into heaps, and the houses built on top of those heaps! When it flooded around all those mounds, while it meant that water didn't enter the houses, it did not allow the inhabitants access to Fitzroy Crossing for their supplies. Again, it is not the aboriginal way of living to provide food ahead for meals, or their other necessities. Now, after repeated floods when Fossil still supplied their needs, all the houses are being rebuilt on stilts, but it still doesn't solve their access issues.

Creating this community required the installation of a proper graded road in from the Great Northern Highway—one hundred years after the Fossil Downs station was established. That was a bonus for the station.

Eventually thirty houses and sundry other buildings were delivered to Muludja, and several other communities around Fitzroy Crossing. But the indigenous people had to live in tents on the reserve for many years before this was achieved.

Aborigine boys

Whenever you drove into Fitzroy Crossing from the station, a group of young native people always came with you, just for the ride. Usually I drove one of the station utes, especially if there were vehicle parts or other freight to collect. Irene and Ruth usually rode in the front with me.

With no legal requirements then for the driver insisting all passengers be seated with their seat belt fastened, a group of youths would leap on the back of the ute at the front gate out of the homestead compound as it was being fastened.

A couple of miles down the track, having traversed the causeway over the Margaret River, there'd be a knock on the roof—that indicated one of the young men wanted to jump off to pee. That achieved, and mobile again, a further few miles down the track there'd be another bang on the roof. Another one wanted to stop for the same reason.

And so this continued for the twenty-six miles into Fitzroy Crossing. There seemed to be no way that these young men could synchronise their biological needs.

No Pot Luck

Mrs. Mac was a product of the more refined 1930s when hospitality and meals were always supplied by the host. But by the late 1960s times had changed regarding hosting social functions. Arrangements had become less rigid—gatherings were more casual. Life was busier. Organising group events had been part of my job at the Junior Farmers organization in Perth prior to my shifting to Kimberley. Colleagues now focused more on the get-together, avoiding making a big job for one or two people.

It occurred to me that the tennis players from Fitzroy Crossing might enjoy a Sunday evening get-together at the station. This could be a change of venue and style of function for the end-of-season championships celebration, thus relieving the nurses at the AIM of that task. Some of the players hadn't been to Fossil Downs, and would enjoy visiting the homestead. But Mrs. Mac thought that would be a lot of work. I indicated that nowadays people were quite happy to 'bring a plate'. If Fossil provided, say, the drinks, plates and cutlery, and set the tables up on the front enclosed verandah, the attendees would bring the food.

That was not Mrs. Mac's style. If it were going to happen at Fossil, she would cater for it and provide everything needed. I was therefore reluctant to persist with my idea—so that event never happened.

Merilee and the Males

Mrs. Mac hated flying in small planes and would only fly in the very early morning before the thermals created air turbulence. On these occasions, the charter plane would be hired from Aerial Enterprises in Derby. The pilot, Dick Roberton, would fly out and stay at the station overnight so that a departure could be made at first light next morning. The plane would be loaded up the night before with whatever was needed for the places being visited—frangipani branches, large containers of lemon squash, and cakes and biscuits baked by Mrs. Mac. This was prior to Fossil acquiring its own Cessna with John as pilot.

Whereas Mrs. Mac hated flying then, I loved it in the small 4-seater plane. Dick made the flight interesting by first lining up over the homestead and station buildings for photos, then over the scenic gorges—Geikie and Windjana. After following the Fitzroy River, we'd arrive at Frazier Downs, south of Broome, then owned and run by Merilee and Rodney Wells, Mrs. Mac's older daughter and son-in-law.

After our visit to Merilee, Dick would fly us up to Broome to stay with Sam and Phyllis Male, long-standing friends of Bill and Maxine. This was still old Broome, corrugated and dusty, not yet discovered by Lord Alistair McAlpine, who came to Broome in 1979 to buy seashells. He ended up purchasing at least 20 homes—he lost count—the outdoor cinema, a caravan park, and built a luxury resort and zoo. Obviously he fell in love with the town and its ramshackle streets and lifestyle, with its location and ambience, and with Cable Beach, which was only sparsely developed. He restored many homes and showed the locals there was beauty in them. Equally he's seen as the man who began Broome's tourist industry.

The house allotments in town were large and the houses built to cope with the extremely hot and sometimes humid Broome weather, as air-conditioning wasn't readily available then. At the Males' home, the outer walls of the sleeping areas were all encased with insect screening to let the evening breezes through but keep the mosquitoes out. Mrs. Mac commented that while this was comfortable for the night, it was not easy to find somewhere private to undress! My sleeping room was the dovecote up the outside stairs above the bathroom. The first night, in ignorance, the mistake was made of not pulling shut the little wooden flaps below the windows, where the bougainvillea was poking through. I didn't know what those flaps were for, but the mosquitoes knew and soon swarmed in, biting mercilessly!

Pearling was one of the businesses Mr. Male was involved with. During World War II, it was reduced to a standstill as the Navy had taken over all the luggers, and the 'Broome-Japanese' people had been quickly interned when war was declared. By 1948, the fleets were gradually being reconditioned to resume operations. However, with the development of plastic buttons in the 1950s, the pearl shell industry fell into decline. Then in 1956 the first pearl farm in the Kimberley was established at Kuri Bay in Camden Sound, 230 miles north of Broome. It was a joint venture between Sam Male and Japanese and American partners following the repeal of the Pearling Act. 'I hope to see pearling become a big and lucrative industry for Broome and Australia again,' Bill had reflected. 'The spell over the war years will have increased the quality and size of the pearls and shells, and should make operations very successful.' By 1973, Kuri Bay was producing 60% of the world's large, cultured South Sea pearls.

'The Sun' open air picture theatre was legendary—still is—and Mrs. Male had reserved tickets for every film, as TV hadn't yet arrived in the north of Western Australia. 'Who's Afraid of Virginia

Wolf', with Richard Burton and Elizabeth Taylor, was showing in 1969 and we all went and reclined under the stars in the canvas deck chairs—an experience to be remembered.

Phyllis Male's curry was renowned. It took several days to make, after she'd been to Chinatown to collect the spices that were specially ground up for her. It was accompanied by a vast array of condiments and additions—and the flavour was significantly improved by the meal being eaten right outside on the lawn, under the moon and stars, in the balmy night air, enhanced by the wafting perfume of the frangipani flowers.

Broome is still a unique town, with an eclectic historical past. It's a wonderful mecca much appreciated by southern residents who flock there to 'winter over' now there's a sealed road all the way.

Maxine and Phyllis were such good friends that after Bill's death Phyllis and Sam offered to purchase the bottom storey of Maxine's dwelling in Perth's Peppermint Grove. Sam, who was an executor of Bill MacDonald's will, suggested this. Was he thinking ahead, making sure Phyllis had a base in Perth, which would be more convenient for her than Broome in her later life? The transaction ensued, but the transfer of the Certificate of Title into strata title, was an ongoing nightmare of administration for all those concerned. The time taken for documents to be drawn up, arrive, be signed, then returned to the solicitors was unbelievably protracted. Was this another 'first' in which a MacDonald was involved? The strata title scheme was first devised in Sydney in 1961, and this was only the middle sixties in Perth. Eventually the transaction was concluded. Sam died in 1976.

Arrangements like this, entered into with the best of intentions and seeming like a good idea at the time, don't always work harmoniously however. Maxine lived in her upstairs unit when she was in Perth. Originally she had acquired, planted and tended rose bushes in the garden that grew well. When she wanted to pick some blooms so she could see them upstairs, Phyllis wouldn't allow it. Each day Maxine struggled into Peppermint Grove to do the shopping for both of them, and carried it back, as she had never learned to drive. Climbing the outside stairs also became a great effort for her. John and Annette had plans drawn up for the installation of an elevator, which would benefit them both, now that they were well into their 70s, plus add value to the property. Sadly, Phyllis refused to allow that to happen.

After Maxine's death in 1988, her portion of this property was left to Merrilee. Had there been some mistake or misunderstanding in the original agreement and paperwork? The expected 50/50 settlement was not what was forthcoming for Merrilee.

Kimberley Wet

Before air-conditioning in cars and houses became standard in the Kimberley, the wet season could be a challenge. Day after day, night after night of clammy, hot, humid conditions could really stretch a person's weather tolerance. Temperatures were typically 115° Fahrenheit and humidity 90-100+%.

The time between September and November is known as the 'build up'. It gets hotter, and more humid and oppressive each day. This may be relieved by spectacular lightning-rich thunderstorms in the late afternoons if they bring rain.

It all gives rise to the legendary sickness called 'troppo', that is, going crazy! Researchers say that hot temperatures and humidity during the monsoon season influence people's behaviour. 'Its normal to feel a bit cranky when it's stinking hot,' they say. 'Dehydration combined with high temperatures and humidity affects some people more than others and can lead to distress, irritability—even aggression. It's probably to do with thermal regulation.'

Going for a swim helped a little bit—you got wet—but the water in the gorges was warm, as was the water in the big tank up on the hill which fed the house and gardens. No gas water heating was needed for showers for several months! The wet season I experienced was challenging, although only 8 inches of rain fell in 1969/70. At 7.30 a.m. perspiration prevailed; it became progressively worse as the day wore on.

Most of the white stockmen and contractors returned to their home region then as the stock camp had finished work for the year, and it was too uncomfortable to carry out much other work. Many station personnel decamped to cooler climates for the wet, heading south to Perth in December for a couple of months, where they'd attend Kimberleyites get-togethers if they could. Lexie Jones on Gogo usually vacated to Perth for the wet. I mentioned to her once that I thought she had the best of both worlds—the beautiful dry season from April to September in the Kimberley, then the summer season in Perth, where the humidity was much lower even on the really hot days there. Her reply was memorable—'No, not really. I think your body needs to experience the four seasons.' She elaborated that she had not encountered an autumn or winter season for over twenty years—and her body ached to sit inside by a log fire on a night when it was miserably cold and wet outside.

Telephone Arrives

At the station there were times when it was necessary to obtain a signature, an answer, or a decision from someone, or deliver the contents of a telegram to a recipient. Only—where were they? Looking for a particular person could necessitate walking around for ages. Would Mrs. Mac be in the kitchen, at the laundry, upstairs, in the hall or front lobby, or down at the cookhouse, or even over at the Court House. Annette might be in the main store—or garage, or supervising cleaning at the men's quarters, or over at the head stockman's house talking to his wife, or grooming and medicating her horse—or any other place. She might even have gone with John on a station run. It could take ages to locate someone.

The 20th century was moving forward. In the 1980s telephone wires were installed between Derby and Fitzroy Crossing and Halls Creek. 'We think we can get a phone line out to you', said the young, enthusiastic techos from Telecom who were thriving on their Kimberley experience. Seconded to the area from southern states to hook up cattle stations to the network, they were living a life their compatriots down south could barely imagine. All the stories they relayed to their mates, about staying on stations, in camps, or in isolated townships and the situations they encountered, were no doubt heavily embroidered, but started out with a modicum of truth. These stories would be filed away in their brain's database, to be retrieved eventually to regale to their grandchildren.

Fossil Down's telephone line would head northeast from Fitzroy Crossing, being strung from living tree to tree to tree, deviating via

Brooking Springs station. Twice it crossed over the massive 100-yard wide Fitzroy River. It was a party line—that is, it was used by more than one subscriber, with each phone having its own unique ring, like three short rings, or long-short-long. There was no privacy on a party line. If you were conversing, anyone on your line could pick up their receiver and listen. Also, if anyone was using the phone, no one else could make a call—even in an emergency situation although common sense usually prevailed then. It was a good method, though, of quickly alerting entire neighbourhoods of emergencies such as fires and floods. With copper wire in short supply at times, this system provided at least some means of communication, even if not entirely ideal.

For the stations in the Kimberley, it was close to heaven. Being able to call a business, friend or relative, and talk, plus receive an instant response or answer, was a distinct improvement on sending telegrams and waiting for a reply—although that Royal Flying Doctor service had been much better than no service at all.

Was the Kimberley the last area on the Australian mainland to receive a telephone service? While the techos were in the area, they provided a good, prompt service, whenever cyclones, storms or lightning strikes disrupted the line. They'd come as soon as they could to repair damage. But after they returned to their home bases the resulting service emanating from Broome was not nearly so obliging.

More improvements gradually came. Moving into the 21st century, Fossil eventually acquired its own unique line and installed a Commander system, whereby all the houses, offices and working sheds, were connected. Then you could locate someone simply by pressing a button!

Contract Musterers

Mustering is when all the cattle on the property are rounded up into workable mobs, in different areas of the run. This is when the calves are earmarked, branded, vaccinated in some cases, and the males castrated. It usually takes a good six months for the whole property to be mustered.

Preparing the stock camp to conduct the annual muster became a nightmare for the managers: saddles, stores, personnel, plus shoeing all the horses—and more. The aboriginal people had shifted across the river to Muludja, their own community. How many stockmen would present from there for work at Fossil each day this year? How many would want to return to their community after only a few days on the job? A vehicle and driver would need to be available to collect them, along with their swags. As well as personnel, there was all the saddles and horse tack to repair and maintain after the last muster. Stores for the mustering camps needed organizing. Could they find a good and reliable camp cook? A myriad of tasks needed to be completed for the first day of muster so that it could run reasonably smoothly. Mustering was the hinge on which the finances of the station swung.

Since the advent of the Pastoral Award in 1971 fewer stockmen could be employed, and no longer was there always an experienced head stockman. This role was performed by a variety of people. Each year all these tasks were dreaded. It helped using the Cessna 182, acquired in 1972, to spot where the grazing mobs were, but it still strained everyone's nerves until the muster was underway. Even then it may not run smoothly. The hope, always, was the native people would not be called away for a tribal gathering or someone's funeral. Mustering ceased totally when that occurred.

A native couple, Manly and Sally, were the stock camp cooks in 1970. As well as feeding the numerous ringers, the cooks were responsible for shifting the camp to a new site when the branding was concluding in an area. A tractor and wagon was provided for this purpose, as everything could be loaded easily, including the stockmen's swags. Manly was one of the few aborigines who could drive at that time. His knowledge of the run was invaluable. He knew it intimately, and could recall exactly every campsite they had used previously. As can sometimes happen during busy times with a camp to shift and a lot of people to feed, their meat ran out once. Jimmy, the stockman who was telling us later, added, 'so we blew out a donkey and ate it. It wasn't that bad'.

One day, in the new millennium, a letter for Annette arrived in the Fossil Downs mailbag. It was from a couple that previously had worked in the stock camp at Fossil. Darren and Jacqui Castle advised that they had purchased a small holding in the Northern Territory, but they required off-farm income, so were establishing a contract mustering team. Under this arrangement, they offered to supply all the personnel, gear, and anything else required. The landholder needed only supply meat, diesel, and payment. Would John and Annette be interested in availing themselves of this service? Would they? It sounded like manna from heaven!

Negotiations took place and an agreement worked out. What was previously dreaded as a nightmare undertaking changed and became an extremely amicable, happy arrangement. It worked like a dream and lasted for 12 years until the Castles retired.

Drive to Kununurra

Iron ore mining in the Pilbara and Kimberley eventually brought improvement—a dubious word in this context—to regional infrastructure, especially bridges and roads. A 2,500 mile bitumen road all the way from Perth to Broome to Darwin and beyond had only ever been a dream. As I drove down it from Kununurra to Halls Creek in 2009, the fascinating scenery mystified me—I hadn't remembered weaving through all those mauve and pink multicoloured hills in 1970 on my only other drive along this road.

In 1970 it was a memorable drive. Ros, a nurse at Fitzroy AIM, and I were driving the Fossil Downs Perth bank manager, Mr. Hodgson, and his wife the 650 kms from Fossil Downs to catch their plane at Kununurra. Halls Creek and Turkey Creek were the only townships along the way. It was Mr. Hodgson's driving shift—he and I took turns. The Holden Kingswood was my responsibility, and about 80 miles prior to reaching Halls Creek it jerked slightly. Nothing was said. The rules at Fossil were that you were not permitted to take a vehicle beyond the ZV5 front gate unless you'd checked the tyre pressures, oil, water and fuel. No exceptions! That had all been done the previous evening so we could get an early start. We were still rolling along the dirt road. Maybe this hiccup was imagined and it had been a small pothole, or dirty fuel, or.... From the back seat I took a discreet look over Mr. Hodgson's shoulder at the fuel gauge on the dashboard. It was showing full. Horrors! We'd come 200 miles and it was still showing full. It must have been jammed when it was checked. How much fuel did we really have? How far were we from a fuel supply? Another cough from the car and it was confession time as we gradually rolled to a halt. Everyone put a positive spin on the situation.

A map was rolled up to make a funnel and the 5 gallons of petrol we had in a jerry can in the boot was poured into the fuel tank. Would this get us to Halls Creek? This V8 Holden Kingswood was thirsty and seventy-five more miles along the track we slowly rolled to another halt. 'We'll eat an early lunch and wait for someone to come along' suggested Mrs. Hodgson cheerfully. Lunch duly eaten, no one had come along, so Ros and I said we'd take the empty jerrycan and walk into Halls Creek, get some fuel, and see if someone from the servo would drive us back. Mr. Hodgson, who found shade for them to wait in, suggested we wave when we got to the bend in the road up ahead if we could see the township from there. Mercifully we didn't need to. Half a mile along the road, coming towards us was a Land Rover towing a caravan—commonplace nowadays but not then. Amazed at the sight of two young women in shorts, walking with a jerry can, they quickly realised our plight. They were gem fossickers, two brothers, a wife and a little Chihuahua dog being cuddled. They'd been fossicking in the area now known as the Bungle Bungle, which wasn't a National Park or a tourist destination then. 'I'll unhook the 'van and take you back to Hall's Creek', volunteered the sympathetic driver who'd been heading the opposite direction. They drove us into Halls Creek and saved us an hour's walk in the broiling sun. After obtaining the fuel, just 5 minutes before the servo closed for lunch hour, they drove us back to our vehicle. Then they hitched up their 'van and gave us a cheery wave as they continued on their way.

The mauve tinted shades of the Carr-Boyd Ranges over to the east were memorable, but on that drive in 1970 I didn't remember winding through hills between Halls Creek and Kununurra. Analysis revealed how much the road had been raised when it was upgraded and bitumen laid to allow for wet season monsoonal conditions. In 2009 we were travelling much higher than the surrounding plains. The added height of a 4WD over the Kingswood also enabled a better view. Maybe the road was realigned that way to cater for the ever-increasing number of grey nomad tourists.

This raised road giving a more scenic view of the surrounding plains has had mixed blessings. When the track from Halls Creek to Fitzroy Crossing was originally created in the 1880s, naturally it followed close to creeks and rivers providing overlanders, drovers and gold prospectors easy access to water. It still mainly follows that course today, albeit elevated several metres in places.

Time to go

The 1970/71 wet season was approaching. Would the conditions be the same as last year? Probably. Would only five of us be at the station, with no conversational input from the outside world? Probably. Would the same scenario as last year be repeated and would we play the same rain game again? Probably. Since continually learning and experiencing new things was my forte, my mind was considering these questions when a letter arrived from June, a friend in New Zealand. There was someone waiting for me to visit New Zealand, she claimed. It helped make up my mind. With reluctance, it was time for me to move on.

A Week of Drama, Hell, and High Water

Wednesday 16 March 1983

The wet season was delivering this year! It rained all night! It was still raining at 5.00 in the morning. How many cyclones are up in those hills? Floodwater was already lapping the cattle yards outside the homestead front gates. It had never been that high before! John discovered a leak in their house, so Annette inspected the Big House, but she discovered no leaks there. Drains and gutters were blocked though—a major cleanup will be needed.

Delys, the housekeeper, cleaned the bedrooms and bathrooms upstairs in the Big House. Stockman John Forrester continued making horse tack repairs in the saddle shed, while stockman Sprocket assembled shoeing kits ready for the stock camp. 'I'm glad I don't have to irrigate anywhere today', cousin Bob remarked—after which the rain started pelting down!

Thursday 17 March 1983

Very early in the morning, water from the Margaret River had risen up to Fossil's native store, and also reached the sand at the front of the Big House. It had never been there before! This commenced a major project—Operation Move Out! At 3.00 am, John, Danny the general factotum, and the other men emptied the welding shed and helped Scotty, a general station hand, evacuate his camp.

Everything from the native store, and the saddle shed, was moved nearer the range into a higher, more secure location. John rotated the propeller on the Cessna to start it, then took off and flew along the river. On return, he alerted everyone that the Margaret had burst its banks. That spelt disaster. The black soil plains alongside the Margaret River were the station's most fertile land. It was being swilled out and washed away. Hundreds of tons of premium topsoil were spewing into the raging torrent! Sadly Fossil's cattle were being swept down the river too, and a mob was stranded in the Nhillabublica paddock.

Pitifully eighty-seven stud Percheron horses were trying to save themselves and swim to safety—but they were still fenced in. Back at the homestead now and swapping the plane for the tinny, John boated out and opened the gates in the hope the horses would help themselves and head to higher ground. He and John Forrester were trying everything to save those horses.

The black muddy water kept gathering speed all morning, rising unbelievably fast—it rose from ankle deep to knee deep in ten minutes. Something nobody ever believed could happen was happening—a flood in the Big House! This was a first not needed. The water approached from the front and the back, and collided in the beautiful main hall. By nightfall it was chest deep, and the force was so great it was impossible to keep upright in it, so nothing could be grabbed and saved from the hall.

Everyone was trying to save whatever they could from other rooms by stacking items higher and higher in the billiard room, which seemed to be the safest place, until there were no more shelves or railings to stack things on. Attempts to beat the rising water level were abandoned when the shelves collapsed and everything just fell down into the thick, gluggy torrent.

Out on the run, gates were opened and cattle were chased to higher ground via the boat. The sight of the Margaret overflowing along its entire length was like water rushing out of an overfull bathtub—but with incredibly more force. 'It was tragic', Annette winced, the memory still hurting. 'There was absolutely nothing we could do about it. To keep everyone safe, we all climbed up the Geikie Range and sat on the rocks. A lifetime's planning, efforts and hard back-breaking work, was getting swept away with those beautiful cattle and horses. We were powerless to prevent any of it.'

As darkness fell, the last sight was of the chooks being swept off the chook shed roof—those hens never to be seen again. All the buildings, including the big machinery shed, were more than half submerged. Only the rooftops of the two Nissen huts and the welding shed were visible. The Big House, plus Henwood's Court House, and the main store, were copping the full force of the current. The engine room and the cool room were now under water. Fuel drums and gas bottles were being swept away. Valiant efforts were being made by John and the men to save them by trying to drag them into the tinny. The cookhouse was knee-deep in sludgy water, making it difficult for Lynda, the cook, to keep upright so she could feed everyone. At least she could still grab food from the main store and the cold room.

It was another miserable night spent on top of the rocky range. Danny and Marti were the only ones to have rescued a swag. Everyone else huddled on saddlecloths. Everyone's feet were rubbed raw from walking barefoot over the uneven, gouged out paths and broken glass. Everyone was utterly exhausted.

Then at midnight the floodwater peaked.

Friday 18 March 1983

At dawn, everyone sat on the range and watched the utter devastation of everything. No one could express his or her feelings. The team all felt the loss personally as they watched everything getting washed away. Too much was doused out of the machinery and implement sheds to ever be accounted for. A hundred-year collection of unique tools was gone—some were items from the historic overland trek.

Also gone were the picturesque saddlery, barn and native store. From the office many historic mementos, significant business files and documents, and long lists of inventory, which were irreplaceable records, were being sluiced out and shredded into useless wet and unreadable papier-mâché.

Everyone was doing their best to help as they waded through the buildings throwing out rotten food. Somehow from somewhere, someone rescued the visitor's book, which included the signatures of Princess Margaret and Lord Snowdon, and many Governors-General and State Governors—a unique history of station events.

Bill, John's brother, and Olive Henwood flew over from Bow River Station near Kununurra and flew round and round but couldn't land on the airstrip—it was still waterlogged and slushy. They relayed by UHF that the stock they saw were in a bad way.

John had tied the tinny to some undergrowth on the range. In the morning he and Annette accessed it from a boulder and floated over and perched it near the pergola outside the office. From there they could use the office UHF radio so they called all the stations further down the Fitzroy, warning them what to expect. Mrs. Mac and Merrilee, in Perth, had the news broken to them via radiotelephone. There were still no telephones in the Yurabi area.

Slowly that morning the water began to drop, and by lunchtime it was falling more rapidly. As darkness approached everyone climbed back up the range, again, to spend another miserable, stormy wet night, exhausted and unhappy. Trying to sleep on saddlecloths on rocks was mightily uncomfortable.

Saturday 19 March 1983

Everything was a sodden muddy mess. At daybreak the water was still ankle deep, making it very slippery and dangerous. The driveway was like a washed-out creek bed. Everywhere floors were slimy with mud, and dangerous with unseen broken glass.

In the Big House, the Beale pianola and the already once-rescued billiard table from Broome, had both been hurled through the ornate leadlight doors now smashed to smithereens. Few of the once impressive book collection from the billiard room, including many first editions, were ever seen again.

In an effort to make 'cleaning up' progress at the homestead, an order of priority was decided. First: Fresh water, then staff accommodation, kitchen cleanup and food for everyone. They split into teams: Bob and Annette to the men's quarters; Lynda the cook, Sonja the governess, and Sprocket to the big kitchen; Debbie the secretary, and Delys to the Big House; Danny and Marti to their house.

John was under enormous pressure trying to be everywhere and flying endlessly in the Cessna looking for horses and cattle. The stockmen were helping out wherever they could, trying to save motors and engines, and salvage as many tools and equipment as possible. Everyone was unstinting in their efforts, supporting each other as well as John and Annette. The damage was colossal, the mess was heartbreaking and the 'dead fish' smell was putrid.

The hall, the billiard room, the store and the office, were very hard for John and Annette to face without breaking down. There was no real bedding anywhere, but a dormitory was rigged up in the insect-wired front veranda with what bedding items had been salvaged.

Bill and Olive flew over again from Bow River station and were able to land this time. They brought donated goods with them, much of it bread and thongs, from Halls Creek people. It was sincerely appreciated. Bill hopped into trying to save motors, and Olive washed up absolutely hundreds of filthy dishes. Geoff McGlasson, the electrician from Halls Creek, arrived to help with the power, fridges, freezers and washing machines. Drs. Sadler and Deckland from Fitzroy Crossing Hospital arrived to see if their services were needed, and Craig, from Helimuster, flew in and was invaluable ferrying people to and from Fitzroy Crossing, while also looking for horses and cattle.

Sunday 20 March 1983

The nightmare continued. Every morning everyone was hoping it was just a terrible dream from which they would wake. The damage out on the run was humungous—eighteen bores were silted up, dozens of water-tanks and troughs were smashed, and a copious number of windmills and holding yards had disintegrated beyond repair. Countless miles of top quality fencing with new posts, standards, and barbed wire, were completely wrecked, gouged out and washed down the river. So far there was no accurate indication of how many cattle and horses had been lost. The damage was so bad out on the run that John could not tell Annette. Danny scored the job of conveying to her the catastrophe they'd seen from the air.

Everyone plodded on through the relentless mess and mud. There were absolutely endless items to be washed—endless scrubbing to be done. A few books had been saved from the office and were laid out to dry. In an effort to eliminate more of the putrid smell, the fermented chook food and rice was gathered up and dumped. In their exhaustion everyone become very tired and strained.

The Hon. Ernie Bridge AM, MP, called briefly to view the damage to enable a report to be filed with the State government. Jamie Gray flew over from Leopold Station and worked on saddles and horse gear, and cleaned out the chook shed that was in a really bad way. Piles of furniture were stacked in sodden heaps ready for burning, after the insurance assessor arrived.

Monday 21 March 1983

Scrubbing. Washing. Sorting. It was endless. Allan Simpson, the horse breaker, who knew the property well, arrived to help. All the women were trying to clean buildings and their contents. Big areas such as floors and walls were not nearly as depressing as the contents of drawers and cupboards, which just had to be tipped out.

'My father moved down to this site on the advice of the local aborigines who told him it never flooded here—and so it was for my parents' lifetimes', Annette emphasized, surveying all the chaos, detritus and destruction. Historically they were right. Continuing, 'For nearly fifty years while my mother was here, no water ever entered a house or shed', she said. These were unprecedented times.

All the men worked from daylight to dark trying to find and sort tools and parts, windmill gear, pumps, troughs, saddlery, and motors, and the general accumulation of a hundred years of cattle grazing, much of it beyond salvage.

The health inspector came to check the water supply for drinking, and said that it should all be boiled. 'Yeah, right. We'll light a fire under the tank stand', was Danny's ironic comment.

It was estimated that six and half thousand head of Fossil's prime beef cattle were flowing down the swollen river—some dead, some alive. Others were still unaccounted for. From their estimates only, approximately eight thousand cattle remained alive on higher ground. The horses were still trying to save themselves and swim to safety where the water levels hadn't yet abated. There was a happy event, though, when Amber and Sprocket walked a mare 'Partytime' home along the range. Someone in a helicopter had spotted her down near the Island Paddock. Although very lame, exhausted and with a deep and frequent cough, it lifted everyone's spirits to see her! Regretfully there was no sign of 'Daisy Bell', 'Pepper', 'Birthday Girl', 'Stormy' or 'Amberetton' the stallion, plus all the other horses.

Tuesday 22 March 1983

Trevor Lunt, loss adjustor for the insurance company, flew in with Mr. Hillman, Fossil's accountant from Perth, to assess damages. Along with Annette, they spent the day working out figures for damages. It was all very depressing. Debbie had done a remarkable job in the office, sorting out some of the chaos, saving some documents, and creating a temporary filing system that was marginally operational. To achieve this, she had transferred everything upstairs into Mrs. Mac's big bedroom.

Offers of help came from lots of local people but Annette felt they would be unable to cope with feeding so many. The big kitchen was in no state to cater, yet! It was difficult for the cook to provide enough food for the people already on the station. Eating arrangements had to be outside the big kitchen on what was left of the muddy lawn.

John flew into Fitzroy and collected the four new stockmen, as previously arranged. They were all very sympathetic and dived in to help wherever they could. Robbie Whyatt, who had worked at Fossil, came out from Fitzroy to assist with cleaning and checking motors, which was a tremendous help.

John was flying all around, as needed. The floods and mud made it impossible to drive anywhere. The seats had been removed from the Cessna to allow cargo and some animals to be shifted. Merve and Jane, the homestead maintenance managers, needed to go into Fitzroy and said they'd sit on the plane's floor—it was a very short flight. When they landed at Fitzroy Crossing there was another plane there. The Air Police! Why were they there? When John returned to the plane with the mail, a note was attached to it—a 'please explain' to these police was necessary. He had to re-sit the exam for his pilot's licence, and redo the practical test before he was permitted to fly again to continue the clean up! Fortunately this delay was short. The $30,000 fine originally imposed was later waived.

Wednesday 23 March 1983

Trevor Lunt, the insurance loss assessor, gave the okay for all the ruined furniture to be burned—it made a very big bonfire! He, Bentley Hillman and Annette continued working out the values of contents for damages, this mammoth task made more unappealing by the assessor being quite difficult at times.

The Industrial Special Risks insurance policy, previously recommended by Fossil's insurance brokers, covered Fossil for disasters, they thought. This policy provided for property damage and loss to protect physical assets including buildings, stock, plant and machinery, plus other property. Reviewing his assessment later, the assessor seemed more familiar with buildings than with the necessity of replacing stock, fences, pumps, yards, troughs, windmills, and the regular items that aid in bringing revenue to a property. For example, it took two fencing teams eleven weeks, working flat out, to restore the fences that had been either damaged or washed away. The final fencing settlement was a long way short of the actual replacement costs.

Will Fossil Downs ever be the same again? Would John and Annette have the heart and courage to pick up the pieces and start all over? How do you replace and restore everything when a third of the cattle, which provide your income, have just been swept down the river?

More floods happened—twice in 1986, and in 1991 and 1993, although the first in 1983 was the worst. Trying to remain positive in these adversities each time it flooded, Annette and John took stock of the buildings at the homestead and decided on a gradual replacement and upgrading policy. Some structures were not reinstated—others were eventually replaced, larger and stronger. The main store, tool shed, and several other buildings were elevated with mezzanine floors installed. Inside the Big House, the billiard and dining-room tables, and the pianola had winches attached for quick elevation to the ceiling, if necessary, along with the dining table in the cookhouse. As well as the homestead buildings all requiring restoration or renewal after each flood event, the fencing, yards, windmills, troughs, pumps and reconstruction of water-bores, required another massive input of both finance and labour. Insurance covered only a minimal portion of the losses, which were substantial with each flood.

Innovation was used in the other houses and sheds to mitigate the effects of flooding now that it seemed to happen regularly. Gradually additional houses, one for the maintenance manager and an 'eco' house for guests, were added and sited above the flood level on the top of a hill adjacent to the front of the Big House, nearer the bore and water tank. This broke with the tradition of all buildings lining up on the street, but was necessary to avoid further inundation. It also gave scenic outlooks north towards the airstrip. A larger generator shed and chilling chamber was located higher up on the foothills of Geikie Range. None of this spoiled the overall layout.

The Big House was built with love, and Annette called it her 'labour of love' to maintain it. 'The homestead seems to endure everything nature throws at it', she said. 'Because the bricks were made by hand I suppose there were variations in the amount of cement used, and how well one person mixed the sand and cement compared to another. I think it says such a lot for the old place that it is still standing, particularly with all the floods that have confronted it. A 6.3 earthquake rocked it in 1999, and a few cracks appeared. But you've got to marvel at the way it withstands it all'.

Reflecting further, she added, 'You have to have an enormous heart to start again,' as she gazed around the complex. She continued, 'after each flood subsides, every part of every inundated building has to be scrubbed. It's easy to think you clean a cement building by squirting a hose at it, but water blasting is too severe on the handmade sand/cement brick structure of the Big House. That gluey mud from the black soil clings and stains—you have to scrub every inch by hand. It's the only way to get rid of the dark stain and mess on the walls and the dank smell—just scrub and scrub and scrub.'

In 1993 Waverley, the housekeeper, and Annette had just finished scrubbing the last building, it having taken three weeks of backbreaking, shoulder wrenching work. It started to rain—and four days later it flooded again. They both sat down and cried.

Bridges or Highway Upgrade?

What caused these floods? Why did they happen? It's claimed two cyclones collided up at the headwaters of the Margaret and the Leopold rivers. Fourteen inches of rain fell in two days in the Mueller Ranges—the annual average is 22 inches. But massive rain events had occurred there previously without causing such devastation.

Did the style of bridging over the three watercourses in Fitzroy Crossing contribute to these occurrences when that road was upgraded in 1982? To reduce the length of the bridges, and therefore the cost, the sides of the two creeks and the mighty Fitzroy River had hundreds of tons of rock and spoil dumped where the bridges were to be sited, and shorter bridges installed. Those buttresses reduced the pace of the flow of the floodwaters, causing a massive bank up. At the usual 30,000 cubic yards of water per second flowing through Fitzroy in the wet season, it didn't take long for the water to back right up the Fitzroy and Margaret Rivers—did this cause the catastrophic disasters for Fossil Downs?

Did the upgrading and significant raising of the Great Northern Highway from Fitzroy Crossing to Halls Creek also contribute? Were insufficient culverts installed? Instead of the floodwater from the Margaret River gradually seeping out into the Great Sandy Desert, or down into the Fitzroy Valley, was it channeled through much of the Fossil Downs black soil plains and homestead complex, being unable to slowly dissipate as it could prior to the raising of the road? Later, when the engineering was challenged, a curt 'Well, can't you shift the homestead to higher ground' was the reply from a bureaucrat at the

Main Roads Department. However, that department did eventually, reluctantly, make some amendments to the Brooking Creek bridge buttresses in Fitzroy Crossing to allow floodwaters to subside more quickly.

The Margaret River has a massive catchment with at least fifteen rivers and creeks running into it from the ranges to its north. Did the road engineering cause the run off from these rivers to become channeled down the Margaret—to storm right through the iconic Fossil Downs homestead? A soil inundation consultant considers this raising of the highway contributed substantially to the damage. What criteria are used to calculate the requirements for the amount of runoff when a road is raised?

In an ironic twist, in 2009 my husband and I were having dinner with friends and their colleagues in Perth and I was seated next to a civil engineer who worked with the Main Roads Department, and had worked in the Kimberley. 'I'm familiar with that road and area,' I said. 'I used to work at Fossil Downs.' Throwing his arms in the air he guiltily admitted, 'It wasn't me. I wasn't responsible! Kununurra to Halls Creek was my patch'—without my saying another word.

> In January 2023 this bridge over the Fitzroy River was washed away when a massive volume of water spilled down both the Margaret and the Fitzroy rivers. The replacement bridge is much longer, and stronger. Of seven spans, it is 370 metres between abutments and 12.8 metres wide with pedestrian walkways on either side. It took only eight months to erect—six months quicker than was contracted or expected.

After each flood Annette and John would survey the disaster in front of them. Putrid muddy water saturated all the downstairs areas of every structure, buildings were tipped off their foundations, machinery would be washed down the street and piled up against fences, trees, and any other barrier still remaining. 'What do we do,' they'd deliberate as they processed in their minds the massive tasks ahead. 'Do we walk away and leave it, or put it all back in order?' Each time, remembering Annette's ancestors and the numerous catastrophes they endured to establish Fossil Downs, while walking away from it was a very tempting option at that point, they decided instead on restoration.

As well as the homestead buildings all requiring restoration or renewal after each massive flood event, the fencing, yards, windmills, pumps and restoration of bores required another massive input of both finance and labour. All new yards were rebuilt in steel, in a convenient user-friendly style, suitable for the modern aerial methods of mustering and holding stock. Absolutely everything was eventually evaluated and renewed.

Maxine Departs

Retaining the Big House and surrounds in the manner Maxine desired required a mighty amount of energy and stamina. There were never-ending chores in this large, 14-room homestead, with no help from the native workforce now. They were all living in their new houses across the Margaret River in Muludja, their new community.

Standing on the veranda, looking around, she reflected, 'I love this house, but sometimes I think it gives the wrong impression. Bill and I built it as the fulfilment of a dream, but keeping it and the property going takes a lot of money and hard work. My million is in acres, not dollars.' Then she added, 'This land can be hard and cruel but it's always irresistibly challenging and beautiful.'

Cattle stations had evolved and changed over the fifty years Maxine had been there. 'The romanticism, resilience and inspired legends of the cattle kings are gone now, consigned to history and memories,' she deliberated, thinking of those years. 'Kimberley has passed from its own total isolation to satellite communication with the rest of the world.'

Battling on with the help of Annette and a cook, but getting older, meant Maxine couldn't achieve as much in a day as she used to. She fought on thinking of the obstacles Bill overcame to erect the homestead. She insisted, to herself, that the dining room table be flawlessly polished; that the silver cutlery and other accoutrements be placed at exactly the correct angle; that the crystal goblets on the table be placed at the tip of the knife, at every meal. She arranged it all impeccably. Then one day while preparing some lunch she suddenly felt a little light-headed, and looked around for something to rest her hand on for support until the feeling passed. But the feeling didn't pass.

After 50 years of calling Fossil Downs home, of morphing from a city sophisticate into a capable chatelaine and station owner/manager, of creating style and elegance in an area where there had been none, Maxine's allotted time was up. She had a stroke and died, while still continuing to uphold the standards she herself had set and maintained for all those years.

In 1988, shortly after Maxine's death, Martin Peirson-Jones, a Director of the Kimberley Accommodation Group, built the Fitzroy River Lodge in Fitzroy Crossing. Such was the esteem in which he held Mrs. MacDonald he named the restaurant after her. 'Maxine's' is now a tourism landmark in Fitzroy Crossing. Portraits of her and the story of the MacDonald's momentous cattle drive and some of Fossil's historic photographs adorn the walls.

(Some Of The) Achievements of Bill & Maxine MacDonald

1931 First sale of herd bulls from West to East Kimberley
1934 First road transport of livestock in Kimberley
1942 Support of Broome freezing and chilling works
1943 Mapping of area for the military; identifying and sketching bush tucker if needed for food if the Japanese invaded
1946 Registration of the Kimberley Poll Shorthorn Stud — the first stud of any breed to be established in North Western Australia
1948 Support of Glenroy Air Beef Project
1948 First large scale attempts at pasture rehabilitation — aerial seeding first time in Australia
1950 First export of bulls to Northern Territory— to Charlie Schultz at Humbert River Station
1950 First in Australia to deliver herd bulls by air. World record airlift 31st July 1950
First to adopt road-transport for delivery of cattle shipments (2,200 trucked)
1951 Experimented with growing lucerne with irrigation from the Margaret River
1959 First in Kimberley to experiment with mineral and hormone supplements
1962 First to agree to cooperate in experimental marketing of chilled beef from the Kimberley

On **2 January 1956**, William Neil Mitchell MacDonald was awarded the Order of the British Empire - Member (Civil) (Imperial), for services to the pastoral industry.

On **13 June 1981**, Maxine Claire MacDonald was awarded The Order of the British Empire - Member (Civil) for community services

Suspension of Live Cattle Trade

Choices and decisions are made in matters over which you have control—sometimes good decisions, sometimes not. Mitigating circumstances can intervene. Then there are those matters over which there is no control.

On 7 June 2011 the Australian Federal Government suspended the live cattle trade with Indonesia. No other region in Australia was more adversely affected by this suspension than the Kimberley, Northern Territory and North Queensland. Since the closure of the abattoirs there in the early 1990s, this region's massive cattle industry relied almost solely on the live export trade to Indonesia.

Right at the time of the suspension, musterers had planes and helicopters in the air, plus ringers and horses in stock camps on the ground. Pastoralists had yards and paddocks full of cattle ready to send on the ships, with thousands more being walked towards their yards. Feedlot managers were in the midst of replacing their stock. Transport operators had hundreds of cattle trains on the road heading out to load those cattle—and suddenly it was all banned right in the thick of the crucial cattle season in the Top End. Nothing could move.

Nil cattle sales equals nil income to the pastoralists or the trucking and mustering operators. Continuing stock health required spending large sums of money. Being interviewed by the ABC at the time as he tried to keep everything functioning on Fossil, John contended, 'the health of the animal is paramount so you just have to keep going. We have a rotational grazing system and you can't just stop and say we're not going to handle or move the cattle; they still have to be branded and treated. It has to be continued for the animal's sake. We (graziers) still have to purchase the necessary products and pay wages. We're living in hope—hope that the "government" will get some sense and reopen the trade.'

In reply to the then calls for abattoirs to be reconstructed in the Kimberley, John was exasperated, explaining 'The three meat works in the Kimberley closed up because of costs, and people are kidding themselves if they think we can build more meat works. All the butchers would want mining-type wages. The returns to the stations would be so low it just wouldn't be feasible.'

In the Kimberley dry season, as many cattle as possible are turned off in preparation for the wet season. That system was then forced completely out of whack for a whole 12-month period. Graziers further south were affected too for the next three to four years as Kimberley cattle, now too heavy to go to Indonesia, were filtered into southern markets. There were some producers who had no income at all until the following season. By the time the ban was lifted on 6 July 2011, many Kimberley cattle producers had quite literally missed the boat—but not through their own decisions.

Was this the final catastrophe after all the flood disasters that convinced John and Annette that their time at Fossil Downs was drawing to a close? How many calamities can you endure? When does your 'psyche' give up and say, 'enough is enough'?

Epilogue 2014

The clear early morning autumn air glowed. Cyclone Ita had visited Queensland's Sunshine Coast, doing little damage but dumping several inches of rain on the dry pastures. Overnight emerald green grass emerged from the still warm soil in the paddocks. In the valley a hint of fog floated over the Mary River, heralding cooler nights. Iconic Queenslander homes, with steeply pitched roofs to disperse the searing summer heat, were nestled contentedly amongst the hills and valleys. The vegetation on the foothills of the Great Dividing Range presented pale blue in the early morning light—the trees soft and rounded, picturesque and beautiful.

It was 2014, and time to revisit the vibrant orange and ochre colours of the jagged, ragged Kimberley. We'd drive slowly, with no particular itinerary or timetable, heading along some of the routes those early overlanders took to reach their grass empires. We'd travel differently though—no bullock teams pulling wagons, or bush bashing a route by longitude and latitude bearings. An air-conditioned four-wheel drive vehicle, with a modest caravan in tow, provides us with comfort. Our GPS is plugged in beside us. We don't need it for directions—it's just interesting to check the altitude sometimes. We can travel on smooth, sealed roads all the way if we choose, with roadhouses, coffee shops and general stores to provide refreshments and supplies at regular intervals along the route. What would those first overlanders have given to resupply their needs along the way instead of hauling everything with them? Would they even recognize the route they traversed now? There's a sealed road from Winton to the Nine-mile Waterhole and a mobile phone signal most of the way. A what? Yet even today, with working communications in many places and defined roads and map directions, some people still hesitate to venture along the early outback droving routes.

Having lived and loved the Kimberley, its magnetism draws you back. The amazing rugged beauty casts a spell on you—geologists call it heaven, photographers call it paradise. Travellers gaze in awe and wonder as they discover yet another magnificent gorge, its colourful sides displaying gold and amber, pink and purple, along with native blue waterlilies. They gaze in wonder at the unique horizontal waterfalls and the stunning coastal features of the Dampier Peninsula and Buccaneer Archipelago occurring as a consequence of the 35-foot tide. The spectacular sunsets are posted endlessly on social media.

Times had changed. Fitzroy Crossing is now an established town, with kerbed and channelled streets. A new hospital and schools are functioning. Service stations, roadhouses, and an information centre along with caravan parks, a grocery store, and an accommodation lodge, have brought the town up to date, very convenient for those living there now, but having lost its unique frontier atmosphere.

Once again our destination is Fossil Downs station. What new initiatives might be merged into its operation? What disasters have occurred since our last visit 15 years ago?

The Fossil Downs road leaves the Great Northern Highway in a different location. It was realigned in 1984. A discreet sign indicates the way to the Muludja aboriginal community on the same road. The Great Northern highway is much closer to the Gogo station headquarters. The Fossil road is actually a formed road now, unlike the assortment of dusty, bumpy tracks, scattered with giant bulldust holes, which underscored the previous access to the station.

Silt is piled up on either side of the 80-yards wide crossing that negotiates the Margaret River, the southeastern boundary of Fossil. It must have run a banker in the last wet season to pile up so much. A cattle grid has been installed near the ZV5 boundary gate. No need to wait for the dust to settle before opening the car door—conveniently you can just keep driving. The road follows the river before diverting left to the station homestead complex. The grass, while generally dry, is abundant—plenty of cattle feed. Efforts to maximise the fodder appear to be working well. Suddenly the gate pillars, displaying that MacDonald coat of arms, are in front of us.

The cool atmosphere beyond the gates draws you into its compound. Everything is green—green grassy lawn, green leaves on the bottle trees *(Adansonia gregorii)*, large leafy-green weeping fig trees *(Ficus benjamina)* and green roofs on buildings, which previously were red. Most buildings are now shaded from the scorching afternoon sun by strategically planted trees. The Australian flag flies proudly overhead, its pole set in a tropical garden bed of frangipani blended with oleanders. Everything is immaculate.

It's a busy time for all Kimberley and Territory stations as thousands of head of cattle are being mustered and trucked to Broome, Wyndham and Darwin, to be loaded aboard ships and delivered mainly to Indonesia and the Middle East. We timed our arrival on a day when Fossil wasn't trucking and for 9.00 am, the traditional time for smoko, when all hands and guests gather at the cookhouse for what is a sumptuous repast—hot chicken pies, toasties and other savoury treats, sandwiches, fruitcake, grapes and watermelon. Jenny, the cook, has raised the bar. No longer just hot buns straight from the oven—of which there was nothing wrong.

Annette joined us for morning tea and graciously answered Norm, my friend from Perth Junior Farmer days, who had come with us and had lots of questions. As a well-travelled West Australian ex-cropping farmer, he was enthralled with the complex. Annette suggested our team, Norm and his wife Gail, and my husband, John, and I, go for a walk around the centre of operations, the huge machinery shed, after which she'd show us what the interior of the Big House looks like now.

The whole complex is even more impressive than it was in 1970. The once dusty street is now grassed over with dual wheel tracks for vehicles to access the Big House. These grassy green lawns have reduced the dust flying into the homestead. They have been extended further down the street, alleviating some of the housekeeper's dusting chores, and contributing to the cooling ambience of the environs. But what determination and effort it must have taken to get grass to grow there. How was lawn achieved on that hot, hard, limestone street surface? All the living quarters along this street now have extensive shade, plus air-conditioning. More bottle trees have been planted and nurtured. We learned later that Annette, using a lightweight crowbar, single-handedly thumped it into that limestone to create the necessary holes to plant those trees.

The Big House, standing sentinel at the top of the street, is even more impressive. The colour scheme has been amended slightly—the green roof is now grey, and the earlier green lintels are aubergine which tones with the purple cushions on the white wooden chairs strategically placed on the flagstoned veranda. The same white tables displaying lace cloths and vases of purple silk flowers are still there. The pink flowering oleanders, originally placed to screen the lawn in front of the house for sleeping, are now trimmed down low allowing a better view of the 'Taj Mahal'.

What a magnificent place! Every year it gets even better now that the flooding is somewhat controlled. Everything Bill and Maxine desired in the homestead is still there, only enhanced several notches. The green room lounge is even more comfortable. A new Beale pianola now resides there. In the billiard room the cues are set out on the table, ready for the next group of players. The office, in deference to the floods that now occur, is comfortably situated upstairs above the previous office. No more is the Flying Doctor radio a pivotal item—it's been replaced by the Commander telephone system to most parts of the complex. Computers, of course, have replaced the old Underwood manual typewriter and the Burroughs adding machine.

The determination, fortitude, and overpowering sense of purpose required after all the calamities has produced a brilliant testament to everyone who has ever had a part in working at Fossil Downs. A different mode of operation from the second generation is station publicity. Bill actively sought newspaper publicity for Fossil Downs and West Kimberley cattle in particular. Annette and John are publicity shy and when Maxine was still alive, she handled it all, having originally had tuition from Bill. 'But we three made a good team. Mum was 'the voice' and John and I just got on with what we do best—the running and improvement of the station', Annette sighed.

Norm voiced his reaction to the complex. 'Arriving at the station homestead,' he said later, 'was like driving into the grounds of Government House only you are way out the back of Fitzroy Crossing in the Kimberley!' Gazing around he continued, 'It's like royalty! I've been to Buckingham Palace and the Vatican, but I haven't experienced anything better than the immaculate presentation of Fossil Downs station homestead and grounds.'

WA veteran real estate executive, Malcolm French, also commented that in 50 years in the industry he had seen nothing that compared to Fossil Downs. Up until 2015 it was the largest property in Australia still in the ownership of the family that settled it—a total of 133 years.

Did my instinct tell me this was most likely my last visit to Fossil? Annette said that she and John, both now in their late 70s, had really enjoyed looking after Fossil Downs, carrying on from her parents, and embracing the chance to upgrade what had been created before them. 'But the disasters we've had to endure torment your spirit, and can challenge your very being,' she recalled scrunching up her face, remembering. 'Now we're getting tired. Maintaining everything on a million acres—the windmills, bores, pumps and troughs, the miles of fencing, plus yards and the machinery plant, the homestead buildings, and the trees, lawns and gardens—requires total love and dedication.'

'One morning John got out of bed and said "I can't do this any more". So we had to mull over our situation and make some decisions'. 'But,' she added, 'following the tradition of those MacDonalds who came here before us, it's been John and my life's work to look after it.' Emotion cracked her voice as she added, 'Walking away after living and working here for seventy-three years was the hardest thing I've ever had to do. I never wanted to be the MacDonald who quit. But you can't roll back the years. It's hard work and there's probably been more tough times than good—but it's a life that we chose and we've really loved it'

One hundred and thirty-three years labour of love was invested into Fossil Downs by three generations of the MacDonald family—but all things (on earth) must eventually come to

An End.

Mrs. Gina Rinehart, a fellow West Australian, purchased the whole of Fossil Downs station in 2015—the first time it was sold out of the MacDonald family.

John & Annette Henwood's 'modus operandi':
In all our dealings we expect and endeavour to return:

Honesty	— in all our dealings
Integrity	— our word is our bond
Reliability	— we deliver whatever the cost
Punctuality	— we get through on time
Fidelity	— we remember our friends

Achievements of John & Annette Henwood

1970s	Commenced changeover to Droughtmaster cattle
1970s	Began purchasing machinery plant to upgrade efficient running of the station: Cessna 182 plane, DC 6 bulldozer, several flat deck Toyota Landcruiser utilities, the Haflinger, all fitted with the necessary equipment for its intended purpose, plus a grader and front-end loader.
1980s	Pasture upgrade. Began new grazing technique, and collection of native plant seeds.
1980s	Upgrade of communications equipment on the station and beyond
1980	Establishment of Fossil Downs cemetery
1980/90	Reinstatement and upgrading of every building after disastrous floods, 5 times in 7 years.
2015	First commercial breeders to receive Life membership from Droughtmaster Cattle Society
2015	PGA of WA Achievement Award
2018	John Henwood is awarded the OAM, Order of Australia Medal, for services to the cattle breeding industry in the Kimberley.

ACCOLADES

Droughtmaster Society

'Over the past 30 years two wonderful people, Annette and John Henwood from Fossil Downs Station in the Kimberley, have been buying bulls from the Droughtmaster National Bull Sale in Rockhampton, Queensland. Many others may have been purchasing as long or longer but there would be none who have tackled the journey across Australia, from west to east, year after year. Over time they continued to lift their sights and purchased bulls, which put extra length and muscle into their steers and could at the same time handle the Kimberley conditions — which aren't always kind.

The Fossil Downs cattle are a credit to their sire selection over the last 30 years. John and Annette are justifiably proud of their cattle, which draw compliments from all parties in the live export supply chain and are keenly sought after by overseas buyers. From what was a herd of Kimberley Shorthorn some 20 years ago, the Fossil Downs cattle are now some of the very best Droughtmaster cattle you could hope to see.

In recognition of the long term significant contribution John and Annette have made to our breed the Board of the Droughtmaster Society has great pleasure in awarding Life Membership to you both.'

Pastoralist Peers

Pastoralists in Western Australia's Kimberley region have paid tribute to John and Annette Henwood, who have sold their iconic Fossil Downs Station. The station had been in Mrs Henwood's family for three generations and is held in high regard by the Kimberley pastoral community. Kimberley Cattlemen's Association chairman and Kalyeeda Station owner, Peter Camp, said the sale was a good outcome for the cattle industry, but the Henwoods' departure was still a huge loss.

'Their contribution to the Kimberley cattle industry over the last 50 or 60 years has just been enormous. Their standards were second to none,' he said. 'The improvements on the property, through to the horses, they've always held a very high profile and it's a credit to John and Annette to have a property of that standard and keep it going.'

Mr. Camp's family worked at Fossil Downs in the early 1970s and the station was one of the first places where he got his start in the cattle industry. 'It certainly had an impact on the way I think now,' he said. 'Someone who imprints those principles at such a young age, certainly has an effect on your life.'

Pastoralists & Graziers Centenary

After a couple of quick drinks at the end of the day it was time for everybody to go and get their gladrags on for the centenary ball at Fossil Downs.

Annette Henwood had spent many, many hours preparing for this centenary ball and this was well and truly evident for the 200 or so souls who attended the ball on arrival at the large shed where the ball was held. The decorations were spectacular! Absolutely breathtaking—I don't think I will see anything like it ever again! Pink and white balls and stars suspended from the rafters were glowing, as were the tables with candles and the dazzling disco ball that hung from the ceiling.

As one looked up to the ceiling they not only saw the glowing decorations but also an old windmill that had been restored and painted silver—it was stunning. Boot and hat cutouts were hung about and even the shed poles were decorated in white. The beer, wine and champagne flowed steadily throughout the night and the food was delicious and there was enough of it to feed an army! Everybody's meal was served up on a PGA Centenary commemorative plate which they got to take home as a memento from the night. There were also commemorative stubby holders and pens to take home too. A large number of items were auctioned off in the celebrity auction at the ball. These donated items included paintings, furniture, animal statues, sculptures, two hides (marked with all the station brands from the Kimberley) and more. Kelvin Hancey from Elders, Broome, took on the role of auctioneer and he had no shortage of bids with the Kimberley locals as well as the visitors showing their great generosity.

Everybody at the ball appeared to have a tremendous time. John and Annette Henwood sure know how to put on a party! The band, Quiver from Broome, played some fantastic tunes to get everybody's feet tapping and up and dancing. They managed to keep playing until the wee hours of the morning before turning in for the night.

However, there were a fair few people who managed to stay up and see the morning in—they along with those who had managed a few hours sleep were all ready for the sausage sizzle in the morning!

All in all the PGA Kimberley Centenary events were hugely successful and will be long remembered. A special thanks to everybody involved in the planning and organizing of the events and I hope everybody is looking forward to and holding off on buying bulls until the 2008 PGA

Bibliography

Anderson, Max. *Digger*

Australian Geographic. *Longest Cattle Drive in the World*

Barron, Greg. *Whistler's Bones*

Bolton, Bert. *Stories of the Outback*

Bell, Kathrine. Cattle Australia – *The Story; the Icons; The Drives, the Big Runs*

Byrne, Geraldine. Fremantle Arts Centre Press 2006. *Tom & Jack: A Frontier Story*

Buchanan, Bobbie. *In the Tracks of Old Bluey*

Buchanan, Gordon. *Packhorse and Waterhole: With the First Overlanders to the Kimberleys*

Durack, Mary. *Kings in Grass Castles*

Durack, Mary. *Sons in the Saddle*

Farwell, George. *Cape York to the Kimberleys*

Griffiths, Max. *Angels in the Outback*

Gugeri, Michael. *God before Gugeri*

Mahood, Marie. *Legends of the Outback*

Margery, Susan and Round, Kerry. *Roma the First*

MacDonald, Charles Kimberley

McDonald, Nan. *Portofino Design Group Pty. Ltd. (1988)*

McHugh, Evan. *The Drovers*

MacKenzie, Gordon. *Fossil Downs: A Saga of the Kimberley*

McKenzie, Keith. *They Paved the Way. Mudgee Guardian, NSW (1980)*

Niall, Barbara. *True North: the Story of Mary and Elizabeth Durack*

Quilty, Edna: *Nothing Prepared Me*

Shultz, Charlie. *Beyond the Big Run*

Register of Heritage Places: *Assessment Documentation*

GLOSSARY

Ant-bed	Termite mound which is crushed and used as flooring in houses, sheds and tennis courts
Bushed	Getting lost, or being sent off a property
Bough shed	A structure, mainly used in the tropics, which consists of pipe uprights, with a chicken-wire roof, over which vegetation is tightly packed. Sometimes a hose is threaded through this roof, and water is allowed to drip. It is designed for coolness.
Cattle unit	One cattle beast
Comptometer	The first key-driven mechanical calculator; invented in 1862.
CSIRO	Commonwealth Scientific and Industrial Research Organisation
ETA	Estimated time of arrival
Found	In salary or wages, 'found' relates to being provided with food and lodging, plus other 'living' incidentals
Founder	A common and very painful condition affecting the feet of horses. Known technically as 'laminitis', founder occurs when there is inflammation of the laminae, i.e. folds of tissue connecting the pedal bone to the hoof
Horse tack	Saddles, stirrups, bridles, halters, reins, bits, and harnesses used on domestic and working horses
Kip	Sleep or rest

Leprosarium	An institution that cares for people suffering from leprosy The Derby Leprosarium opened in 1936, and cared for Aboriginal people
MMA	MacRobertson Miller Airlines, a Western Australian airline
Nissen hut	A large shed, similar to the half-cylinder structures used in military barracks
Petrol rationing	Legislated by the Federal Government during World War II. It concluded in 1948.
Polled cattle	Cattle bred without horns
PTO	Power-take-off, being a shaft which transfers power from a tractor to the PTO-driven machine or implement
Duffing	Rustling, or stealing cattle
RFDS	Royal Flying Doctor Service
Scrape	A two-yard piece of curved pipe, with a 2' piece of pipe welded at right angles on one end. This was drawn (scraped) across the sand 'greens' on the golf course to smooth them.
Servos	Mainly roadhouses, which served fuel and food and sometimes retailed basic vehicle spare parts
Techos	Technicians, who install and repair telephone lines and wires
Turned off	Cattle being driven into grassy paddocks to graze
TSRs	Travelling Stock Routes: Wide roads or easements where it was permitted to drove stock. In Queensland these were gazetted in the late 1880s, of which the Nine-mile Waterhole became part
Scurs	Small horn-like structures in young cattle
Sked	A scheduled UHF radio broadcast from the various headquarters of Royal Flying Doctor Services e.g. 7.00 am for telegrams, 8.00 am for medical issues

Fish falling out of sky phenomenon

Occasionally a fish phenomenon occurs where water commences flowing down a river, which doesn't flow all the time. At the end of February 2010, residents of Lajamanu in the Northern Territory saw hundreds of spangled perch fall from the sky.

Marsden Court Case

There are brief references to Charlie and Willie MacDonald attempting to take Marsden and Plumbs-cattle to Kimberley on a previous trek, but it had to be abandoned because of drought. Apparently a court case ensued which Marsden and Plumb lost, but details are sketchy.

A 'whistle call' was used to call for help in an emergency when the RFDS base was not broadcasting. A V-shaped whistle was used, created by two metal tubes, one being shorter than the other therefore having different pitches. Blowing 6 seconds on the longer tube and 3 on the shorter caused a shutter to drop down at the Flying Doctor base. This alerted the base operators who would answer and instigate the appropriate action.

ABOUT THE AUTHOR

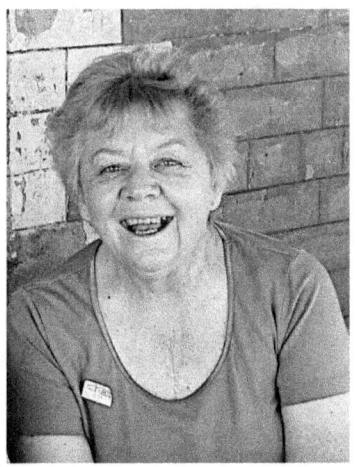

Lyn Caverhill lives on the Sunshine Coast in Queensland. Landscape gardening is a great interest, along with activities at the nearby Goodlife Community Centre – book group, writing group, coffee and cake group!
Previously public speaking was an unlikely interest fostered in Victoria, which resulted in attending conventions In USA for International Toastmistress Clubs. This included a stint judging international speaking competitions and more recently tutoring students at The Pines Institute nearby at Buderim.
Visiting outback places still attracts her.

www.ingramcontent.com/pod-product-compliance
Lightning Source LLC
Chambersburg PA
CBHW052048230426
43671CB00011B/1835